Prisoners of Time

The Misdiagnosis of FDR's 1921 Illness

Prisoners of Time

The Misdiagnosis of FDR's 1921 Illness

Armond S. Goldman, MD

With Daniel A. Goldman, MD, MPH

EHDP Press - 2017

Prisoners of Time
The Misdiagnosis of FDR's 1921 Illness

Armond S. Goldman, MD
With Daniel A. Goldman, MD, MPH

While great care has been taken in the preparation of this book, the authors and publisher assume no responsibility for damages resulting from the use of the information in this book.

The cover shows FDR in a wheelchair at Hill Top Cottage in Hyde Park, NY, along with Ruthie Bie and FDR's Scottish terrier Fala. Ruthie Bie (later Ruth Bautista) was the granddaughter of the cottage caretakers. She was three years old at the time of the photo (1941). Fala was one of the most famous dogs in Presidential history. He was born April 7, 1940 and arrived at the White House November 10, 1940, where he became FDR's constant companion and part of his public image. FDR's distant cousin and close friend Margaret Suckley, a dog breeder, gave Fala to FDR. The dog's original name was "Big Boy", but FDR renamed him "Murray the Outlaw of Fala Hill", or "Fala" for short. Fala's talents for performing tricks, his appealing appearance, and his mention in FDR's humorous 1944 "Fala speech" made the dog popular with the public. After FDR's death, Fala and Eleanor Roosevelt became close companions, but Fala seemed to never stop hoping for his master's return. Fala died on April 5, 1952, and was buried at Springwood, FDR's estate in Hyde Park.

ISBN-10: 1-939824-03-6
ISBN-13: 978-1-939824-03-5

EHDP Press

See http://www.ehdp.com/press/fdr-polio-gbs/ for any errata, and to leave any comments or questions concerning *Prisoners of Time*.

Table of Contents

List of Portraits

List of Figures

List of Tables

Foreword

Among the names of the great Presidents of the United States of America is that of Franklin Delano Roosevelt (FDR) (1882-1945), the subject of whom we read between the covers of this book. A great wartime leader whose judgements generally are accepted as sound, in 1921 Roosevelt suffered an acute neurological illness, diagnosed at the time as paralytic poliomyelitis, which left him with permanent physical disability.

In January 2003, shortly after I became the Editor of the *Journal of Medical Biography*, I received a manuscript with the intriguing title "What was the cause of Franklin Delano Roosevelt's paralytic illness?" sent to me by Dr. Armond Goldman and his colleagues at the University of Texas Medical Branch in Galveston. The paper presented evidence and argued that Roosevelt's 1921 illness was not due to poliomyelitis. Based on my initial assessment, I sent the manuscript out for peer review. The reviewers recommended publication, and the article was therefore published in the November 2003 issue of the *Journal*.

Not surprisingly, the article generated a significant amount of publicity, because the universal belief in 2003 was that Roosevelt's illness had been due to paralytic poliomyelitis. The publication started an ongoing controversy, yet to be resolved, concerning the cause of FDR's illness. Since 2003, several new histories have insisted that poliomyelitis was the cause of Roosevelt's paralytic illness.

Armond Goldman wrote this book to provide additional information concerning the cause of FDR's 1921 illness, extending beyond that possible to present in a scientific journal article. In addition, this book, the first complete telling of FDR's 1921 illness, explains why FDR's doctors might have got the diagnosis wrong and explains why the misdiagnosis may have persisted.

I think it is likely that *Prisoners of Time* will appeal to those interested in Franklin Roosevelt, medical diagnosis, controversy in the sciences, or just a real-life detective story. I welcome historians, physicians and general readers to read the book and weigh the evidence for themselves. I hope this book promotes further debate concerning the cause of FDR's illness.

Let not this foreword-writer spoil the story by saying much more. Let the deductive reasoning of the authors, in Sherlock Holmes fashion, be told as a story that gradually unfolds, analysing evidence as best it can be obtained nearly one century after Roosevelt's illness, and taking into account the views of the treating doctors who actually saw the patient, but in the light of our current best knowledge. I invite readers to assess the evidence that the authors lay out in the coming pages, and to make up their own minds.

Christopher Gardner-Thorpe, MD, FRCP, FRCPE, FACP

Consultant Neurologist in Exeter, UK

History Courses Director, The Worshipful Society of Apothecaries of London

Acknowledgments

Paul Goldman originally discovered that Franklin Delano Roosevelt (FDR) most likely did not have paralytic poliomyelitis (paralytic polio) in 1921, as had been widely believed for many decades. Without Paul's insight, our investigation of FDR's 1921 neurological illness would not have been conducted.

Several excellent colleagues made important contributions to the investigation. They were Frank C. Schmalstieg Jr, MD, PhD, a clinical immunologist; Elisabeth J. Schmalstieg MD and Charles F. Dreyer, MD, clinical neurologists; and Daniel H. Freeman, PhD and Daniel A. Goldman, MD, MPH, biostatisticians.

The following librarians provided important references for the investigation: 1) Lynn Burke, Julie M. Trumble, Anne B. Howard, Alex C. Benkowski, Robert O. Marlin, and Kelly L. Caldwell from the Moody Medical Library at the University of Texas Medical Branch in Galveston; 2) Herman Eberhardt, Curator, and Virginia Lewick, Archivist, at the Franklin D. Roosevelt Presidential Library in Hyde Park, New York; 3) Jessica B. Murphy, Reference Archivist for Public Services from the Center for the History of Medicine, Francis A. Countway Library of Medicine, Harvard Medical School; and 4) librarians at the Groton School Archives in Groton, Massachusetts.

Photographs of famous individuals depicted in this book were obtained from the professional staff of several institutions. 1) Photographs of Franklin Delano Roosevelt and Eleanor Roosevelt from Curator Herman Eberhardt, Archivist Virginia H. Lewick, and Archivist Matthew C. Hanson at the Franklin D. Roosevelt Presidential Library in Hyde Park, New York; 2) Eben Homer Bennet from Ronald Pesha at the Lubec Historical Society in Lubec, Maine; 3) Dr. William Williams Keen from F. Michael Angelo Scott at the Memorial Medical Library of Jefferson University Archives and Special Collections in Philadelphia,

Pennsylvania (Art/Photo Collection, AK-016); 4) Dr. Robert W. Lovett from Reference Librarian Jack Eckert at The Center for the History of Medicine at The Francis A. Countway Library of Medicine in Boston, Massachusetts; and 5) Dr. George W. Draper from Lead Archivist Margaret A. Hogan at the Rockefeller Archive Center in New York City, New York (Rockefeller University, RG 526, Box 5, Folder "Draper, George W."). Ann Newman, Cultural and Interpretation Manager at the Roosevelt Campobello International Park, provided the picture of the bedroom in the Roosevelt cottage where FDR lay ill during August 1921 with a severe neurological illness. Other photographs in the book are to our knowledge in the public domain. Doria Goldman and her son Nicholas helped to create Figures 1, 4, and 6.

Dr. Meredith A. Bennet, a physician at the New England Rehabilitation Hospital of Portland, Maine, provided important information concerning her great-grandfather, Dr. Eben Homer Bennet, who first cared for FDR during his neurological illness in 1921.

Mrs. Sandra Levine, the daughter-in-law of Dr. Samuel A. Levine, provided (through The Francis A. Countway Library of Medicine in Boston, Massachusetts) a previously unpublished document written by her father-in-law regarding FDR's 1921 neurological illness.

Dr. Christopher Gardner-Thorpe, Editor of the *Journal of Medical Biography* where our articles concerning FDR's neurological illness appeared, carefully critiqued and improved the manuscripts of the articles and wrote the foreword for this book. Dr. Charles McClelland, Emeritus Professor of History at the University of New Mexico at Albuquerque, New Mexico; Sandy Sheehy, the previous Director of the Development Office at the University of Texas Medical Branch in Galveston; Dr. Lynn Goldman, Dean of the School of Public Health at George Washington University; Dr. Nadia Hejazi, a neurologist at the FDA; Kim

Palkowetz and Beth Rudloff at the University of Texas Medical Branch in Galveston; and Gene Willard also reviewed and critiqued the book.

Barbara, Lynn, David, Daniel, Paul, Robert, Nadia, Douglas, Doria, and Frances in our family encouraged me to write this book and made helpful suggestions about certain aspects of the work. I could not have completed the book without Daniel's countless hours of formatting, editing, revising, indexing, and proofreading.

I dedicate this book to my wife, Barbara, who encouraged me from the beginning of my efforts five years ago to write the book. Whenever I became discouraged, she reminded me that I could learn from FDR's tenacity to recover and from his ability to accomplish so much for so many people. Barbara's love of life and learning was an even more important lesson to me. I wish that she could have lived to see the completed work.

Most Important People in This Story

Franklin Delano Roosevelt (FDR) - Stricken with paralysis in 1921.
Anna Eleanor Roosevelt - FDR's wife. Nursed him early in the illness.

Physicians Who Had a Role in FDR's Case

Eben Homer Bennet - Family physician. First saw FDR for his illness.
William W. Keen - Neurosurgeon. Saw FDR early in the illness.
Samuel A. Levine - Cardiologist. First suggested that FDR had polio.
Robert W. Lovett - Orthopedist. First diagnosed that FDR had polio.
George C. Draper - Internist. Cared for FDR during his hospitalization.

Scientists Involved in the Study of Poliomyelitis

Karl Landsteiner - First experimentally transmitted polioviruses.
Simon Flexner - Verified Landsteiner's discovery.
John Enders - Found how to culture polioviruses in the laboratory.
Hilary Koprowski - Made the first safe, effective live poliovirus vaccine.
Jonas Salk - Made the first safe, effective inactivated poliovirus vaccine.
Albert Sabin - Made the widely used live poliovirus vaccine.

Discoverers of Guillain-Barré Syndrome

Octave Landry - First described the disease (Landry's ascending paralysis).
Georges Guillain - Further elucidated the disease Landry described.
Jean Alexandre Barré - Colleague of Georges Guillain.
André Strohl - Colleague of Georges Guillain.

Other Important Figures

Francis Bacon - Philosopher. Described confirmation bias.
Thomas Bayes - Clergyman. Formulated "Bayes' Theorem".
Frederic Delano - FDR's uncle. Contacted Samuel Levine.
Louis Howe - FDR's advisor. Helped during the illness.

Timeline of Main Events in FDR's 1921 Illness

July 27 (Wednesday). (Day -14) FDR visits Boy Scout Jamboree.

August 5 (Friday). (Day -5) FDR begins to sail to Campobello on the *Sabalo*.

August 9 (Tuesday). (Day -1) FDR falls into the Bay of Fundy. Arrives at Campobello the same day.

August 10 (Wednesday) (Day 1). FDR sails on the *Vireo*. Helps put out a fire on nearby island. Jogs and swims. That evening, has lumbago, fatigue and chills.

August 11 (Thursday) (Day 2). FDR has fever. One leg becomes paralyzed. Then, the other leg becomes weak. Dr. Bennet diagnoses a *"heavy cold"*.

August 12 (Friday) (Day 3). Fever continues. Both legs are paralyzed. Numbness of legs is replaced by extreme pain. Unable to urinate or defecate.

August 13 (Saturday) (Day 4). FDR is paralyzed from the chest down. Arms are weak. Thumb muscles are weak. Fever, urinary retention, constipation and extreme pain continue. Dr. Keen examines FDR and diagnoses *"a clot of blood from a sudden congestion --- settled in the lower spinal cord."*

August 14 (Sunday) (Day 5). Eleanor fears that FDR has polio. She asks Louis Howe to write to Frederic Delano to find a medical specialist who might come quickly to see FDR.

August 17 (Wednesday) (Day 8). Fever is gone.

August 18 (Thursday) (Day 9). FDR has a brief period of delirium.

August 20 (Saturday) (Day 11). Delano consults Dr. Levine in Boston. Levine says, *"unquestionably Infantile Paralysis."* Delano recommends that FDR be seen by Levine. Instead, it is decided to have Dr. Lovett see FDR.

August 23 (Tuesday) (Day 14). Lovett meets with Levine in Boston. Both agree that FDR has polio. Lovett mentions in a telegram to Keen that a spinal tap would be useful, but makes clear that he cannot not do it.

August 24 (Wednesday) (Day 15). FDR paralyzed from the waist down. Back muscles, facial muscles, and muscles at the base of his left thumb weak. Lovett sees FDR, diagnoses paralytic polio. Lovett never mentions doing a spinal tap.

September 1 (Thursday) (Day 23). Still unable to urinate. Leg pain continues.

September 14 (Wednesday) (Day 36). FDR is improved but still paralyzed and in great pain. Taken by train to New York-Presbyterian Hospital. There, Dr. Draper agrees with polio diagnosis.

October 28 (Saturday). FDR somewhat improved. Discharged to home.

December. FDR remains paralyzed in the lower extremities.

Chapter 1. Prologue

"What's past is prologue." ~ William Shakespeare, *The Tempest*

ROOSEVELT DEAD AT 39

"It was learned yesterday that Mr. Franklin Delano Roosevelt, a past New York State Senator, the Assistant Secretary of the United States Navy during President Woodrow Wilson's Administration and World War I, and the nominee by the Democratic Party for Vice-President of the United States in 1920, died recently at his summer home on Campobello Island at age 39 due to infantile paralysis.

It was widely believed because of his service in the government and his recent candidacy for Vice-President of the United States that Mr. Roosevelt would be nominated for the office of the President of the United States in the near future.

Mr. Roosevelt's wife Anna Eleanor Roosevelt and his mother Sara Roosevelt are planning a memorial service for Mr. Roosevelt. As we learn the details of Mr. Roosevelt's illness and death and the time and location of the memorial service, an announcement will appear in The New York Times."

New York Times. August 27, 1921

The reason for this fictional introduction is because the future thirty-second president of the United States, Franklin Delano Roosevelt (FDR) (1882-1945) (Portrait 1), came close to dying when he was age 39, from a severe neurological illness characterized by an alarming, symmetric, ascending paralysis and severe protracted pains to the slightest touch.[1,2]

At the peak of his illness in August 1921, one of FDR's physicians, a national expert on infantile paralysis (paralytic poliomyelitis, alias paralytic polio), decided that FDR had paralytic polio.[1,2] Several weeks after the onset of his illness, FDR gradually recovered strength in the upper parts of his body, and most of the other manifestations of his illness slowly lessened and then disappeared. However, his lower extremities remained paralyzed. Without the aid of leg braces, crutches or other supports, he was unable to stand or walk. A few years after his illness and despite his extensive residual motor impairments, he re-entered politics. In 1932, eleven years after his illness, FDR was elected President of the United States.

Portrait 1.

Franklin Delano Roosevelt.

Franklin Roosevelt (1882-1945) was stricken with paralysis at age 39 in August 1921.

Re-examination of FDR's 1921 Illness in 2000

For eight decades following FDR's 1921 neurological illness, physicians and historians who wrote about him or poliomyelitis agreed that his illness was paralytic polio. Like countless others before me, I did not doubt the diagnosis. Then, around the year 2000, I unexpectedly became aware that the diagnosis was probably incorrect. That initiated a retrospective investigation of FDR's 1921 neurological illness that culminated in an article published in the *Journal of Medical Biography* in 2003.[2]

Even before the exploration of FDR's neurological illness began, my colleagues and I realized that the task might be difficult. That was because FDR, the members of his family (including his wife Anna Eleanor Roosevelt who was with him throughout his illness), and the physicians who cared for him, had long since passed away.

The problem was how to explore the possible cause of FDR's illness. I wondered whether "medical archeology" might help. Indeed, genetic analyses of tissue or other physical remains sometimes reveals definitive information concerning the nature of diseases in humans who have been deceased for hundreds (or even thousands) of years. Unfortunately, it would not have helped even if structurally intact genes from FDR's tissues were available, since no genes predict the most likely neurological diseases, including poliomyelitis, that were considered in his case. Furthermore, the genetic code for polioviruses (poliovirus RNA) does not persist in survivors of poliomyelitis.[3,4] And even if it did, it would not have distinguished between non-paralytic and paralytic polio.

However, we were fortunate that sufficient archival records from FDR, his family, and his physicians concerning his case permitted a retrospective investigation of the cause of his 1921 neurological illness.

In addition, our reappraisal was greatly aided by a wealth of discoveries in the intervening years regarding neurology, microbiology, immunology, and the diseases that were potential causes of his illness.

Publication of the Investigation and Its Impact (2003)

After we completed exploring FDR's devastating neurological illness, we concluded that the illness was not paralytic polio, but was most likely a different neurological disease caused by an autoimmune mechanism. Because of the historical and medical importance of the discovery, we prepared a report of our investigations for a peer-reviewed journal, the *Journal of Medical Biography*. The manuscript was accepted and published in November 2003.[2]

On the day of publication, the article was the most featured health news item on Yahoo News and Google News. For several weeks afterwards, accounts of our findings appeared in *The New York Times*, *USA Today*, and many other major newspapers in the United States and abroad, on National Public Radio in the United States, in the research journal *Science*, and on three major American national television news programs. There were also many online commentaries concerning our article. I was interviewed briefly on CBS Television and more extensively on National Public Radio in the United States. In addition, a few historians and physicians commented in the public media about the article.

Reactions to the Publication

Some commentators agreed with our analysis; most did not. Negative comments gained the most media attention. Most commentators were confident that Roosevelt had paralytic polio. However, the scientific basis for their beliefs was not expressed. No specific pros or cons concerning our article were presented.

By the first part of 2004, the controversy concerning the results of our published investigation of FDR's illness seemed to fade. But then our study was questioned in a peer-reviewed journal publication, in a number of books concerning FDR, in a few histories of poliomyelitis, and in a book concerning the neurological disease that we felt was the cause of his illness. These physicians and historians held fast to the notion that FDR contracted paralytic polio in 1921.

Some newer historical works concerning FDR mentioned our views on the diagnosis of his neurological disease, but they did not deal with it in any detail. In essence, many historians and physicians still believed that FDR had paralytic polio. Some histories stated without a doubt that the polio diagnosis was correct.

In some others, the possibility of an alternative diagnosis based upon our analysis was mentioned in passing.

Since we did not respond to the critics, some of our fellow physicians and other colleagues asked whether we had come to believe that FDR had paralytic polio. We had not, since none of the critics had made any kind of a convincing case that FDR had paralytic polio in 1921. To make this clear, my colleagues and I wrote a rebuttal (published in 2016) concerning the criticisms of our initial article for the same peer-reviewed journal where the first article appeared.[5]

Why This Book Was Written

Once our second article was accepted for publication, I realized that a book about the cause of FDR's neurological illness was worthwhile to prepare for several reasons.

1. Although the story of FDR's 1921 illness had been told many times, the medical aspects of the case had never been completely revealed. In addition to overturning the polio diagnosis, this book is the first complete account of his illness.

2. The book format allows a wider audience to read about the misdiagnosis of FDR's neurological disease, permits the story to be told in a more informal way than is required in a scientific article, allows the inclusion of relevant side stories that may be interesting to readers, and allows me to give more information that helps to understand why FDR likely did not have paralytic polio.

3. It had not previously been revealed how close FDR came to dying, and how his wife Eleanor (Portrait 2) most likely saved his life.

4. It could be explained why the geographic site where FDR became ill, Campobello Island in Canada (Figure 1), set the stage for the diagnostic dilemma and his near demise.

5. Others had claimed that FDR had a lumbar puncture at the time of his illness, based on an "unpublished note" by a physician consulted in 1921, and that the cerebrospinal fluid findings must have been consistent with paralytic polio, since that was the diagnosis made at the time. It was therefore important to publish the "unpublished note", and assess whether it provides evidence that a lumbar puncture was done. As explained in detail later (see page 183), there is no historical evidence that a lumbar puncture was done, and an analysis of the cerebrospinal fluid at the time of the supposed tap would likely not have been of diagnostic value anyway.

Portrait 2.

Anna Eleanor Roosevelt.

Eleanor Roosevelt (1884-1962), through her nursing, helped to save FDR's life during his 1921 illness.

6. It could be explained why a change in the diagnosis of FDR's neurological illness in 1921 would not have altered the medical management of his illness or the extent of his final recovery.

7. It was important to explain why setting the record straight concerning the cause of FDR's illness matters, even beyond the obvious requirement for historical accuracy.

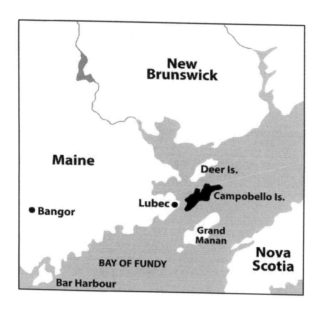

Figure 1. Location of Campobello Island. Campobello Island, in black, was where FDR and his family were vacationing when his 1921 illness began.

8. As this book was being written, a concerted, serious (though not peer-reviewed) article, written by three physicians, appeared in the medical literature attempting to *"put this debate to rest"* by proving that FDR had paralytic polio. The article did not put the debate to rest. This book allowed me the chance to fully respond to their detailed, but faulty, arguments.

9. I did not sense another reason for this book until the work neared completion. The physicians who cared for FDR during his near-fatal illness in August 1921 were trapped in the time in which they practiced medicine, when comparatively little was known about the biological and medical sciences needed to understand the cause of FDR's illness. That was even more so in the United States than in Western Europe. The theme that all of us are trapped in the circumstances of our time inspired the book title *Prisoners of Time.*

Chapter 2. Prelude to the Illness

"Men are not prisoners of fate, but only prisoners of their own minds." ~
Franklin Delano Roosevelt

Before FDR became ill in August of 1921, he was well known for his service in the New York State Senate, his role as the Assistant Secretary of The Navy just before and during World War I, and his campaign for the Vice-Presidency of the United States in 1920.[1,6,7] This earlier part of FDR's life is recounted because it is a reminder that he was exposed to many thousands of people in the United States and Western Europe long before 1921. Those exposures are potentially important in considering the cause of his 1921 neurological illness.

FDR's Childhood and Early Adulthood

Some historians have argued that FDR contracted paralytic polio comparatively late in life because he had a sheltered childhood. It is true that Franklin was exposed to few children during his preschool period. Franklin was tutored at home until age eight. Then he traveled with his parents to Germany, where his father sought to improve his own health by using salt springs through which carbon dioxide bubbled. At Bad Nauheim in Germany, Franklin was in school with children his own age. In the summer of 1896, when he was age 14, he and his tutor, Mr. Arthur Dumper, bicycled extensively in the area around Strasbourg, then part of Germany. Besides being arrested four times in one day for minor offenses, Franklin undoubtedly was exposed to many people during that time, including children.

After his last stay in Germany during the summer of 1896, Franklin entered an exclusive private school at Groton, Connecticut. For the next four years, he led a Spartan life at Groton. Except for a bout of scarlet fever, he was well during that period. At age 18, he entered Harvard College, where he was with many students in their late teens and early twenties. After graduating from Harvard and attending law school at Columbia University, he briefly worked in a law firm before running for the New York State Senate.

FDR's Political Career Begins (1910)

Although he was a lawyer, FDR was not very interested in the practice of law. Instead, he wished to enter politics. He greatly admired Theodore Roosevelt, who was his fifth cousin and had become his step-uncle after his marriage to Anna Eleanor Roosevelt in 1905. FDR wished to emulate him by eventually becoming President of the United States. His subsequent career closely paralleled Theodore Roosevelt's (New York Senate, Assistant Secretary of the Navy, Governor of New York).

Election to New York Senate - "Typhoid Fever"

The first step in FDR's political career was to run for the New York State Senate. At age 28 (1910), he was easily elected after a spirited campaign. He did well as a senator. Two years later, when he was campaigning for re-election, he and Eleanor were struck by "typhoid fever". The details concerning the illness are lacking, but it may have helped trigger his 1921 neurological illness, as discussed later in this book.

FDR quickly recovered from the illness and was readily re-elected to the New York State Senate. His progressive political stances did not always agree with those taken by the leadership of the Democratic Party in the Senate. He was at odds with "Tammany Hall", the powerful New York City Democratic Party political machine. Despite those differences, his influence in the New York State Senate grew over time. Indeed, in 1913, FDR led an effort for the Democratic

Party to nominate Woodrow Wilson (1856-1924) for President of the United States.

Assistant Secretary of the Navy (1913)

Soon after Woodrow Wilson became President in 1913, he appointed FDR to the office of Assistant Secretary of the Navy at the suggestion of the Secretary of the Navy, Josephus Daniels (1862-1948). Daniels handled the formalities of the Department, whereas FDR was responsible for the major policy decisions. As the Assistant Secretary, he took a more vigorous stance to strengthen the Navy than most others in the Administration, including Secretary Daniels and President Wilson. Because he felt that it was likely that the United States would be drawn into World War I,[8] he initiated a number of important reforms. He helped to revise the system of promotion of naval personnel, how civilian personnel were directed, and the administration of the United States Naval Docks. More importantly, he led the effort to create the Navy Reserve. He envisioned that the 50,000 reservists could be readily activated during an emergency, such as the war that was to come.

Acute Abdominal Illness (1915)

In 1915, FDR experienced sudden abdominal pains that were suspected to be due to acute appendicitis. However, because the pains subsided within a few days, no surgery was performed. It is therefore doubtful that he had acute appendicitis. Instead, the illness was more likely a self-limited inflammation of the intestinal tract, such as mesenteric adenitis, viral enteritis, or bacterial enteritis. The potential relevance of both his bout of severe abdominal pains in 1915 and his "typhoid fever" in 1912, as causative factors for his 1921 neurological illness, will be considered later in this book.

United States Enters World War I (1917)

During the first part of FDR's service as Assistant Secretary of the Navy, it was feared that the country would be drawn into World War I.[8] The possibility heightened on January 16, 1917, when Arthur Zimmermann (1864-1940), the Foreign Secretary of the German Empire, sent an encrypted telegram to Heinrich von Eckardt, the German Ambassador in Mexico City.[9] In the telegram, Zimmermann instructed von Eckardt to ask Mexico to join Germany if the United States entered the war on the side of the Allies. In turn, the Germans promised Mexico military aid, and if Germany prevailed, Mexico was to be given territories in Texas, New Mexico, and Arizona. Von Eckardt also urged Mexico to broker an alliance between Germany and Japan. The Mexican Government rejected the proposal because they did not believe that Germany would be able to defeat the United States.

British Intelligence deciphered the Zimmerman telegram on January 17, 1917. Two days later, a translation was given to Edward Bell, Secretary of the U.S. Embassy in Britain. Bell sent the telegram to the United States Ambassador, Walter Page, who in turn gave it to President Wilson. The revelation helped to set the stage for the entrance of the United States into the First World War.

The United States went to war because of the sinking of the British ocean liner RMS *Lusitania* in 1915 by a German U-boat that killed 128 Americans, the inflammatory nature of the Zimmermann telegram, and the sinking of several United States merchant vessels in 1917.[8,9]

The United States Navy was quickly marshaled to protect ships carrying soldiers, arms, and other supplies to the allied nations in Western Europe from German U-boats. The American Navy joined the British Grand Fleet in December 1917 to blockade the German coast and thus bottle up the German Navy. The blockade also reduced the importation of foods into Germany and thereby intensified the food shortages in that country.[10]

FDR in Europe during World War I (1918)

As World War I was winding down in the summer of 1918, FDR crossed the Atlantic Ocean on the USS Destroyer *Dyer*.[6,7] In England, he inspected the American naval facilities and met with Winston Churchill. FDR then visited several battlefields and saw the carnage of the war being waged on the Western Front in France. In that respect, he was briefly under fire at *La Citadelle* in Verdun on August 6, 1918.

After visiting Italy to investigate the inactivity of the Italian fleet moored in Taranto harbor, he returned to England. On September 8, 1918, FDR left from Brest, France for New York City on a large troop carrier, USS *Leviathan*.

FDR Contracts Influenza (1918)

Some 6,000 military personnel were commonly on trans-Atlantic voyages of *Leviathan*. During previous voyages of *Leviathan* in the summer of 1918, the pandemic influenza virus infected and killed great numbers of passengers. On the September voyage that Roosevelt took from France to New York City, the virus struck the ship's personnel and travelers. Many died and were buried at sea during the eleven-day voyage. The exact death toll is unknown, although according to the Department of the Navy, on the return trip to Europe that began on September 29, 1918, out of 9,000 on the ship, about 3,000 became ill and 91 died. It is likely that the toll was similar during FDR's trip. During the voyage, Roosevelt became very ill with influenza and a complicating pneumonia.[7] When *Leviathan* landed in New York City, his illness had largely resolved.

Near End of FDR's Marriage (1918)

Shortly after FDR landed in New York City on September 20, Eleanor discovered in FDR's luggage a package of love letters from Eleanor's social secretary, Lucy Mercer. In keeping with her high moral principles, Eleanor immediately demanded a divorce.

Heated discussions ensued between Eleanor, Franklin, and Franklin's mother Sara. Sara argued that a divorce would ruin Franklin's political career and that Eleanor would have to raise their five children on her own. Furthermore, Sara threatened to disinherit Franklin if he and Eleanor divorced – to cut him off from her considerable financial fortune and his birthright to the 900-acre estate of Springwood at Hyde Park. Louis Howe, Roosevelt's closest advisor, also went to great lengths to persuade Eleanor and Franklin to keep the marriage together.

Finally, Eleanor relented. Although it is doubtful that Eleanor and Franklin ever completely reconciled, the marriage worked to their mutual advantage. Eleanor not only rescued FDR's political future, but also probably saved his life in August 1921 when he was felled by a neurological illness that was diagnosed as paralytic polio.

Mission to Europe - Tonsillectomy (1919)

In January 1919, while leaders of the Allied Nations were negotiating the end of World War I and the creation of the League of Nations, FDR went abroad to sell off the remaining United States naval assets in Europe. Afterwards, he returned to the United States.

In December 1919, FDR had a tonsillectomy, apparently because of recurrent upper respiratory infections. The details of the upper respiratory illnesses and the surgery are lacking, except that his recovery from the surgery was uneventful.

How others have mistakenly suggested that the tonsillectomy may have predisposed FDR to polio will be discussed later in this book.

Vice Presidential Campaign (1920)

In June 1920, the delegates of the Democratic Party met at their convention and chose FDR to run for Vice President of the United States. He accepted the nomination and accordingly resigned as the Assistant Secretary of the Navy. During the rest of the summer and autumn of 1920, Roosevelt conducted a spirited electoral campaign. Roosevelt gave as many as 800 speeches during August through October of 1920. His campaign that summer and fall exposed him to tens of thousands of people including children and young adults who were potentially infected with polioviruses.

The Republicans Warren Harding and Calvin Coolidge handily defeated the Democratic ticket of James Cox and Franklin Roosevelt. However, because of the campaign, Roosevelt became well known to the public and to the leaders of the Democratic Party.

Thus, many leaders in the Democratic Party predicted that Franklin Roosevelt would be a future Democratic nominee for the President of the United States. However, at the end of 1920 FDR retired from politics, began a law practice in New York City, and became Vice President of the Fidelity and Deposit Company of Maryland.

Chapter 3. Campobello Island

"Canada is a place of infinite promise." ~ John Maynard Keynes

It was ironic that FDR became ill at a place where the Roosevelt family had so much pleasure. It was a long-standing tradition of Roosevelt's family to spend their summer vacation on Campobello Island in Canada in the Bay of Fundy (Figure 1, page 10).

Figure 2. The Roosevelt Cottage on Campobello Island. FDR became ill and nearly died there in August 1921.

Environment of the Island

Campobello still is a thinly populated island located just south of New Brunswick and northeast of the northern tip of Maine. The temperatures on the island are usually pleasant during the summer. The mild summers are ideal for outdoor activities.

In 1921, Campobello Island could only be reached by boat and was not connected to the mainland by telephone. The island had no medical facilities. The closest physician lived in nearby Lubec, Maine. The nearest American hospital was the Eastern Maine General Hospital in Bangor, Maine, which was about 114 miles (about 183 kilometers) from Lubec.

Franklin and Eleanor Roosevelt had a 34-room "Cottage" on Campobello Island (Figure 2) that was well equipped for family and friends.

Journey to Campobello - Summer of 1921

In June 1921, Eleanor and the Roosevelt's five children arrived for their vacation. FDR was delayed because of business commitments and because of the congressional investigation of the infamous "Newport Sex Scandal" that happened when he was the Assistant Secretary of the Navy.[11] After the matter was laid to rest and other items of business were settled, FDR briefly visited a Boy Scout Jamboree held at Bear Mountain in the upper part of New York State on July 27.

On August 5, 1921, he embarked on the last part of his journey to Campobello by sailing on his friend Van Lear Black's steam-powered yacht, the *Sabalo*. Four days later, while sailing on the Bay of Fundy, FDR slipped off the deck of the *Sabalo* into the cold waters of the Bay.[1,6,7,12] He quickly came back on board. He was uninjured but chilled,[1,12] for the water temperature in the Bay during the summer was usually about 45 °F (7 °C).[13] (In an odd turn of fate, Van Lear Black fell off the *Sabalo* in 1930 while yachting off the coast of New Jersey. His body was never recovered.)

Undaunted, the next day (August 10) FDR, Eleanor, and two of their sons sailed on the Bay on their 24-foot boat, the *Vireo*. During the sail, they spotted a fire on a nearby small, uninhabited island and landed to put it out. After some hours, the blaze was extinguished. They then sailed back across Cobscook Bay, to a long wooden slip that jutted out into Friar's Bay in front of the Roosevelt Cottage. Afterwards, they jogged a few miles across Campobello to swim in Lake Glen Severn and in Herring Cove at the Bay.

Chapter 4. Acute Neurological Illness

"I didn't get the usual reaction, the glow I'd expected." ~ FDR

Figure 3. FDR's Bedroom on the Second Floor of the "Cottage". He lay ill there from August 10 until September 14, 1921.

The neurological illness that struck FDR occurred while he and his family were vacationing on Campobello Island in August 1921.

Onset (August 10, 1921)

After his swim, FDR returned to their cottage on the evening of August 10. He later remarked, *"I didn't get the usual reaction, the glow I'd expected"*.[14] As he walked slowly back to the house, he complained of a *"slight case of lumbago"*,[1] felt *"too tired even to dress"*,[1,14] and had chills.[1,14,15] FDR was quite exhausted and immediately tried to rest. Finally, because of intense fatigue, early that evening he retired to sleep. He slowly climbed the stairs to his bedroom (Figure 3), undressed, and went to sleep. It was the last time that he walked unaided.

He experienced chills that *"lasted practically all night"*.[1,14] The next morning (August 11), he had fever and profound weakness in one leg. It is unclear from the historical accounts whether it was the right or left leg. That afternoon, the leg was completely paralyzed (Figure 4).[1,12,14] That evening, the other leg weakened.[1,12,14] The next morning, both legs were completely paralyzed (Figure 4).[1,12,14]

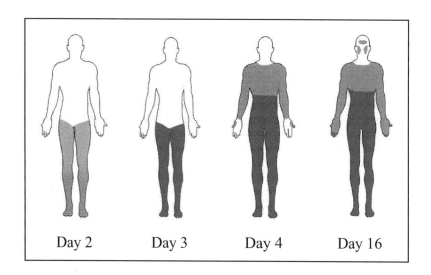

| Day 2 | Day 3 | Day 4 | Day 16 |

Figure 4. Progression of FDR's Muscle Weakness and Paralysis. Day 2 of Illness. Lower extremities weak. *Day 3.* Lower extremities paralyzed. *Day 4.* Weakness and paralysis ascend to the upper chest and thumbs. *Day 16.* Paralysis increased; facial muscles involved.

That same day (August 12, the third day of the illness), his temperature was 102 °F (38.9 °C).[1,14] He *"felt thoroughly achy all over"*.[1,14] *"There was no special pain along the spine and no rigidity of the neck"*.[1,14] FDR had transient numbness of his legs at that time,[15] but that was quickly replaced by extreme pains in those sites. In that respect, *"His skin and muscles had developed a sensitivity to touch so painful that he could not stand the pressure of the bedclothes, and even the movement of the slightest breeze across his skin caused acute distress"*.[1] In a letter that Eleanor sent to James R. Roosevelt (FDR's older half-brother, referred to as "Rosy" in the letter) on August 14, she reported that FDR *"had so much pain in his back and legs"*.[15] FDR stated in a letter to Dr. William Egleston dated October 11, 1924 that *"all the muscles from the hips down were extremely sensitive to the touch and I had to have the knees supported by pillows. This condition of extreme discomfort lasted about three weeks."*[14]

Portrait 3.

Dr. Eben Homer Bennet.

A family physician from Lubec, Maine, Bennet (1848-1944) was the first physician to see FDR during his 1921 illness. His diagnosis was a *"heavy cold"*.

Dr. Eben Bennet's Examination and Diagnosis

Eleanor was alarmed by the illness and sent a member of the community, Captain Calder, to the nearby town of Lubec, Maine to ask Dr. Eben Homer Bennet (1848-1944), a family physician (Portrait 3), to see Franklin. That same day (August 11), Dr. Bennet traveled by boat over the "Narrows", a short stretch of ocean water between Lubec and Campobello, to examine FDR. In 1921, travel by boat was the only way to come to Campobello.

Bennet was very familiar with the Roosevelt family. He tended to Eleanor after the birth of her son Franklin Jr. in 1914, and to other members of the Roosevelt family for minor illnesses when they were vacationing on the island. Bennet's diagnosis was a "*heavy cold*".[1] However, by the next day (August 12), Franklin could not sit unaided because of the ascending muscular weakness that included the lower half of his body (Figure 4).[1,14]

By the fourth day of the illness (August 13), FDR was paralyzed from the chest down. Moreover, his arms, shoulders, and thumbs were weak (Figure 4, page 22).[1,14,15] The fever continued. Because Eleanor was very distressed by the steady worsening of her husband's illness, an additional medical opinion was sought.

Portrait 4.

Dr. William Williams Keen.

Keen (1837-1932), a famous neurosurgeon, examined FDR on day four of his illness. His diagnosis was "*a clot of blood from a sudden congestion --- settled in the lower spinal cord.*"

Dr. William Keen's Examination and Diagnosis

Eleanor consequently asked Dr. Bennet to see whether a suitable expert concerning such medical problems was vacationing on the nearby mainland of Maine and whether such a physician would come to Campobello Island to examine FDR. Bennet quickly discovered that Dr. William Williams Keen (Portrait 4) (1837-1932), an 84-year old retired famous neurosurgeon from Philadelphia, was vacationing in nearby Bar Harbor on the northern coast of Maine.

Keen was famous for his pioneering surgical methods to remove brain tumors, and for his discovery of causalgia, a constant, burning pain following an injury to a peripheral nerve. Furthermore, Keen had assisted in removing an epithelioma (abnormal growth of epithelium) of the hard palate of President Grover Cleveland in 1893.[16] Because of his knowledge and experience with neurological diseases, Keen was seemingly an ideal choice to examine Franklin and determine what was wrong and what to do about it.

Keen travelled approximately 100 miles by boat to Campobello that same day (August 13, the fourth day of FDR's illness).

After his examination, Keen concluded that FDR had *"a clot of blood from a sudden congestion --- settled in the lower spinal cord"*.[1,15] Keen did not explain how such a condition could have occurred. Indeed, the diagnosis was peculiar since there was no history or physical evidence of trauma to FDR's back, and there was no evidence of a systemic disease that could have produced congestion or clot formation. Regardless, Keen was confident of his diagnosis. Unfortunately, he advised deep muscle massages that must have produced considerable pain because of FDR's great sensitivity to pain (hyperesthesia).

The Illness Worsens

During the next few days, FDR's hands, arms, and shoulders progressively weakened. Because of marked difficulty in defecation, frequent enemas were required.[1,14] From August 12 (the third day of the illness) throughout the next two weeks, he could not urinate.[1,14] To deal with the urinary retention, Bennet supplied Eleanor with thin glass catheters and instructed her how to insert them into Franklin's bladder through the urethra.[1] With little nursing background, Eleanor was suddenly thrust into the role of providing highly skilled patient care. Her actions could save her husband's life, or lead to potentially fatal complications.

By the seventh to eighth day of the illness, the fever was gone.[1,15] Except for a brief period of "delirium" on the ninth day of the illness (August 18) that might have been due to sleep deprivation, FDR's mental state was unimpaired.[2,15] The "delirium" was not described, but apparently it was brief, because it was not mentioned again in the records of the illness.

Fears for the Family

Because of the paralysis, Eleanor greatly feared that Franklin had paralytic polio.[1,15] If that were the case, their children, Anna (15 years), James (14 years), Elliot (11 years), Franklin Jr. (7 years), and John (5 years) were in danger of contracting the disease. Consequently, she kept the children away from their father, except to let them speak briefly to him from his bedroom door.

Eleanor was increasingly alarmed by Franklin's deterioration, the growing prospect of permanent paralysis, Dr. Keen's unusual diagnosis, and his exorbitant $600 fee (equivalent to about $7,300 in 2010 dollars).[17] Franklin and Eleanor were also greatly troubled because the paralysis was progressing and the involved skeletal muscles were wasting away.

Eleanor continued to be concerned that Franklin had paralytic polio. That was very understandable. The fear of paralytic polio was very strong at that time because of the severe epidemic of polio that had struck New York City and some areas of New England in 1916. In that epidemic, more fully described in Chapter 8, 23,900 cases of paralytic polio with 5,000 deaths occurred, mostly in young children.

Portrait 5.

Dr. Samuel A. Levine.

Levine (1891-1966) was the first physician to declare that FDR had paralytic polio.

Dr. Samuel A. Levine's Role in the Diagnosis of Polio

Because of her doubts and fears, Eleanor asked Louis Howe, FDR's close confidant, to get more medical help. On August 14, Howe wrote to Sara Roosevelt's brother Frederic Adrian Delano, about FDR's illness and asked him to find a medical specialist who might come quickly to see FDR. Delano spoke with Dr. Parker in Washington, DC, who suspected paralytic polio. On August 20, Delano contacted the Harvard Infantile Paralysis Commission to see if one of their physicians could see FDR, since paralytic polio was suspected. Neither Dr. Francis W. Peabody, an internist, nor Dr. Robert W. Lovett, an orthopedist, was immediately available. Instead, Delano was advised to consult an internist / cardiologist in Boston, Dr. Samuel A. Levine (1891-1966) (Portrait 5) of the Peter Brent Brigham Hospital, who had seen many children with paralytic polio earlier in his medical career.[18] On August 20, Delano wrote to Eleanor that Levine said, *"it was unquestionably Infantile Paralysis"*.[19] Levine's opinion provided even more reason to believe that FDR had been struck by paralytic polio. Although Levine did not see FDR, he thus played an important role in establishing the diagnosis of paralytic polio.

Dr. Robert W. Lovett Diagnoses Paralytic Polio

After Eleanor was told about Levine's diagnosis, she asked Bennet and Keen to
seek an expert on polio to come as soon as possible to see FDR. In his letter to
Eleanor, dated August 20, Delano had recommended that Levine be called for.
Instead, the decision was made to contact Dr. Robert W. Lovett (1859-1925)
(Portrait 6), from the Infantile Paralysis Commission at Harvard. Lovett, a
respected orthopedist, had written an influential book about paralytic polio in
1917.[20] As fate would have it, Keen found that Lovett was planning to vacation
in Newport, Maine in the next few days. Keen thus arranged for Lovett to see
FDR as soon as possible. On the day before his visit, Lovett telegraphed Keen
from Boston. *"Have telegraphed wife of patient – unless already done spinal
tapping, cell count, & globular reaction[†] would be useful. This I cannot do
personally"*.[21] The question whether a spinal tap was done then or at any other
period during FDR's illness will be considered later in this book.

Portrait 6.

Dr. Robert W. Lovett.

Lovett (1859-1925) diagnosed *"infantile
paralysis"* in FDR's case on day 16 of his
illness.

[†] "Globular reaction" means protein measurement.

Before he left Boston to see FDR, Lovett met with Dr. Samuel Levine to discuss FDR's case. Levine expressed no doubt that FDR had paralytic polio. Further details of that meeting will be recounted in Chapter 20 when the question of a spinal tap will be considered further.

The next day (August 24, the fifteenth day of the illness), Lovett arrived at Campobello Island by boat after traveling by train from Boston to Eastport in Northern Maine. In a letter to Dr. George Draper that was sent on September 12, 1921, he stated the following. *"I saw him with Dr. W. W. Keen of Philadelphia . . . There was some uncertainty in their minds about the diagnosis, but I thought it was perfectly clear so far as the physical findings were concerned and I never feel that the history is of much value anyway. . . . he was tender when I examined him, but not excessively so, so that my examination had to be more or less superficial."*[21]

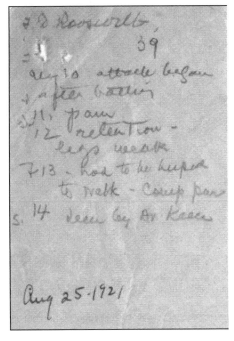

Figure 5.

Robert Lovett's History of FDR's Illness.

Lovett's case notes from his August 24, 1921 examination of FDR. From the FDR Library.

Lovett found that FDR's body temperature was 100 °F (37.8 °C), slightly elevated, assuming that the temperature was taken orally. Although the fever was gone, Lovett found (September 12, 1921 letter to Draper) that FDR was paralyzed from the waist down, and that his back muscles, facial muscles, and the muscles at the base of his left thumb were weak (Figure 4, page 22).[21] Lovett also noted that FDR continued to experience intense pain in the lower extremities in reaction to the slightest touch, and could not urinate. Lovett's diagnosis was paralytic polio.[21] Much to Franklin and Eleanor's relief, the muscle massages were stopped because of FDR's exquisite, protracted sensitivity to pain.

Although Lovett felt that FDR had *"a mild case within the range of possible complete recovery"*, his prognosis was possibly more guarded in other parts of the September 12, 1921 letter to Draper.[21]

Further Progression of the Illness

The symmetrical paralysis had ascended, and the involved muscles continued to atrophy (Figure 4, page 22). Severe pains to the slightest touch persisted in the lower extremities. Because of the progression of the illness, FDR's physicians advised FDR and Eleanor that he was too ill to be moved to a major hospital in the United States.

Regression to an Infantile State

It must have been a nightmarish situation for Franklin and Eleanor. Although Franklin's physicians reassured them that he would recover, the progression of the illness must have been alarming. Franklin was reduced to an infantile state. He was unable to tend to his most elementary needs – personal hygiene, eating, drinking, dressing, urinating, and defecating. Furthermore, the intense pains after the slightest movement must have been a trial for him and Eleanor. Repeated catheterizations of the bladder with thin glass catheters for two weeks must have been very difficult and probably demeaning. Moreover, the paralysis ascended to involve more of Franklin's body (Figure 4), including the intercostals (muscles between the ribs) responsible for voluntary respirations and the muscles of the upper extremities including his hands.

In August 1921, the days at Campobello were long and sunny, but the scene in Roosevelt's bedroom was in sharp contrast, given FDR's progressive illness, helplessness, and unrelenting pains. Except for brief periods of relief by FDR's closest advisor, Louis Howe, Eleanor was Franklin's full-time nurse. During the most dangerous period of his illness, the first two weeks, she slept on a couch in Franklin's bedroom to tend to her husband's needs. She encouraged Franklin, fed him to maintain his nutrition, washed him to keep him clean and prevent skin infections, turned him frequently to prevent pressure sores (decubitus ulcers) that are prone to become infected, moved him frequently to prevent clot formation in his lower limbs, gave him enemas to evacuate his lower intestinal tract, and repeatedly catheterized his bladder.

Dangers of Bladder Catheterizations

Eleanor was instructed by FDR's physicians to insert thin glass catheters to empty Franklin's bladder because he could not urinate. That was necessary, but the catheterizations could have caused a urinary tract infection due to the introduction of bacterial contaminants during the procedures. A urinary tract infection would have been potentially fatal, since antibiotics were not available for treating such infections in 1921. In addition, the thin glass catheters were fragile and prone to break when they were inserted into or removed from the bladder.[22,23] In that event, the bladder or urethra might have been perforated, which would have led to bleeding, a severe urinary tract infection, or a fatal abdominal infection. It was all the more remarkable that Eleanor had never catheterized a patient before. Except for a brief appearance of leukocytes in the urine,[21] (Bennet letter to Lovett, September 6, 1921), there was no indication of a urinary infection.

Possibility of Nutritional Deficiencies

Malnutrition was a potential threat because FDR could not feed himself. However, the danger was minimal for several reasons. 1) FDR's nutritional state immediately before the start of the illness was apparently excellent. 2) The chance of a deficiency in vitamin D was low given that he had been exposed to abundant sunlight for several days before the illness. That should have provided ample synthesis in the skin of vitamin D1 (the precursor of the bioactive form, vitamin D3).[24] 3) The chance of a symptomatic vitamin C (ascorbic acid) deficiency was also low given the adequacy of his diet and that the clinical manifestations of ascorbic acid deficiency do not usually appear until some weeks after body stores of ascorbic acid are depleted.[25] 4) Other nutrient deficiencies were improbable except for a protein or calorie deficiency. However, Eleanor went to great lengths to feed Franklin during the height of his illness. The reports from his physicians suggest that there were no clinical signs of malnutrition.

Eleanor's Nursing Care

Eleanor's past provides some indication how she was able to nurse FDR so expertly during the most dangerous part of his illness. Her need to care for others was evident during the early part of her marriage when she spent a great deal of time caring for the sick and needy.[26] She also received informal training in nursing from Miss Blanche Spring, an excellent nurse at St. Luke's Hospital in New York City who helped with the birth of her third child, Franklin Jr., who lived less than eight months, and cared for him during his fatal illness. During World War I, Eleanor spent much of her time visiting hospitalized American soldiers, working in canteens for soldiers who were departing for the war, and campaigning to raise funds to improve the care of soldiers who had sustained severe mental disorders from combat.

Many years later, when she was famous in her own right, Eleanor revealed her feelings about service to others. *"You must do the thing you think you cannot do."*[27]

Even more telling to the strength of her character was that just three years before Franklin's illness, she discovered Franklin's marital infidelity that nearly ended their marriage. Now, Eleanor devotedly cared for her desperately ill husband who had once betrayed her.

As will be discussed later, the care of seriously ill patients even in modern intensive care units is beset with many difficulties, even though the facilities are staffed with expert healthcare personnel and equipped with sophisticated medical devices. However, in August 1921, FDR's survival depended principally upon Eleanor's unrelenting efforts.

Eleanor was directed and advised by FDR's physicians, but she was the one who carried out his care. Her success was evidence of her character, her intelligence, and her empathy for less fortunate people. Surely, she was largely responsible for FDR's survival.

Eleanor, with the help of FDR's closest advisor, Louis Howe, also communicated with the rest of the family, FDR's physicians, and close friends. Indeed, she initiated the effort to find a leading expert in paralytic polio to examine him. During the long travail, Eleanor also encouraged Franklin to keep up his spirits despite the gravity of the situation. Except for a brief period of "delirium" on the ninth day of the illness, FDR's mental faculties were unimpaired.

Eleanor reassured the children that their father would recover. Lovett also expressed that view when he first saw FDR. However, after several weeks, it must have been clear that a full recovery was improbable.

Fears for the Roosevelt Family during August 1921

There was considerable concern that one or more of the Roosevelt children might come down with polio. There were several reasons for that concern. 1) FDR's physicians believed that he had paralytic polio. 2) Summer was the peak season for polio in the United States. 3) It seemed likely that if FDR had polio, the polioviruses could spread from him to his children from close contact.

Because of that apprehension, the children were kept away from their father for at least the first three weeks of his illness. A tutor (Jean Sherwood), her mother (Sidney Sherwood), Louis Howe's wife (Grace Howe), and a governess (Seline Thiel) were in charge of the children while Eleanor cared for their father. Several of the Roosevelt children became ill in the latter part of August 1921, but their illnesses were mild, consisting of slight fever, a runny nose, and minor aches.[28,29] The illnesses were in keeping with non-paralytic polio or a common respiratory viral infection.

The Roosevelt children were told that their father had *"an infectious fever"*, even after he was diagnosed with paralytic polio. Long after they became adults, some of them believed that they contracted a mild form of poliomyelitis during August 1921. Their beliefs may have added to the persistent notion that their father contracted paralytic polio in 1921.

Franklin's mother, Sara, who had been on vacation in Europe, came as quickly as possible toward the end of August 1921 to see her son. Despite Franklin's serious situation, Franklin and Eleanor reassured her that he would recover completely. However, Bennet indicated in a telegram to Lovett sent on August 31, 1921 that *"atrophy increasing and power lessening causing patient much anxiety"*.[21]

Plans to Transfer FDR to a New York Hospital

After the first few weeks of the illness, an excellent nurse, Miss Edna Rockey, came to assist with Franklin's care. Since FDR's neurological abnormalities had stabilized, his physicians decided that he should be transferred to a medical center in the United States. The Roosevelts preferred a major hospital in New York City where they lived. Arrangements were therefore made to transfer FDR to the New York-Presbyterian Hospital. Dr. George C. Draper (Portrait 7), a physician who specialized in poliomyelitis, would care for him there.

In preparation for the transfer, Lovett recounted FDR's clinical findings in a September 12th letter to Draper.[21] It is significant that a spinal tap (lumbar puncture) was not mentioned. Lovett stated that FDR had paralytic polio.

The proposed move of FDR to New York City caused some consternation among public health officials in Northern Maine because they feared that FDR would transmit the poliovirus to the local population. To reassure Bennet and the health authorities in Northern Maine, Lovett provided a signed certificate indicating that FDR was no longer contagious. The public health officials were satisfied; the transfer from Canada to the United States was begun.

Portrait 7.

Dr. George C. Draper.

Draper (1880-1959) cared for FDR in New York-Presbyterian Hospital for one and one half months.

Chapter 5. Hospitalization in New York

"Out of the jaws of death." ~ William Shakespeare, *Twelfth Night*

Transfer to New York-Presbyterian Hospital

On September 14, thirty-four days after the onset of his neurological illness, FDR was placed on an improvised stretcher and moved onto a small motorboat that carried him across the waters to nearby Eastport in Northern Maine. Every bump along the journey caused FDR extreme pain. In Eastport, he was carried on a luggage cart and loaded through a window into a compartment of a private train bound for New York City. Bennet accompanied him throughout the journey.

Several newspaper reporters had learned that FDR was to be transferred to a New York City hospital. To shield him from being interviewed, and prevent the reporters from learning about the gravity of his illness, FDR was surreptitiously placed onto the train. After FDR was positioned comfortably in a train compartment, the reporters were allowed to see him through a window. FDR seemed optimistic, but the reporters barely saw his face. When the train arrived in New York City, he was met by Draper, immediately placed in an ambulance and driven to the hospital.

An article published in the New York Times shortly after his admission to New York-Presbyterian Hospital indicated that Draper agreed with the diagnosis of poliomyelitis, but was confident that FDR would not be permanently crippled.[30] However, in a private communication, Draper presented an opposite, very gloomy view of FDR's physical condition.

Draper's Assessment Letter to Lovett (September 24)

After FDR was hospitalized for ten days (one and a half months after the onset of the illness), Draper wrote the following letter dated September 24, 1921 to Lovett.[21]

"I am much concerned at the very slow recovery both as regards the disappearance of pain . . . and as to the recovery of even light power to twitch the muscles. There is marked falling away of the muscle masses on either side of the spine in the lower lumbar region, likewise the buttocks. There is marked weakness of the right triceps, and an unusual amount of gross muscular twitching in the muscles of both forearms. He coordinates on the fine motion of his hands very well now so that he can sign his name and write a little better than before.

The lower extremities present a most depressing picture. There is little action in the long extensors of the toes of each foot; a little in the perinei (sic); a little ability to twitch the bellies of the gastrocnemii, but not really extend the feet. There is little similar power in the left vastus, and on both sides similar voluntary twitches of the hamstring masses can be accomplished."

The facial paralysis disappeared, and the weakness of his upper extremities and chest lessened (Figure 6). However, the hyperesthesia (pain to the slightest touch) continued in the lower extremities. Other neurological findings (such as the quality of deep tendon reflexes) and the results of laboratory studies, if they were conducted, were not mentioned. During the next six weeks, the muscles of his upper extremities and trunk gradually improved (Figure 6). Consequently, FDR could sit unaided, feed himself unassisted, defecate, and urinate.

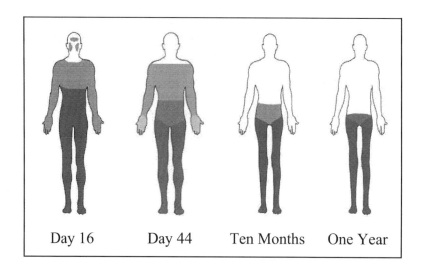

Figure 6. Regression of FDR's Muscle Weakness and Paralysis. Day 16. Maximal involvement. Day 44. Weakness and paralysis regress. *Ten Months.* Continued regression. *One Year.* Lower abdominal muscles weak. Lower extremities paralyzed and atrophic.

An attempt was made to recover the medical records from FDR's stay at the New York-Presbyterian Hospital, but those documents could not be found. Therefore, no other information was available about that phase of FDR's illness.

Post-Hospitalization – Partial Recovery (10/21 - 1/22)

Because of his modest improvement, FDR was discharged from the hospital on October 28, 1921. He was taken to his home in New York City where he received physical therapy, mainly in the form of stretching from a nurse Mrs. Katherine Lake. Some improvement in his lower abdominal muscles was observed (Lake letter to Lovett, February 12, 1922), but pains in the hips and legs continued.[21]

In January 1922, his lower legs suddenly hyperflexed and *"locked"*,[1,6] probably because of shortening of the gastrocnemius and biceps femoris tendons and muscles due to fibrosis after atrophy. His lower extremities were consequently placed in casts for three weeks. FDR's legs were gradually extended by *"insertion of wedges behind the knees"*.[1,6] After the casts were removed, his legs were fitted with heavy metal braces, a lower abdominal sling was applied, and he was supplied with crutches. He could stand, but only with those aids. FDR never walked unaided again.

Over the next six months, the hyperesthesia gradually disappeared, and the lower abdominal and lower back muscles strengthened. However, his lower extremities remained paralyzed (Figure 6).[1,14]

When Draper examined FDR on March 25, 1922, he found little, if any, further recovery from the paralysis.[21] The cause of FDR's paralysis was never stated in Draper's letters to Lovett.[21] Perhaps he assumed that it was unnecessary to restate the diagnosis of paralytic polio. However, in the New York Times article dated September 12, 1921, Draper did say that FDR had polio.[30]

Draper never discussed FDR's case in his 1935 book *Infantile Paralysis,*[31] possibly out of deference to the then President of the United States. Another reason may have been that FDR's clinical findings did not fit Draper's peculiar notions of the features of children who were prone to contract paralytic polio.

The first was an asthenic body habitus (a spare or slender body build) that was the opposite of FDR, who was well built and reasonably muscular. Also, Draper indicated that children with severe paralytic polio were more likely to have brown hair (brunette), delicate dark skin, small deeply pigmented facial moles, and protrusion of the lower jaw. Draper further wrote that children with paralytic polio had wide-set eyes, increased spacing between the incisors, broad hands, and a mongoloid slant to the eyelids – sometimes with an epicanthal fold (a particular skin fold of the upper eyelid). He also indicated that certain subtle features of polio patients required considerable experience to detect. They included puffiness around the eyes, a glazed porcelain quality to the cornea, and a look of mixed apprehension and resentfulness. Finally, he reported that boys with paralytic polio had feminine features, including small external genitalia and a non-descended testicle.

Other investigators in the fields of clinical neurology and infectious diseases never reported that the physical features (phenotypic features) mentioned by Draper were characteristic of paralytic polio.

It is unclear how Draper's notions concerning paralytic polio came about. Perhaps his ideas were based upon his care of the most serious victims of paralytic polio – those who required prolonged hospitalizations and had considerable muscle atrophy. In addition, some of the phenotypic features, such as puffiness about the eyes and corneal abnormalities, may have been secondary to malnutrition (hypoalbuminemia and vitamin A deficiency, respectively). In that respect, when Draper first cared for hospitalized children with paralytic polio, there was little appreciation of the importance of vitamin A and its dietary sources. Furthermore, it was impossible to detect serum albumin or other major types of proteins until the mid-twentieth century. Thus, Draper and others who cared for very sick children during the early part of the twentieth century were *"prisoners of time"*.

FDR ended up moving to his home in Hyde Park for further recovery. Bed rest was insisted upon by Franklin's mother Sara, but he continued to do some physical therapy. His nurse thought that he was slowly improving, but that the progress was minimal (Lake letter to Lovett, January 22, 1922).[21]

FDR also spent some time in his New York City home in May 1922 entertaining friends. By that time, he was able to *"walk"* short distances with canes or crutches (Lake letter to Lovett, May 24, 1922).[21]

On May 28, 1923, about a year and 10 months after the onset of FDR's neurological illness, Lovett reexamined FDR. "*His arms and face and neck were normal. His bowel, bladder, and sexual functions were normal. His abdominal muscles were weak. His ability to flex from the hips was poor. From the waist down, he remained paralyzed. There was no motion in his hamstrings. His toes showed no more than a trace of motion."*[21]

In a letter to Lovett on February 11, 1924, Draper *"could not help feeling that he [FDR] has almost reached the limits of his possibilities"*.[21]

In 1933, eleven and a half years after his paralytic illness, FDR became the thirty-second President of the United States. Soon after his inauguration, a record was made of the strength of his anterior abdominal and lower extremity muscles by the medical staff assigned to the White House. *"The strength in the upper abdominal muscles and the right lower anterior abdominal muscles was normal, whereas most muscles of the buttocks and lower extremities were weak except for the right first flexor digitorum brevis and the left first, second, and third flexor digitorum longus."*[1] The conclusion was that the profound, symmetrical muscle weakness in his lower extremities persisted.

Chapter 6. Rehabilitation

"It is common sense to take a method and try it. If it fails, admit it frankly and try another. But above all, try something." ~ FDR

Figure 7. The Roosevelt Springwood Estate. FDR began his rehabilitation there in early 1922.

In early 1922, FDR faced a difficult situation. He had regained almost complete motor function in his upper body, but his lower extremities were still almost totally paralyzed. As his mother Sara desired, he could have repeated what his father James did when he became incapacitated, and retire to the family estate in Springwood (Figure 7). FDR was independently wealthy, and on the off chance that additional funds were required, Sara, who was even richer, would assist him. Furthermore, if she died, he would inherit Sara's considerable fortune including the Springwood estate. In such a life of leisure, Franklin could devote himself to his family, friends, and hobbies. Also, he and his family would have ample time to travel to interesting places and visit friends in the United States, Europe, or elsewhere.

Decision to Rehabilitate and Re-enter Politics

Instead, FDR chose a different option – perhaps the only one, given his optimistic view of life and his determination to emulate his fifth cousin Theodore Roosevelt, who had been the Assistant Secretary of the Navy, the Governor of New York State, the Vice-President of the United States, and the twenty-sixth President of the United States.[32] He therefore attempted a complete rehabilitation – to be able to stand, walk unassisted, and return to the political arena.

In January 1922, five months after the onset of his neurological illness, FDR began a rehabilitation program under the supervision of a physiotherapist, Mrs. Kathleen Lake.[7] However, the illness left FDR in a terribly weakened state, a state accompanied by fears of dependency and death. When FDR was alone and not in a wheel chair, he feared he would be trapped in his bedroom or some other part of his home because of an unexpected fire. His fear was so great that he practiced getting out of bed onto the floor unaided and crawling to the door to escape the imagined smoke and flames.[1] The fear lessened as the strength in his arms, chest, and abdomen increased, and as FDR learned how to ascend and descend stairs in a sitting position.

Efforts to Rehabilitate (1922)

Despite his extensive paralysis, FDR was determined to rehabilitate and return to his prior state of good health. For many months, he doggedly tried new as well as old methods, even when they were not medically recommended. When one treatment failed, he tried another. Deep massages of wasted muscles, immersion in hot or cold water, prolonged immersion in salt water, repeated exposure to ultraviolet light, and repeated electrical stimulation of weakened muscles were all tried to no avail. FDR practiced for long hours standing and attempting to walk with the aid of braces, canes, crutches, and parallel bars. He could walk short distances with the support of braces and crutches. His upper body strength increased. However, despite these many different measures, the muscles of his lower extremities remained atrophic and useless.

During the first two winters following his illness, FDR sailed on his 71-foot houseboat on the ocean waters that bordered Western Florida and the Florida Keys. During those voyages, he socialized with friends and family, fished, swam, and did some physical therapy while escaping the cold winters of New York State. Although he was outwardly optimistic, he was sometimes discouraged because of his physical infirmity and lack of improvement.[33]

Long Stay at Warm Springs (1924)

In 1924, FDR learned about Warm Springs, Georgia from George Foster Peabody, a wealthy friend who owned part of the Meriwether Inn at that site. The mineral springs at Warm Springs flowed constantly. The temperature of the waters was about 88 °F (31 °C) year round.

Peabody told FDR about a young man whose legs had been paralyzed since early childhood because of poliomyelitis, and who was much improved from swimming in the waters of Warm Springs.[7,34] Because of that purported benefit, FDR thought that the waters of Warm Springs might improve his weakened muscles. Franklin's remembrances of the visits of his father to the therapeutic warm mineral springs in Germany, where many crippled people went to recuperate, may have also influenced his decision. FDR therefore moved to Warm Springs in October 1924 to test the effects of the warm mineral waters.[1,7,34]

After a few weeks, FDR was convinced that the magnesium-rich waters were helping his leg muscles. He accordingly wrote the following enthusiastic letter to his wife Eleanor in 1924.[35]

". . . The legs are really improving a great deal. The walking and general exercising in the water is fine and I have worked out some special exercises also. This is really a discovery of a place and there is no doubt that I've got to do it some more . . ."

In addition, he was convinced that prolonged exposure to sunshine was very important. That was evidenced by his following remarks.

"The best infantile paralysis specialist in New York told me that the only way to overcome the effects of the disease was to swim as much as possible, and bask in the sunlight. Conditions here are ideal for both prescriptions. The water in some way relaxes muscles drawn taut by the disease, and gives the limbs much greater action. The sunshine has curative effects, I understand."

Portrait 8.

FDR at Warm Springs, Georgia in 1924.

His upper extremities and chest muscles were well developed. His leg muscles were atrophied.

A newspaper story was soon published concerning FDR's improvement at Warm Springs. Soon afterwards, FDR received many letters from people who had read the story and were seeking to restore function to their paralyzed limbs. Shortly thereafter, some paralytic polio victims arrived without notice at Warm Springs for the "cure". This surge of interest encouraged FDR to establish a treatment center for victims of paralytic polio at Warm Springs.[34]

Despite FDR's conviction that he was improving, a photograph (Portrait 8) of FDR taken at Warm Springs in 1924 reveals that even though the muscles of his chest and upper extremities were well developed, his lower extremities were atrophied. As the months and years passed, it became evident that the muscles of FDR's lower extremities would not recover.

Development of Warm Springs Institute (1925)

Given FDR's demonstrated leadership abilities, it was unsurprising that he quickly took charge of the facility at Warm Springs. FDR's drive to create a therapeutic center for victims of paralytic polio was described in detail by Hugh Gallagher in his book *FDR's Splendid Deception*.[1] The Inn at Warm Springs was revamped to accommodate handicapped people. Cottages were built to house an increasing number of disabled people who were seeking rehabilitation. In time, part of the swimming area was covered by a glass dome, so it could be used during the winter as well as the summer.

When the owner Tom Loyless died in 1925, FDR decided to purchase the site, so that he could extend the treatment and recreational facilities. The next year, over the objections of his family and close advisors, FDR bought the site for about 200,000 dollars (about 2.5 million in 2010 dollars),[17] which was about two-thirds of his financial worth.[1] An orthopedist, a physiotherapist, and other health care professionals were hired to staff the center.

FDR convinced leaders of the American Orthopedic Association to investigate the effects of the warm mineral waters upon patients who suffered from paralytic polio. Dr. LeRoy Hubbard, an orthopedic surgeon from the New York State Department of Health, headed the study. Hubbard and his colleagues studied twenty-three patients at Warm Springs for six months, and noted improvement in muscle function in each case. The study was not controlled by including untreated as well as treated victims of paralytic polio. Indeed, such a study would have been difficult to perform. But the uncontrolled observations were encouraging. The American Orthopedic Association subsequently recommended establishing a permanent hydrotherapy center at Warm Springs.

FDR closely identified with the victims of paralytic polio – most of whom had become ill in childhood. Because of their plight and the belief that the warm mineral waters were therapeutic, in 1927 Roosevelt formally established a rehabilitation hospital at Warm Springs.[34] It still exists as Roosevelt Warm Springs.

FDR took a major role in the care of the patients at Warm Springs. He often devised new types of exercises, and aided in their social as well as their physical rehabilitation. In that respect, he thought of himself as "The Doctor", and indeed that was how many of the patients saw him. This was despite the fact that he had little education in biological sciences and no formal training in medicine or in medical care.

Although we will never know exactly how FDR assumed the leadership role at Warm Springs, he was remarkably persuasive and skilled in extracting the best efforts from those who worked with him. Those personal attributes allowed him to positively influence patients, staff, and prospective financial donors. The beneficial effects on the disabled people who came to Warm Springs may have been due to the physical therapy and other supportive measures, including the placebo effect, [36,37] but the salutary effect of Roosevelt's encouragements cannot be discounted.

FDR's vision of a center for the rehabilitation of victims of paralytic polio began to take shape, and soon came to fruition. After much of the center was built, the members of the professional staff were recruited. The facility was subsequently accredited as a rehabilitation center.[34]

All of the above was consistent with FDR's optimistic view of life, but other factors may also have been at work. Since he was probably the oldest victim of a paralytic disease at Warm Springs, Roosevelt was most likely the only one who could garner sufficient funds to build a rehabilitation center. Finally, as previously suggested, he had a spirit that refused to admit defeat and that drove him to rehabilitate himself and others with a similar affliction. Those attributes served him well when he was President of the United States during the difficult years of the Great Depression and the Second World War.

Chapter 7. Return to Public Life

"It is surmounting difficulties that makes heroes." ~ Louis Pasteur

During the first few years of FDR's recuperation, his wife Eleanor led the effort for his re-entry into public life by meeting with leaders of the Democratic Party of New York State, speaking frequently at public and political gatherings, and serving in many important social and political organizations in New York State. Her efforts succeeded. Democratic Party leaders in New York State and elsewhere in the country looked forward to FDR's return to national politics. By 1924, FDR appeared in public in a way that partly disguised the extent of his physical impairment.[1] On June 26, 1924, he walked (with the aid of crutches) across a stage at the Democratic National Convention to nominate Al Smith, Governor of New York, to be President of the United States. In later years, FDR and his aides sought to further conceal his disability.

Governor of New York (1928)

In 1924 and 1926, FDR actively supported the election of Al Smith (Alfred Emanuel Smith Jr.) to Governor of New York. Therefore, when Smith ran as the Democratic candidate for President of the United States in 1928, he chose FDR to run for Governor of New York. At that time, FDR was still preoccupied with his rehabilitation and with the development of the treatment facility at Warm Springs.

Although seven years had passed since his illness, and there was very little chance that he could recover strength in his legs, Roosevelt continued to try. Finally, after considerable vacillation, and great pressure from Governor Al Smith and other important leaders of the New York State Democratic Party, FDR agreed to be their candidate for Governor of New York. Despite a banner year for the Republican Party at the national polls and Al Smith's defeat by Herbert Hoover, FDR narrowly won the New York gubernatorial election in 1928.

During his first term as Governor of New York, the stock market crash of 1929 triggered the Great Depression. To aid the suffering populace in New York State, Governor Roosevelt, his advisors (some of whom joined him in the White House in 1933), and his supporters in the New York State Legislature established remedial social programs, which in some ways were the harbinger of the New Deal in the 1930s.

FDR's performance as Governor was deemed by most citizens of New York to be excellent. Two years later (1930), FDR was readily re-elected.[1,6,7] As FDR's reputation as Governor of the most populous state in the union rose, he became the leading contender for nomination by the Democratic Party for President of the United States.

Health Assessment before First Presidential Run (1931)

Because of the physical decline of President Woodrow Wilson during his last years in office,[38] the death of Warren G. Harding during his Presidency,[38] and FDR's prolonged physical problems, many important people in politics and the news media questioned whether FDR was physically and emotionally up to the task of holding the office of President of the United States. FDR was aware of the potential public concerns about his fitness to run for the office. He therefore took a number of steps to reassure the public.[39] In 1930, he obtained a $500,000 life insurance policy from the Equitable Life Insurance Society as a testimonial to his excellent health. The Medical Director of the insurance company, Dr. Edward W. Beckwith, stated to a group of reporters that he was pleased *"to see such a splendid physical specimen as yourself, and I trust that your remarkable vitality will stand you in good stead throughout your arduous campaign."* Though the gubernatorial campaign of 1930 put the governor *"under very great strain,*" Beckwith stated that Roosevelt "*passed a better examination than the average individual.*"

In 1931, Reginald Earle Looker, a magazine editor and public relations consultant, who later wrote a book about FDR that perhaps helped him get elected to the Presidency,[12] asked FDR's wife Eleanor whether her husband would be able to handle the stress of the office. Her response was, "*If the infantile paralysis didn't kill him, the Presidency won't*".[12]

To test whether FDR could withstand the pressures of the Presidency, Looker asked Governor Roosevelt for his permission to convene a panel of noted physicians to examine his physical and emotional fitness for the office. FDR immediately agreed to the request. In fact, it is likely that FDR encouraged Looker to initiate the plan and very likely paid the participating physicians.[39]

Looker asked the Director of the New York Academy of Medicine, Dr. Linsly R. Williams, to select a panel of experts to conduct the evaluation. The panel included Dr. Samuel Waldron Lambert, a noted medical diagnostician; Dr. Russell Aubra Gibbs, Surgeon-in-Chief of the New York Dispensary and Hospital; and Dr. Robert Foster Kennedy, Professor of Neurology at Cornell University.

After the physicians examined FDR on April 29, 1931, they stated the following:[12]

"*We have today carefully examined Governor Roosevelt. We believe that his health and endurance are such as to allow him to meet any demand of private or public life. We find his organs and functions are sound in all respects. There is no anemia. The chest is exceptionally well developed, and the spinal cord is absolutely normal; all of its segments are in perfect alignment and free from disease. He has neither pain nor ache at any time. Governor Roosevelt can walk all necessary distances and can maintain a standing position without fatigue.*"

The report concluded, *"There has been progressive recovery of power in the legs since contracting polio in 1921"*, and that *"this restoration continues and will continue."*

The details of the examinations conducted by the physicians and how they arrived at their conclusion were not revealed. The statement *"can walk all necessary distances"* was inappropriate, since FDR could not walk unaided and required considerable assistance, even when he covered short distances. The physical findings that pertained to his neurological state, such as the muscle strength and deep tendon reflexes in his legs, were not mentioned. Moreover, the chance of further recovery from the paralysis a decade after the illness was negligible.

The member of the panel who was best able to assess FDR's neurological state was Dr. Kennedy, who was famous because of his discoveries in clinical neurology. But the disease that FDR most likely had in 1921 was not well understood in the United States until the late 1940s.[40,41]

It is unknown whether Kennedy or other members of the panel reviewed FDR's prior medical records and correspondence, spoke with him concerning the details of his paralytic illness, or performed a thorough neurological examination on him. Indeed, the neurological findings were not included in the report. The upshot was that the panel of physicians reported that FDR had substantially recovered from his 1921 illness and that he could carry out the duties of the President of the United States. By today's standards, the report of the panel seems incomplete, even beyond the implausible conclusion that FDR had recovered from his paralysis. For example, the physicians stated that there was no anemia, but they did not include any results from a blood count. Similarly, the report implies that other laboratory tests were performed to test the functions of his organs, but no results were included. Regardless of the rationale for their unwarranted conclusions, the cause of FDR's 1921 paralytic illness remained unquestioned.

Elected President Four Times (1932-1945)

In 1932, FDR was elected to the Presidency of the United States. He was re-elected in 1936, 1940, and 1944. He died on April 12, 1945 from a stroke that was likely due a cerebral hemorrhage.[42] He was by far the longest serving President of the United States. Furthermore, he served during some of the most tumultuous periods in American history – the Great Depression of the 1930s, the institution of key socio-economic reforms, entrance and participation in the Second World War, and the plans to form the United Nations. So despite the paralysis of his lower extremities and uncontrolled arterial hypertension, FDR provided the leadership – the inspiration – for the nation during those critical years. As Stephen Jay Gould remarked in his book *Full House*,[43] *"he (FDR) did not govern with his legs."*

Chapter 8. Polio: Mid 19th to Early 20th Century

"Little children seem to age in a few hours." ~ Dr. Frances Peabody

To better understand why FDR was diagnosed with paralytic polio in 1921, and the preoccupation of the American public with that disease, it is necessary to go back to the mid-nineteenth century. At that time, Louis Pasteur disproved spontaneous generation of microbial life, and simultaneously established the germ theory. Those discoveries had many important ramifications. One principal result was that certain infectious diseases could be prevented by providing clean water and food and by establishing septic systems to dispose of human wastes. Consequently, the general health of much of the population improved in industrialized countries. But paradoxically, in countries where these advances were first made, epidemics of paralytic polio emerged. Why these frightening epidemics appeared and left scores of infants and children crippled and some dead was not well understood. However, as more has been learned about polio, a clearer understanding of the reasons for the epidemics emerged.

Polio Epidemics Emerge in the Nineteenth Century

In retrospect, it appears that the combination of poor sanitary conditions, maternally transmitted antibodies, and natural immunization during early infancy can explain why comparatively few cases of paralytic polio occurred before the nineteenth century. This came about in the following way.

1. Humans were the only natural host for polioviruses.

2. The fecal to oral route was the most common route of transmission.

3. Infants and children were thus often exposed to polioviruses from their parents or other members of their family.

4. However, because of maternal antibodies that combined with the polioviruses, infants exposed to polioviruses did not develop clinical evidence of infection. The infants received IgG antibodies to polioviruses from their mothers during the intrauterine period via the placenta, and received secretory IgA antibodies to polioviruses from their mother's milk. The secretory IgA antibodies neutralized the viruses in the alimentary tract but permitted them to act as immunizing agents. In effect, they were naturally attenuated viruses. Afterwards, immunity to polioviruses was boosted by repeated exposures to the viruses. When women reached sexual maturity, the vast majority produced specific antibodies to polioviruses. Thus, each new generation was protected and naturally immunized against polioviruses.

5. The few individuals not exposed to polioviruses during infancy might have been protected later in life by naturally immunized people who surrounded them. The extent to which "herd immunity" for polio occurred at that time is impossible to determine, but it occurs with many infectious diseases.[44]

Beginning in the late nineteenth century, as exposures to polioviruses in infancy lessened because of improved sanitation, children became vulnerable to poliovirus infections after weaning. The protection further waned in the early twentieth century, as the frequency of breastfeeding declined because of the introduction of artificial milk formulas.

Experimental Transmission of Poliomyelitis (1908)

The first step to understanding the pathogenesis of poliomyelitis epidemics was to determine whether the disease could be transmitted to experimental animals. In 1908, an Austrian physician-scientist, Dr. Karl Landsteiner (1868-1943) (Portrait 9), and his assistant, Dr. Erwin Popper, experimentally transmitted paralytic polio to Old World monkeys (monkeys native only to Africa and Asia).

Portrait 9.

Dr. Karl Landsteiner

Landsteiner (1868-1943), an Austrian physician, and his assistant, Dr. Erwin Popper, demonstrated in 1908 that polioviruses could be transmitted to Old World monkeys.

Because epidemics of paralytic polio were raging in Austria and nearby countries, the leaders of the hospital at *Universität von Wien* asked Landsteiner to try to determine the cause of paralytic polio. Based upon the vaccines against chicken cholera, sheep anthrax, and human rabies developed by Louis Pasteur, they hoped that once the cause of polio was determined, a vaccine could be developed to prevent the disease.

Landsteiner was chosen because he was a careful clinical scientist, as exemplified by his discovery of the major human blood group antigens in 1900.[45] Although others had reported that bacteria had been cultured from spinal cords or cerebrospinal fluid from cases of paralytic polio, Landsteiner discounted those findings since no bacteria were seen (by light microscopy) in the stained affected tissues. His interpretation was that the bacteria were contaminants, rather than pathogens. He thus raised the possibility that polio was due to a microbial agent smaller than bacteria. But first he had to establish whether the infection could be transmitted to experimental animals.

In November 1908, Landsteiner obtained spinal cord tissues from a nine-year old boy who had died of poliomyelitis. No bacteria were detected in the child's spinal fluid or spinal cord by direct microscopy or bacterial culture. Landsteiner tried unsuccessfully to transmit human poliomyelitis into mice, rabbits and guinea pigs by injecting them with a preparation of the boy's spinal cord tissue. After those failures, Landsteiner tried to infect two Old World monkeys (a *Cynocephalus hamadryas* and a *Macaca rhesus*), species that are closely related to humans.[46]

A bacteriologically sterile suspension of the child's spinal cord was injected into the abdominal cavity of both animals. The *Cynocephalus hamadryas* became ill six days after the injection and died two days later. The histological findings were consistent with bulbospinal poliomyelitis. The *Macaca rhesus* lived but developed complete flaccid paralysis of the legs 12 days after the injection. The animal was euthanized seven days later. The ventral spinal cord neurons in the *Macaca* were damaged or destroyed. The transmissible agents in either animal were not detected by light microscopy or by *in vitro* cultures for bacteria or fungi.[46]

Landsteiner reasoned that the infecting agents were viruses. To test that possibility, he designed experiments using filters that would exclude bacteria and fungi from passage, but would allow microorganisms too small to see by light microscopy to pass through the filters. However, no Old World monkeys were left in the *Universität von Wien* for those experiments. Furthermore, the directors of the hospital refused to purchase more monkeys for the research.

Consequently, Landsteiner wrote to the director of *l'Institut de Pasteur de Paris,* Dr. Emile Roux, for help. Dr. Constantin Levaditi (1874-1953), a Romanian physician-microbiologist at *l'Institut de Pasteur,* quickly agreed to help with the filtration experiments. Landsteiner was permitted by the leaders of the *Universität von Wien* to conduct the experiments with Levaditi in Paris. Macaque monkeys were used in the transmission experiments conducted in the laboratory of the discoverer of cellular immunology, Ilya Ilich Metchnikoff. The infecting agent passed through the filter, and was thus smaller than bacteria or fungi. Landsteiner therefore concluded that poliomyelitis was caused by a virus.[47,48]

Portrait 10.

Dr. Simon Flexner.

Flexner (1863-1946), an American physician, confirmed that polioviruses could be transmitted to experimental non-human primates.

Simon Flexner Confirms Landsteiner's Discovery (1908)

Also in 1908, Dr. Simon Flexner (1863–1946) (Portrait 10), the director of the Rockefeller Institute for Medical Research in New York City, and his colleague Dr. Paul Aldin Lewis (1879-1929), confirmed Landsteiner's findings by conducting similar experiments in Old World monkeys.[49,50]

What Happened After Those Discoveries

The transmission of poliomyelitis by very small microorganisms to experimental animals was thus demonstrated. However, the other characteristics of polioviruses, including their genetic composition,[3,4] their size and morphology, their transmission via the alimentary tract,[51,52] and their dependence upon host cells to replicate,[3,4] would not be established for many years. But at least the infective nature of polioviruses was discovered thirteen years before FDR developed his neurological illness.

Landsteiner did not attempt to transfer poliomyelitis from an infected monkey to a non-infected one. It was a logical next step, but the leaders of the *Universität von Wien* did not fund additional investigations, perhaps because of the high cost of purchasing Old World monkeys. Also, Landsteiner probably understood that it was unlikely a way to prevent poliomyelitis would be discovered in the near future, because of the lack of an *in vitro* method of culturing the virus.

Landsteiner may have encountered one other obstacle that interfered with his ability to continue his research concerning poliomyelitis. There was a rising tide of anti-Semitism in Austria and in nearby countries. That was exemplified by the popular book written in 1899 by Houston Stewart Chamberlain, *Die Grundlage des Neunzehnten Jahrhunderts* (The Foundations of the Nineteenth Century), that proclaimed the superiority of Teutonic people and the inferiority of Jews.[53] Although Landsteiner converted from Judaism to Catholicism to obtain an academic position, his Jewish ancestry was well known.

As support for his research dwindled after World War I, Landsteiner moved from Austria to the Netherlands, where he worked as a prosector (prepares dissections for anatomy demonstrations) in the small *Ziekenhuis Catholic Hospital* in The Hague. He published several articles on haptens (small molecules that elicit an immune response when combined with a much larger molecule, such as a protein) during that period. To augment his meager income, he also worked in a small factory that produced "old tuberculin" that was thought by the German microbiologist Robert Koch to immunologically cure tuberculosis. Later it was determined that the treatment was useless.

Landsteiner was frustrated by his meager income and his limited opportunities to conduct research in the Netherlands. When Simon Flexner learned of Landsteiner's circumstances, he invited him to join the Rockefeller Center for

Medical Research, which Flexner headed. Landsteiner promptly accepted the invitation and moved to New York City in 1923, where he made further investigations concerning immunohematology.

Table 1. A Death Tabulation from the 1916 Polio Epidemic. A contemporary listing of polio deaths in New York City in 1916.

POLIOMYELITIC DEATHS, CITY OF NEW YORK, EPIDEMIC, 1916.

	Males.	Females.	Total, both sexes.
Total all ages	1119	803	1922
Under 1 year	182	134	316
1 year	240	162	402
2 years	208	149	357
3 years	156	105	261
4 years	105	58	163
Total under 5 years	891	608	1499
5 to 9 years	171	150	321
10 to 14 years	30	24	54
15 to 19 years	7	11	18
20 to 24 years	6	3	9
25 to 29 years	8	3	11
30 to 34 years	2	2	4
35 to 39 years	2	1	3
40 to 44 years	2	1	3
45 years and over	..	..	..
Colored	15	7	22

Tragic 1916 Epidemic of Paralytic Polio

After Landsteiner discovered that paralytic polio was due to a virus, he never investigated polioviruses again, perhaps because it was difficult at that time to envision a way of culturing the virus *in vitro* and rendering it into a safe and effective vaccine. Moreover, he wished to reopen his investigations concerning human blood group antigens.

In contrast, Flexner and Lewis continued to study polioviruses in the hope of creating a protective poliovirus vaccine. In 1911, they produced antibodies to polioviruses in experimental monkeys, but they failed to create a protective vaccine, probably because of the complexities of using infected monkey brain tissues. However, the investigations may have inadvertently produced a strain of poliovirus more virulent than the wild strain. The research may have been responsible for a particularly severe epidemic of paralytic polio in 1916.

The 1916 epidemic was especially tragic. In that year, 23,900 cases of paralysis with 5,000 deaths due to poliomyelitis occurred in New England and the Mid-Atlantic states. The outbreak was especially deadly in New York City, with 8,900 cases and 1,922 deaths (Table 1).[54] The case fatality rate was the highest ever reported for poliomyelitis. The fearsome toll of the epidemic was widely reported in national newspapers. Undoubtedly, FDR, Eleanor, and FDR's physicians were aware in 1921 of the severity of the 1916 epidemic.

The fear of paralytic polio was further heightened by the uncertainty of how the infection was transmitted. Did the virus spread through the air or contaminated surroundings? Did the virus spread though infected water or food? Did it spread from person to person, or were animals other than humans also infected? Did flies or other insects carry the virus?

In 2011, Dr. H. V. Wyatt, a microbiologist at the University of Leeds, first raised the possibility that the severe 1916 epidemic of poliomyelitis in New York City[54] was due to a laboratory strain of poliovirus that targeted motor neurons more effectively than the wild strain of the virus.[55] Wyatt suggested that the more virulent strain was inadvertently created by the experiments that Flexner, Lewis and their colleagues had carried out with Rhesus monkeys in the Rockefeller Center for Medical Research since 1908.[55] Indeed, the Rockefeller Center was just three miles from the epicenter (point of origin) of the 1916 outbreak of paralytic polio in New York City. Furthermore, Wyatt noted that individuals with paralytic polio who were furthest from the epicenter were least likely to experience severe paralysis or to die. That may have been because the virus had reverted to its less virulent wild state by the time it spread farther away.

It was also germane that autopsies on many of the fatal cases revealed extensive inflammation in the basal ganglia, situated at the base of the forebrain.[56] This was important because the basal ganglia are rarely affected in poliomyelitis. Thus, the 1916 polio epidemic in New York City was unusual in its epidemiologic pattern, its clinical severity, its histopathology, and the possibility that it was due to a laboratory strain of the virus. Moreover, the 1916 epidemic in New York City greatly heightened the fear of poliomyelitis in the United States for many years.

What Was Known About Poliomyelitis in 1921

Because in the United States paralytic polio was perhaps the only known cause of non-traumatic flaccid paralysis, when physicians were confronted with a patient with a non-traumatic flaccid paralysis, they assumed that the paralysis was due to poliomyelitis. This was the case in 1921 when FDR developed his neurological illness.

The discovery of the transmissibility of polioviruses to experimental animals also opened up the possibility that a protective vaccine against poliomyelitis could be developed. However, it was difficult to proceed with the development of a vaccine because polioviruses could only be obtained from the brains of artificially infected monkeys. Furthermore, the virus could not be visualized by light microscopy because of its very small size. Moreover, the few investigators who were studying poliovirus detected it by injecting infected spinal cord or brain tissue into the brains of uninfected monkeys. The method was cumbersome and expensive. Polioviruses could neither be quantified nor their virulence reduced until the virus could be cultured *in vitro*. Moreover, as described later in this book, in an attempt to create a poliovirus vaccine in the 1930s, the injection of spinal cord tissue from experimentally infected monkeys into humans caused autoimmune damage to the brain.

The bottom line was that in 1921 there was no way to prevent poliomyelitis, and knowledge concerning polio was still very incomplete. The fear of polio was high in the thoughts of physicians and the public.

Seasonal Occurrence of Poliomyelitis

Another reason for the diagnosis of paralytic polio in FDR's case was that he became ill during the peak of the poliomyelitis season – the summer months. Moreover, he had recently visited a large group of teenage boys at the Boy Scout Jamboree at Bear Mountain, New York. It was conceivable that some of them were infected with the poliovirus. There are no reports that any scouts or personnel at the camp were ill during FDR's visit, although some could have had a minor or asymptomatic poliovirus infection. On the other hand, a certain bacterial infection could also have occurred, leading to a disease other than polio. That possibility will be considered later in this book (see page 115).

Chapter 9. The Diagnosis of Polio Persisted

"Those who cannot remember the past are condemned to repeat it." ~ George Santayana

There are many reasons why the public and physicians believed for many decades that FDR contracted paralytic polio in 1921.

Expertise of FDR's Physicians

As previously noted, Dr. Samuel A. Levine concluded that FDR had paralytic polio, even though he never saw FDR during his illness. Dr. Robert Lovett, a leading expert on the orthopedic management of children paralyzed from poliomyelitis who later saw FDR during his illness at Campobello, concurred with Levine's opinion. Moreover, Lovett had written a book in 1917 about polio that was considered authoritative on the subject.[20] In addition, Dr. George Draper, a clinical expert on paralytic polio and FDR's physician during his hospitalization in New York City, agreed with Lovett's diagnosis of paralytic polio. Until recently, all historians and others who wrote about FDR's illness accepted the diagnosis of paralytic polio made by Lovett and Draper.

However, the reliance on that diagnosis was problematic. Although Lovett and Draper were experts on paralytic polio, they and other physicians in the United States in 1921 were significantly limited by the state of medical knowledge at that time. Many neurological diseases, including paralytic polio, were poorly or not at all understood. In that respect, as will be explained in detail later in this book, FDR most likely had a disease that was apparently not considered as a diagnostic possibility by his physicians.

No Neurological Consultation in FDR's Case

Another reason for the misdiagnosis may have been that a neurologist did not see FDR during his illness or for several years thereafter. A neurologist who was aware of the distinctions between paralytic polio and Landry's ascending paralysis would have considered that FDR had contracted the peripheral neuropathy that Dr. Octave Landry had originally described. However, the failure to consult a neurologist in FDR's case was not surprising. There were very few neurologists in the United States at that time. Furthermore, the initial assumption in patients with a non-traumatic flaccid paralysis was that the disease was poliomyelitis. In 1921, non-neurologist physicians who saw practically all patients with suspected paralytic polio in all likelihood did not have much knowledge of neurological disorders. In contrast, in the last half of the twentieth century, well-informed neurologists in major metropolitan areas were usually available to see patients with paralytic diseases within a short period of time.

Fears of Paralytic Polio

Until the development of effective poliovirus vaccines in the mid-twentieth century, there were great fears that the virus was silently stalking defenseless children. The anxiety about the summer storms of poliomyelitis spread across the United States. Consequently, children of all ages were often excluded from public places – such as swimming pools, movie theaters, libraries, and sporting events – during the summer months. Furthermore, to escape paralytic polio, public and private schools in many locales closed in early May and did not open until late September. Moreover, poliomyelitis was often in the news because of the dread concerning the infection and the uncertainty about how it was spread. Virtually no other disease was discussed in such detail then and for many years to come.

Closer to home, in the 1960s, students in a Texas public school marched out of doors during recess singing:

"My daddy told me to beware,
'Cause polio was in the air.
My mommy told me to wash my hands,
And also pay attention to my glands.

But I was a bad boy and didn't listen.
Now I'm a sufferin' and a limpin'.
'Cause I got the polio from a toilet seat.
So you'd better listen up and repeat:

It's the polio, polio, polio, roly-poly polio,
It gonna kill you cowhands and many more,
So get on your pony and ride far away.
And if you do, you'll beat the polio every day – yeah every day."

I had heard a variation of that same song over the radio when I was a young child in West Texas during the 1940s. Thus, the dread of paralytic polio was profound in rural and urban communities across the United States for much of the twentieth century.

In the United States and many other countries, polio was the "Ebola virus" of its day. Indeed, the Ebola virus, which has been indigenous to parts of West-Central Africa since 1976, is extremely contagious and often fatal (about a fifty percent mortality rate).[57,58] About 28,638 cases of Ebola occurred in Guinea, Liberia, and Sierra Leone from March 2014 through December 2015. In 2015, several infected people went to a few European locations and the USA, but no secondary cases occurred. The Ebola epidemic was halted by isolating suspected cases, using protective clothing for health care personnel, and disposing or disinfecting all potentially contaminated materials.

In contrast, there was seemingly no way to avoid or to treat poliomyelitis. Furthermore, fear of the malady was heightened because of the uncertainty how the infection was spread. That was particularly vexing because the epidemics continued despite advances in sanitation.

Figure 8.

March of Dimes 1946 Publicity Photo.

A model hands the famous performer Eddie Cantor a dime. A portrait of FDR hangs on the wall.

Development of Poliovirus Vaccines

FDR's role in the development of the poliovirus vaccines further associated him in the public mind with paralytic polio. In his second term of office as President of the United States, FDR was one of the principal founders of a large private foundation, The National Foundation for Infantile Paralysis. The Foundation not only supported the care and rehabilitation of patients disabled from paralytic polio, but also funded the research that led to the development of the first safe, effective poliovirus vaccine, and soon thereafter funded the first mass trials of the vaccine. The eradication of poliomyelitis was thus started by a private foundation that successfully gathered financial support from millions of citizens in the country (Figure 8).

Unsuccessful First Efforts to Develop a Vaccine (1936)

In 1934, Dr. John Albert Kolmer, Professor of Medicine at Temple University, developed a poliovirus vaccine from infected monkey brain tissues treated with the emulsifying agent sodium ricinoleate.[59] Kolmer chose ricinoleate because it was believed at that time to be a detoxifying agent. He felt that the treatment would produce an attenuated poliovirus vaccine that would be more immunogenic than an inactivated viral vaccine.

Kolmer's ideas were incorrect. After he injected the experimental vaccine into the brains of non-infected monkeys, the animals seemed well and did not develop paralytic polio when they were subsequently injected with live polioviruses. Consequently, in 1935 Kolmer carried out a large-scale trial of the vaccine in children. Tragically, many vaccinated children developed paralytic polio. Nine died, probably of bulbospinal or bulbar poliomyelitis.[52,60] In retrospect, the vaccines must have contained live polioviruses.

In 1934, Dr. Maurice Brodie at New York University produced a formaldehyde-inactivated poliomyelitis vaccine from ground-up spinal cords obtained from monkeys infected with polioviruses. Formaldehyde was chosen because it was a widely used tissue fixative. The tissue preparation produced some specific antibodies to polioviruses when injected into uninfected monkeys. He then injected the experimental poliovirus vaccine into himself and several of his laboratory assistants. No untoward effects occurred. Consequently, Brodie organized an extensive trial of his experimental poliovirus vaccine.

In 1935, three thousand children received Brodie's experimental vaccine. Unfortunately, the vaccine was not protective, many injected children became ill, and one died.[52] The nature of their illnesses following the administration of the vaccine was never revealed, but it may have been an autoimmune encephalopathy due to systemic exposures to antigens from monkey spinal cords that cross-reacted with human brain antigens.

Those two disastrous trials brought research into poliovirus vaccines to a halt, and ended Brodie's work at New York University. He died a few years later, possibly due to suicide. It is somewhat ironic that the first successful poliovirus vaccine was patterned after Brodie's, and that the developer of that vaccine, Jonas Salk, was a medical student at New York University when Brodie was experimenting with his poliovirus vaccine.

Portrait 11. Drs. Enders, Weller, and Robbins. John Enders (1897-1985), Thomas Weller (1915-2008), and Frederick Robbins (1916-2003) grew polioviruses in human embryonic cell cultures. The discovery led to the development of poliovirus vaccines.

Discovery of How Poliovirus is Transmitted (1941)

It was originally thought that polio was transmitted through the nasal membranes to the brain. As part of his experiments around 1911, Simon Flexner transmitted the virus by introducing washings from the nose and throat of polio victims into the nasal passages of monkeys. For decades thereafter, it was universally accepted that polio spread via the nasal route. This was incorrect.

In 1941, Albert Sabin found polioviruses in the digestive tract, brain, and spinal cord from fatal cases of polio.[61] However, polioviruses were not found in nasal membranes. Sabin's findings, soon confirmed by other researchers, led to the important realization that the poliovirus usually spread by being ingested, and initially infected the digestive tract.[51]

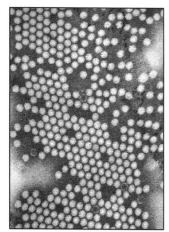

Figure 9.

Electron Micrograph of Cultured Polioviruses.

Polioviruses Cultured *In Vitro* (1948)

A new impetus to develop a poliovirus vaccine occurred in 1948, when Dr. John Franklin Enders (Portrait 11), Dr. Thomas Huckle Weller, and Dr. Frederick Chapman Robbins at Boston Children's Hospital found that polioviruses could be cultured in human embryonic tissues.[62]

Before then, no one thought that polioviruses would grow in non-neural tissue, because the most dangerous clinical effects of polioviruses were upon motor neurons. The idea to culture polioviruses in non-neural tissues came about when Enders, Weller, and Robbins were culturing varicella (chickenpox) viruses in skin tissues that varicella normally invaded. Human embryonic skin was chosen because it grew rapidly in culture, and because Enders and his colleagues had used the method successfully to culture the mumps virus.[63] As Enders commented in his 1954 Nobel Prize Address[64] concerning their 1949 discovery,

"In this way such cultures were made available while close at hand in the storage cabinet was the Lansing strain of poliomyelitis virus. Thereupon it suddenly occurred to us that everything had been prepared almost without conscious effort on our part for a new attempt to cultivate the agent in extraneural tissue."

The results were a huge advance. Injections of polioviruses from human embryonic tissue cultures into brains of non-infected monkeys quickly led to flaccid paralysis. Thus, polioviruses were not only neurotropic (target motor neurons), but they also target certain other cells. Furthermore, the viruses were able to kill cultured cells (cytopathic effect), and the cytopathic effect could be prevented by using neutralizing antibodies to poliovirus. Thus, the first advance was an *in vitro* method for quickly and reliably detecting poliovirus. The second advance was an *in vitro* method for detecting serum antibodies to poliovirus, as evidence of past infection. The third advance was that large quantities of polioviruses could be grown to further determine their nature (Figure 9) and devise a vaccine against them.

Salk's Killed Poliovirus Vaccine (Early 1950s)

With the availability of polioviruses cultured in human embryonic tissue, safe and effective poliovirus vaccines could be developed. One might have thought that Enders and his colleagues would have developed the vaccine. Enders was disappointed that he and his colleagues did not. Instead, the innovator of the first safe, effective poliovirus vaccine was Dr. Jonas Edward Salk (1914-1995) (Portrait 12).

Salk's parents, Daniel and Dora, were Ashkenazi Jewish Russian immigrants who settled in New York City. Jonas was born there in 1914. Thankfully, he was not affected during the severe epidemic of polio that struck New York City in 1916.

Portrait 12.

Dr. Jonas Edward Salk.

Salk (1914-1995), an American physician, developed the first effective inactivated poliovirus vaccine.

Early on, it was evident that Salk was a perfectionist. After excelling at Townsend Harris High School, a public school for intellectually gifted students, at age 15 years Jonas went to City College of New York where the tuition was free. Five years later, he earned a Bachelor of Science degree in chemistry.

Salk chose a career in medicine, with the intention of becoming a medical scientist. Because of limiting quotas for Jewish students in many major medical schools in the 1930s, prestigious medical schools were unlikely to accept him. However, New York University School of Medicine did not have such a quota, and their tuition was low. The latter was very important, since his family was financially strapped during the midst of the Great Depression. Hence, Salk entered New York University School of Medicine in 1935. He was an outstanding student and consequently he was elected to the Alpha Omega Alpha Honor Medical Society. After graduating in 1939, he began his internship and residency at New York's Mount Sinai Hospital. Afterwards, he sought a medical research position in an academic institution, but that seemed to be precluded because of his religion.

Salk had previously worked in the laboratory of Dr. Thomas Francis Jr., when Francis was discovering the Type B influenza virus at the Rockefeller Medical Research Institute in New York City. Afterwards, Francis led the School of Public Health at the University of Michigan. Salk understandably turned to him for help, and Francis found funds from the Federal Government for Salk to join him at the University of Michigan. In 1938, Francis and Salk devised an effective influenza virus vaccine.

In 1947, Salk sought repeatedly to establish his own laboratory for vaccine research. Finally, he was offered a position and a laboratory at the University of Pittsburgh. However, Salk found to his dismay that the laboratory was small and poorly equipped. Undeterred, he sought funds to properly equip and staff the laboratory. Andrew W. Mellon, the famous philanthropist from Pittsburgh, provided the financial support for the laboratory. Soon afterwards, the leaders of the National Foundation for Infantile Paralysis asked Salk to join them in their quest to develop a safe, effective poliovirus vaccine.

By using ample amounts of cultured wild poliovirus, Salk produced a formalin-inactivated preparation of all three serotypes of polioviruses. It is curious that the vaccine was patterned after the unsuccessful one that Brodie had devised in the 1930s while Salk was attending the same medical school where Brodie worked.

Preliminary studies of the vaccine in non-human primates and in a few human subjects were promising. In 1954, five years after the discovery by Enders, Weller, and Robbins of how to culture poliovirus *in vitro*, the inactivated poliovirus vaccine was tested at Arsenal Elementary School and the Watson Home for Children in Pittsburgh, Pennsylvania. Injections of the vaccine into the children produced no untoward effects, and gave rise to neutralizing serum antibodies to polioviruses.

Preparations for Clinical Trials of Salk's Vaccine

Many scientists criticized Salk's work and feared another disaster, as had occurred in the mid-1930s during the Kolmer and Brodie poliovirus vaccine trials. The critics may have been particularly concerned because Salk's vaccine was patterned after Brodie's disastrous preparation. Understandably, certain virologists on the Advisory Committee of the Foundation for Infantile Paralysis raised questions about the safety and lasting effectiveness of Salk's vaccine. They accordingly advised Salk to conduct human trials with small numbers of children before embarking on a large-scale trial. However, Basil O'Connor, the Director and co-founder with FDR of the Foundation for Infantile Paralysis, and Dr. Harry Weaver, the Director of Research at the Foundation, disagreed with the Advisory Committee. O'Connor apparently feared that a poliovirus vaccine created by a scientist not supported by the Foundation might be tested first if trials for Salk's formalin-inactivated poliovirus vaccine were delayed. The race was on. In May 1953, O'Connor created a committee of public health authorities to advise the Foundation on a field trial of Salk's vaccine.[65]

Field Trials of Salk's Poliovirus Vaccine (1954)

Three pharmaceutical companies (Parke-Davis, Eli Lilly and Connaught Laboratories) were recruited to produce large enough quantities of the vaccine for the field trial. However, Salk worried whether each lot of the vaccine would exclude live polioviruses. Dr. William Workman, the Director of the National Institutes of Health's Laboratory of Biological Controls, insisted that Merthiolate (thimerosal), an organomercury compound, be added to the poliovirus vaccine to eliminate bacterial contaminants. However, since Salk feared Merthiolate would weaken the protection of the vaccine against type I poliovirus, it was not added.

Dr. Joseph Bell from the United States Public Health Service was selected to direct the trials. He advocated a randomized positive-control trial, in which the control group received an injection of influenza vaccine to ensure the credibility of the vaccine trial. Salk disagreed, because he felt that the influenza vaccine injections would be expensive and might be injurious. Salk advised to recruit children in primary school grades one and three as controls, and to use second graders as the recipients of the experimental vaccine. O'Connor agreed with Salk.

Salk's past mentor, Dr. Thomas Francis Jr., subsequently replaced Bell as the director of the field trials. Francis recommended a double-blind trial with randomized controls, and he advised that the controls should receive saline injections. Salk and the leaders of the National Foundation agreed.

However, a randomized, placebo-controlled trial could not be conducted until a great number of physicians and local and state health officials agreed to participate. After considerable negotiations with local public health groups, the medical leaders at some locations opted for the randomized, placebo-controlled study, while the remainder chose observational controls.[65]

A few weeks before the field trials began in 1954, the famous radio news commentator, Walter Winchell, broadcast that the new vaccine might be a killer, in that some recently tested lots killed several monkeys. Consequently, some states withdrew from the field trials. It was not until the Public Health Service and an expert panel of virologists pronounced that the poliovirus vaccine was safe that the trials proceeded.

In the design of the field trials, cases of paralytic and non-paralytic polio had to be confirmed.[65] The vaccine's ability to elicit specific antibodies against each poliovirus strain was also tested. Communities with fewer than 50,000 people were generally excluded, because their public health and medical resources were usually insufficient. Therefore, most of the trials occurred in more heavily populated areas. Over 400,000 children were vaccinated in the field trials, and there were even more controls.

Despite considerable efforts to standardize the reporting of paralytic polio, the quality of the clinical assessments post-vaccination varied. To resolve the issue, a small number of specialists in poliomyelitis revised the classification scheme, and reviewed many of the diagnoses during the final analysis of the clinical data.

Table 2. Key Results from the Salk Field Trials. The Salk vaccine greatly reduced the rate of paralytic polio in vaccinated children.

Experiment	Group	Population	Paralytic Polio	
			Cases	Rate / 100,000
Saline Injection Controls	**Vaccinated**	200,745	33	16.4
	Controls	201,229	115	57.1
Observed Controls	**Vaccinated**	221,998	38	17.1
	Controls	725,173	330	45.5

People around the world waited with great anticipation for the results of the vaccine trials. Would the vaccine prevent the disease that physically disabled many thousands of children and was believed to have struck Franklin Delano Roosevelt in 1921? The results were announced on April 12, 1955,[66] the tenth anniversary of the death of FDR.

The Salk vaccine was sixty to seventy percent effective against type 1 poliovirus and over ninety percent effective against the somewhat less virulent type 2 and 3 polioviruses. In the "saline placebo" areas (poliovirus vaccine versus saline injection controls), the paralytic polio rate was 16.4 per 100,000 in the vaccinated group, and 57.1 per 100,000 in the control group (Table 2).[66]

Results in the "observed" areas (poliovirus vaccine versus observed controls) were similar. The paralytic polio rate was 17.1 per 100,000 in the vaccinated children, and 45.5 per 100,000 in the observed controls.

Approval and Widespread Use of Salk's Vaccine (1955)

On the day the results of the field trials were announced, Dr. William Workman, the Chief of the Bureau of Biological Standards of the National Institutes of Health, met with a group of expert virologists in Ann Arbor, Michigan to discuss whether the poliovirus vaccine should be federally licensed. After a two-hour discussion, Workman phoned the Surgeon-General of the United States to tell him that the experts unanimously recommended that the vaccine be licensed. It was the quickest federal approval ever for a vaccine, or perhaps for any therapy, by the federal government of the United States.

In July of the previous year, O'Connor had spent nine million dollars (equivalent to about 73 million dollars in the year 2010) from the Foundation for Infantile Paralysis to underwrite the production of the Salk poliovirus vaccine.[17] More than ten million doses of the vaccine were stockpiled for future use if the vaccine field trials were successful. A massive poliovirus immunization program was rapidly deployed once the federal government approved the Salk vaccine.

Salk Vaccines Contain Live Virus - Remedial Measures

All went well during the first several days of the national poliovirus vaccine campaign. Then, on April 25, 1955, Workman's office was informed that some children in Illinois and California who had received the poliovirus vaccine became partially or completely paralyzed.[67] Consequently, one manufacturer, Cutter Laboratories, voluntarily suspended the distribution and production of the vaccine.

Afterwards, the unfortunate occurrence was called the Cutter Incident,[67] although the other pharmaceutical firms that produced the vaccine had similar difficulties in completely inactivating polioviruses. There were 200 or more cases of vaccine-related paralytic polio. Public confidence in the poliovirus vaccine abruptly diminished. Consequently, immunization rates fell significantly.

Over the next month, manufacturers, federal authorities, and virologists determined what had gone wrong and remedied the problem by figuring out how to ensure that live polioviruses were excluded from the vaccines. The director of the field trial, Dr. Francis, declared that the revised poliovirus vaccine was safe and effective.[67] Over the next several years, the production and testing of the vaccines were modified many times to make the vaccines safer and more effective in preventing polio.

Success of Revised Killed Poliovirus Vaccine

As a result of the mass poliovirus immunization campaign, the annual number of cases of paralytic polio in the United States plummeted from 35,000 in 1953 to 5,600 by 1957.[68] By 1961, only 161 cases were recorded in the United States.[69] By 1979, poliomyelitis was eliminated from the United States, and soon thereafter, the infection disappeared in many other industrialized countries.[60] The striking success of the inactivated poliovirus vaccine further underscored the positive role that FDR had played in the development of the vaccine. The association of FDR with the successful effort reinforced the public perception that he had suffered from paralytic polio.

Portrait 13.

Dr. Hilary Koprowski.

Koprowski (1916-2013) developed the first live attenuated poliovirus vaccine.

First Live Attenuated Poliovirus Vaccine

Hilary Koprowski (1916-2013) (Portrait 13) was born in Warsaw, Poland to a Jewish family. He received his medical degree from Warsaw University in 1939. That same year, he and his wife fled Poland because of the German invasion that triggered World War II. They eventually settled in the United States, where he became a researcher at Lederle Laboratories located in Pearl River, New York. There he began experimenting with polioviruses.

By 1948, Koprowski had produced an attenuated strain of polioviruses by injecting the virus into brains of cotton rats (*Sigmodon hispidus*), a New World species that was found to be susceptible to experimental polio. The harvested attenuated strain from those animals was not pathogenic in other animals. In

1948, he administered a small oral dose of the attenuated poliovirus to himself. He experienced no ill effects.

An opportunity to test the experimental vaccine in a small number of children came about when he was approached in 1950 by Dr. George Jervis, the director of Letchworth Village, a home for disabled persons in Rockland County, New York, very close to where Koprowski worked. Jervis wished for a trial to be conducted because he feared that a polio epidemic might occur in the children because of their unsanitary behaviors.

Portrait 14.

Dr. Albert Bruce Sabin.

Sabin (1906-1993), an American physician, developed an oral live attenuated poliovirus vaccine that temporarily replaced the Salk vaccine because of the ease of its administration.

In 1950, an attenuated type II strain of the virus was given to 20 disabled children at Letchworth. None developed adverse reactions to the experimental vaccine. Seventeen of the children developed serum antibodies to polioviruses; the others apparently already had antibodies to the viruses. Soon thereafter, several hundred children in the United States received Koprowski's vaccine against type I and type II strains of the virus without ill effects. Koprowski and his colleagues confirmed the results during a mass field trial in the Belgian Congo carried out between 1957 to 1960.[70] It was the first oral attenuated poliovirus vaccine and was the basis of Sabin's live attenuated poliovirus vaccine.

Sabin's Live Attenuated Poliovirus Vaccine

Albert Bruce Sabin (Portrait 14) (original surname, Saperstein) was born into a Jewish family in Bialystok, Russia, an area primarily populated by Jews at that time. However, largely to avoid religious persecution that was escalating throughout Eastern Europe, his family immigrated to America in 1921 when Albert was 15 years of age. Nine years later, Albert became a naturalized citizen of the United States, and changed his surname to Sabin.

Sabin was an excellent student. To please his parents he briefly studied dentistry, before becoming interested in medical research. He received a medical degree from New York University in 1931, four years before Salk entered the same medical school. Sabin trained in internal medicine, pathology, and surgery at Bellevue Hospital in New York City from 1931 through 1933. In 1934, he conducted research at The Lister Institute for Preventive Medicine in the University of London. He then joined the Rockefeller Institute for Medical Research, where the discoverers of the poliovirus, Karl Landsteiner and Simon Flexner, were working. This association most likely profoundly influenced the course of Sabin's future career, as he eventually succeeded in developing a safe, effective oral vaccine to polioviruses.

In 1939, Sabin moved to Cincinnati Children's Hospital where he continued his investigations into infectious diseases. When the United States entered the Second World War in 1941, Sabin became a Lieutenant Colonel in the United States Army Medical Corps, and helped to develop a formalin-inactivated vaccine against the Japanese encephalitis virus to protect military personnel in the Pacific theater.

After the war, he rejoined the Children's Hospital in Cincinnati, and by 1946 became the head of Pediatric Research at the University of Cincinnati. It was there that Sabin further developed the attenuated oral poliovirus vaccine, by culturing an attenuated strain (obtained from Koprowski) in non-human cells at sub-physiological temperatures.

Sabin's oral attenuated poliovirus vaccine was safe and effective. A massive uncontrolled field trial of the oral poliovirus vaccine was conducted in the USSR in 1959. Ten to fifteen million people, principally young children, received the vaccine.[71] No adverse reactions were reported. However, it is likely that the live oral vaccine was inadvertently given to some immunodeficient (deficient in some part of the immune system) children. Therefore, at least a few cases of paralytic polio should have occurred.

The mass immunization campaign was uncontrolled and no data were published. Nevertheless, the precipitous drop in cases of paralytic polio in the USSR laid the foundation for the universal acceptance of the oral poliovirus vaccine.[72] Today, the lack of a large, controlled study for a new vaccine would not be acceptable.

Since no adverse effects were reported and the vaccine was immunogenic, Sabin's vaccine was approved for human use. For many years, it was the principal poliovirus vaccine, because it could be given orally rather than by injection. Sabin's live attenuated oral poliovirus vaccine was particularly useful in underdeveloped countries in Africa and Asia, because of logistical problems with the transport and administration of the injectable inactivated virus vaccine.

The eradication of poliomyelitis in most of the world was in large part due to the support of the Foundation for Infantile Paralysis (The March of Dimes) founded by President Roosevelt. At every step in the development, testing, and implementation of the poliovirus vaccines, the public was reminded of FDR's poliomyelitis diagnosis, his struggles to overcome paralysis, his great accomplishments as President, and his role in providing support for the development of polio vaccines.

Portrait 15.

Barbara Jean Goldman.

She and many thousands of other nurses immunized millions of children against polio in the 1960s.

The successful deployment of protective polio vaccines had an enormous positive impact upon the American public. My wife Barbara (Portrait 15), who was an excellent nurse, and I helped to immunize hundreds of infants and children at one of the local schools. The event was duplicated many times by many volunteer nurses and physicians across the country (Figure 10).

The memories of the looks of gratification on the faces of parents, knowing that the deadly, crippling polio was to be a thing of the past – that their child was not going to be at risk from that feared malady – are still vivid. Because this was occurring only a little more than a decade after the death of FDR, it was a reminder of his efforts to prevent poliomyelitis. Also wrapped in this package were the realizations that the country had come out of the depths of the Great Depression, that we with our allies had won the Second World War, and that the United Nations had been largely created because of the leadership of FDR. It was heady times for the United States, and somewhat of a deification of the past leader of the country.

Figure 10.

People in Line for Polio Vaccines.

Hundreds of people lined up in San Antonio, Texas to get oral polio vaccinations in 1962.

Public Reminders of FDR's Poliomyelitis

Most people in the United States were greatly impressed with FDR's courage in overcoming what they believed was the crippling effect of paralytic polio. That in turn encouraged victims of that disease to rehabilitate and to return to a more normal life. The published pictures and newsreels of President Roosevelt's upturned face and infectious smile, and his statement at his first presidential inaugural address *"the only thing we have to fear is fear itself – nameless, unreasoning, unjustified terror*" were heartening, and continued to remind the public that he had overcome the dreaded poliomyelitis.

Even after poliomyelitis disappeared from the United States because of the widespread application of the poliovirus vaccines, the public was repeatedly reminded about the past burdens imposed by polio. One of the major writers on this important subject was Dr. Marc Shell, Professor of English at Harvard University. When Shell was age six years, he developed what was believed to be paralytic polio. In Shell's somewhat autobiographical book *Polio and Its Aftermath*,[73] published in 2005, he commented in detail about the personal costs, cultural implications, and historical significance of paralytic polio. He depicted the disease as one of most deadly diseases in recent history. In that respect, he described the broad cultural impact of paralytic polio upon the American public. Indeed, many Americans became engrossed with the disease. Poliomyelitis became the subject of many books and movies concerning the polio victims, and gave rise to many autobiographical accounts of paralytic polio. In the minds of the public, poliomyelitis was considered not just an infectious disease, but also a scourge.

Of equal importance, Shell revealed how the crippling effects of poliomyelitis preempted a discussion of other pressing infectious diseases, until the plague of poliomyelitis ended with the widespread application of poliovirus vaccines.

Famous People with Poliomyelitis

The preoccupation of the American public with paralytic polio was further intensified by the diagnosis of paralytic polio in other famous Americans, including the classical music violinist Itzhak Perlman,[74] the film director Francis Ford Coppola,[75] the actress Mia Farrow,[76] the actor - director - writer Alan Alda,[77] the singer and talk show host Dinah Shore,[78] the US Senator from Kentucky Mitch McConnell,[79] and the champion Olympic runner Wilma

Rudolph.[80] The stories of how Rudolph and Perlman overcame paralytic polio to reach the highest levels of accomplishment in athletics and classical music, respectively, are briefly presented below.

Wilma Rudolph was struck down by paralytic polio at age four years. Her left foot became twisted, due to a disparity in the strength of the muscles in her partially paralyzed left leg. Consequently, her left leg and foot were fitted with a special brace that she wore for the next five years. Her disability lessened. But Rudolph needed to wear an orthopedic shoe to support her left foot for another two years.

When she discarded the orthopedic shoe in her teenage years, she became a basketball star, set state scoring records, and led her team to a state basketball championship. But Rudolph's forte was running. At age 16, she won a berth on the United States Olympic track and field team, and at the 1956 Melbourne Summer Olympic Games, she earned an Olympic bronze medal in the 4 x 100 meter relay. Four years later, she won three gold medals (100 meter, 200 meter, and 4 x 100 meter relay) and set two world records in the 1960 Summer Olympics in Rome.

The second inspiring example, Itzhak Perlman, developed what was believed to be paralytic polio at age four years (1949), and remained paralyzed in his lower extremities. Even before his paralysis, Itzhak wished to play the violin, but he was denied entrance to the Shulamit Conservatory in Israel because he was too small to hold the smallest sized violin. Instead, Itzhak taught himself how to play by using a toy fiddle.

Despite the permanent paralysis of his lower extremities and his inability to walk without the aid of crutches, Itzhak began to study violin in the Shulamit Conservatory in Jaffa and the Academy of Music in Tel Aviv. It was soon recognized that he had the potential to become a great violinist. Consequently, when Itzhak was in his late childhood, his family moved to the United States so that he could study at the Juilliard School of Music. His tutor, Ivan Galamian (1903-1981), was a noted violin teacher who combined the French and Russian schools of violin technique. In time, Perlman became one of the premier concert violinists of the twentieth century,[74] despite the permanent paralysis in his lower extremities.

Figure 11.

Movie Star Ralph Bellamy as FDR.

Movies such as *Sunrise at Campobello* played a powerful role in reinforcing the public perception that FDR had paralytic polio.

Sunrise at Campobello

After the death of President Franklin Delano Roosevelt, the public was reminded vividly of his heroic struggle to overcome the paralysis attributed to polio by the Broadway play *Sunrise at Campobello*, and the adaptation of the play into the moving, very popular motion picture of the same name. The 1960 motion picture starred Ralph Bellamy (Figure 11), who literally became FDR, and Greer Garson, who depicted Eleanor Roosevelt so effectively that she was nominated for the Academy Award for Best Actress, and won the Golden Globe Award for Best Actress – Motion Picture Drama and the National Board of Review Award for Best Actress.[81]

The film *Sunrise at Campobello* depicted scenes before, during, and immediately after the paralytic illness that struck FDR. The film masterfully captured FDR's struggle to regain the use of his lower extremities, the anxieties generated in his family, and Eleanor's pivotal role in Franklin's recovery. The movie's climax, FDR's re-entrance into politics, came as he reached the podium with the aids of leg braces and crutches to nominate Al Smith for the Democratic Party candidate for President of the United States in 1924.

Sunrise at Campobello was seen in movie theaters by many millions of Americans in 1960, just when the newly developed poliovirus vaccines were defeating poliomyelitis. The messages from the movie were powerful, and the intermingling of FDR and paralytic polio made an indelible impression upon viewers.

The many replays of *Sunrise at Campobello* on television reinforced the message of FDR's victory over that dread disease. Moreover, in 2005, Home Box Office (HBO) produced the highly praised made-for-television film *Warm Springs*, which was based on FDR's struggle to overcome paralytic polio. It too had a dramatic ending at the 1924 National Democratic Convention. The film won several Emmy Awards, including one for Best Made-for-Television Film.

Thus, in the eye of the public, there was never the slightest doubt that FDR had paralytic polio, and that he won the battle against that terrible disease. The corollary was that FDR, who had contracted paralytic polio, played a decisive role in the development of the vaccines that put an end to that affliction in the United States and in the vast majority of other countries.

Thus, at the end of the twentieth century, there was universal agreement that FDR was crippled by paralytic polio in the summer of 1921.

"The Waltons –An Easter Story"

The diagnosis of paralytic polio in FDR was again reinforced by the highly rated, emotionally packed 1973 television episode of *The Waltons* entitled "An Easter Story", the last episode of the first season of that television series.[82] The series was created by Earl Henry Hammer Jr., and patterned after his book *Spencer's Mountain*. I accidently saw a replay of the episode in 2015. In the story, set in the mid 1930s during the Great Depression, Olivia Walton – the still young mother of the seven Walton children – developed a sudden symmetrical paralysis of her legs that ascended to her lower abdominal muscles. She also had transient neck and back pain. Very soon, she lost feeling in her legs, which was replaced by pain. Afterwards, the feeling in her legs again diminished. She had fever during the first several days of the illness.

The illness was diagnosed as polio by the family physician. A spinal tap was not done and apparently was not considered. Olivia was cared for at home by her family and their family physician. She was poignantly portrayed, as she vacillated between depression over her illness and a determination to recover. Over a few weeks, her husband and her mother-in-law feared that she would not recover and would have to use a wheelchair. But Grandpa Walton admonished the family not to give up, and pointed out that President Franklin Roosevelt overcame the same affliction. Olivia's eldest son, John Robert "John-Boy" Walton Jr, also adamantly refused to accept that his mother would be permanently paralyzed. At one point, Olivia was visited by Dr. Miller, a physician from a medical school in Virginia, whose legs were severely paralyzed from polio when he was age 18. That visit served to further emphasize the diagnosis of polio and the possible fate that awaited Olivia - permanent paralysis of her legs - confined to a bed, a chair, or a wheelchair.

After some weeks, the paralysis and pains receded in the reverse direction. After a few trying months, she recovered almost completely, in time to celebrate the rebirth of life as exemplified by the coming of spring and Easter.

Olivia's case was not in keeping with polio. 1) Her age (about 32) made it unlikely she would contract polio. 2) The illness began in February, rather than in the summer when polio characteristically struck. 3) There was no evidence of a febrile, pre-paralytic phase that occurs in paralytic polio. 4) The symmetric, ascending paralysis and the prolonged hyperesthesia were not in keeping with paralytic polio.

The creator of *The Waltons* television series, Earl Henry Hammer Jr., inadvertently used many major features of Guillain-Barré syndrome to describe the illness. Given the strong association in the public mind between FDR and polio, it is likely that Olivia's illness was based on what Hammer had read about FDR's 1921 neurological illness or what he had seen in the movie, *Sunrise at Campobello*. Or perhaps Hammer had witnessed an adult with a similar illness who was incorrectly diagnosed with paralytic polio. Regardless of the reasons, the television program reinforced the belief that FDR had paralytic polio. And as with the case of the *Sunrise at Campobello* movie produced 13 years earlier, the diagnosis was incorrect, but the story was compelling and uplifting.

"American Experience – The Polio Crusade"

On February 1, 2009, PBS broadcast a program on their *American Experience* history series concerning the blight of polio, the intense fear generated by the disease, and the attempts to control it by the development of the first polio vaccine. FDR's polio diagnosis, his work to restore his body and his career, and his efforts to find support for the development of the inactivated polio vaccine were highlighted during the one-hour program.

The Roosevelts: An Intimate History

The notion that FDR had paralytic polio in 1921 was again emphasized in a popular television series produced by Ken Burns and his associates for the Public Broadcasting System. In the fourth episode, which aired on September 17, 2014, the fact that FDR had poliomyelitis was stated without reservation over twenty times. The phrase *"right diagnosis"* was stressed in that regard. No other diagnostic possibilities were mentioned. The remaining episodes of the series continued to declare that Roosevelt had poliomyelitis.

It was of interest that the televised series was produced with the aid of several outstanding historians, who were very knowledgeable about the life of FDR. However, the purpose of the television series was not to discuss the cause of FDR's neurological illness, but to indicate how he dealt with the illness and its permanent damage, and to examine the life, character, accomplishments, and lasting impacts of FDR, his wife Eleanor, and his fifth cousin Theodore Roosevelt.

This very powerful depiction of the life and times of Theodore, Franklin, and Eleanor Roosevelt was viewed by many millions in the United States and in other countries where the program was broadcast. An estimated 9.1 million viewers saw the first episode. The series was shown again in May 2015, adding even more viewers.

I admired the presentation. On the negative side, the incorrect polio diagnosis was presented unchallenged, it was not discussed how close FDR came to dying, and Eleanor's role in his nursing care was not mentioned. It was, however, a further impetus to write a book explaining why the diagnosis of paralytic polio was incorrect, and why a different disease caused FDR's neurological illness in 1921.

Chapter 10. Cause of FDR's Illness Questioned

"The true delight is in the finding out rather than in the knowing." ~ Isaac Asimov

Until the end of the twentieth century, I assumed that FDR was disabled by paralytic polio. Then, by chance, I was led to question the diagnosis. It was serendipity – the accidental discovery of something of value. The problems with the polio diagnosis were pointed out to me late one autumn afternoon in 2000 by a member of my family. It happened in the following way.

Discovery at Windy Hill

My wife Barbara and I had a ranch called "Windy Hill" that was located in the eastern part of the Texas Hill country, a few miles from the Colorado River. Because of its rolling terrain, natural beauty, and abundant wildlife, it was the best place we ever lived. When I was not on call, one of our sons, Paul (Portrait 16), and I drove from Galveston to Windy Hill each Friday evening, to help with the longhorn cattle, repair fences, mow the pastures, and tend to other chores. Paul and I were the proverbial unhired hands. The experience was good, for I saw many interesting native plants and animals and was able to escape for a little while the stress of playing doctor. And during the evenings, I had a chance to write, study, listen to classical music, talk with Barbara, or admire the clear, star-filled night skies. And I had the pleasure to be with Paul.

Now Paul, who is not a physician or a biologist, asked me one late October afternoon, after we had finished mowing the west pasture in preparation for the spring wildflower season, to read a chapter in a biography of FDR concerning *"his paralytic illness"*. I innocently replied, *"You mean his poliomyelitis"*. Paul gently corrected me. *"No Father, his paralytic illness"*. I briefly puzzled over

Paul's correction, and agreed to read the chapter. Afterwards, I understood why Paul had said, *"his paralytic illness"*.

Portrait 16.

Paul Goldman.

Paul Goldman was the first to determine that the diagnosis of FDR's 1921 paralytic illness was incorrect.

After I read the chapter a number of times, I was stunned. Almost unconsciously, I walked onto the porch of our little frame house and looked to the west over the rolling plain that sloped down toward the Colorado River. I had conflicting thoughts. If what I read was correct, why had it taken me so long to discover this strange medical story? I went back inside to reread the chapter. After Paul returned, I asked him what he thought about Roosevelt's illness. He told me that Roosevelt did not have poliomyelitis. When I asked him why, he promptly gave several reasons why he doubted the diagnosis of paralytic polio. Paul pointed out that it was very unusual for someone FDR's age (39 years) to get poliomyelitis, and that certain of his symptoms, such as the symmetric, ascending paralysis, did not fit paralytic polio. I agreed with his analysis. Now that my mind was open to other possibilities, I also realized that FDR probably had another disease, one that I had encountered once in an older child and four times in middle-aged adults.

You might ask how Paul, who was not a physician or a scientist, quickly and coherently analyzed FDR's clinical case. Paul was and is an avid reader of science, mathematics, medicine, and history. He probably learned a great deal about medicine indirectly from me, for I often brought home medical books and journals to read. Sometimes I needed time off from medicine, so I left them "temporarily" unattended. At least that was my rationalization. Paul read my books and journals from cover to cover, and in some ways understood their contents as much as I did. He does to this day.

Paul's discovery was in a sense serendipity, but it was also a reminder that serendipity is only successful when one is seeking new information, and when one is prepared to examine and interpret the accidental finding. This is an important, fundamental concept in science. Accidental discoveries have often led researchers to question long-standing beliefs. That is one important way science advances.

What to Do With the Discovery

After the revelation that FDR most likely did not have paralytic polio, but instead had a different neurological disease, I was in a dilemma. Along with hundreds of millions of other people and many thousands of physicians, I had never doubted that FDR had paralytic polio. Therefore, it was difficult to believe otherwise. I felt conflicted. If the description in the FDR biography was correct, why was it that I had never heard that the diagnosis of paralytic polio might be incorrect, and that a different disease might have caused FDR's permanent paralysis? Surely there were many excellent physicians, including neurologists and experts in poliomyelitis, who must have read accounts of FDR's 1921 illness, at the very least in his biographies. It struck me that the account of the illness in the book

Paul and I read might be incorrect. To be more certain, Paul found several other biographies of FDR at the public library in Houston. The descriptions of the 1921 neurological illness in those biographies were virtually the same as what was described in the first book.

Plans to Reappraise FDR's 1921 Neurological Illness

To be more certain about the clinical features of FDR's 1921 illness and to determine its cause, the original descriptions of the disease had to be found and studied. I sought help from the excellent librarians at the Moody Medical Library at the University of Texas Medical Branch in Galveston. With their generous assistance, the clinical facts of FDR's case were gathered from primary sources. The sources included letters from FDR,[14] his wife Eleanor,[15] and his uncle Frederic Adrian Delano;[19] Earle Looker's book concerning FDR;[12] and communications concerning FDR written by his physicians, Lovett and Draper.[21] Other published books concerning FDR, and the few medical journal articles that dealt with FDR's illness, were studied. All said that FDR had paralytic polio.

The counsel of several senior physicians who had seen many cases of paralytic polio was sought. They were puzzled by my question, and each said without hesitation that FDR had paralytic polio. That was a presage of events that were to come once our study was published.

At the same time, an in-depth review was conducted of the non-traumatic causes of flaccid paralysis and of the other clinical features of FDR's illness. That was particularly important, since I was not a neurologist. However, I had cared for several children with paralytic polio before the poliovirus vaccines were widely used, and I had seen several adults and one teenaged boy with the disease we suspected caused FDR's neurological illness. Being a clinical immunologist was also advantageous, as you will learn later in this book.

The diagnostic reappraisal of FDR's 1921 neurological illness was greatly aided by a wealth of discoveries in the last half of the twentieth century concerning microbiology, immunology, neurology, and the diseases that might have been responsible for FDR's neurological illness. It was important that four professional colleagues provided needed skills and expertise for the investigation. They were 1) Dr. Elisabeth J. Schmalstieg, an excellent clinical neurologist; 2) Dr. Frank C. Schmalstieg Jr., a nationally recognized expert in basic and clinical immunology; and 3) Dr. Daniel H. Freeman Jr., an epidemiologist and biomedical statistician. In 2001, each independently analyzed the clinical data and concluded that FDR likely did not have paralytic polio. Later on, Dr. Daniel A. Goldman, a physician, epidemiologist, statistician, and computer programmer, joined the study. He also agreed with the revision in the diagnosis.

Dr. Charles Dreyer, another excellent clinical neurologist, aided us in our second investigation of this subject nearly a decade later. He took a fresh approach to the question, and provided some valuable insights regarding the cerebrospinal fluid abnormalities in two of the diseases in question. After his analysis was completed, he agreed with us concerning the cause of FDR's 1921 neurological disease.

I asked Paul to co-author a manuscript concerning the investigation of FDR's neurological illness. To my disappointment, he declined. When I asked him why, he calmly stated he was satisfied that the diagnosis of paralytic polio was incorrect. He therefore felt that his help was no longer needed. It was enough in his mind that he had initiated the investigation. Furthermore, he explained that his attention had turned to other important historical figures, a study of some mathematical puzzles, and a book regarding theoretical physics. I reluctantly accepted his polite refusal, but credited him for the initial discovery in the articles that we published, as well as in this book.

Paul's insight was the key first step in the analysis of FDR's illness. Without Paul's questioning mind and his ability to read the FDR biography free of preconceived notions, the issue would not have been raised. Perhaps others privately questioned the diagnosis and kept quiet. To my knowledge, Paul was the first to raise the issue.

Without Paul's prompting, the question of the polio diagnosis would almost certainly have never occurred to me, just as it never occurred to countless other physicians. I could have dismissed Paul's conclusions with a brusque "Everyone knows FDR had polio" and the matter would have died. Instead, I took Paul seriously, and read the FDR biography chapter as if I were consulting on a patient.

After reading the chapter, it was clear that the polio diagnosis was likely wrong. However, even at that point, most might have given up, since overcoming the pervasive conventional wisdom that FDR had polio would be extremely difficult, regardless of the facts. Unfortunately, that has proven to be the case.

Finally, without help from others, it is unlikely that I would have undertaken a detailed analysis of FDR's 1921 illness.

Without this special set of circumstances, the diagnosis of FDR's 1921 illness would perhaps never have been questioned, as the continued repetition that "FDR had polio" in books, TV programs, films, and other powerful media would have made it ever harder to challenge the conventional wisdom.

Chapter 11. Diagnostic Methods

"Most of the fundamental ideas of science are essentially simple." ~ Albert Einstein

Illnesses from the distant past are often difficult to reappraise. That pertained to FDR's 1921 neurological illness in several ways. 1) FDR, his wife, others in his family, and his physicians, who were the principal sources of information, had long since departed. Therefore, it was impossible to directly confirm the medical history and the physical findings, as we would do with a living patient. 2) FDR's hospital records in the New York-Presbyterian Hospital could not be found. That was unfortunate, since it is likely these medical records included case notes and the results of laboratory studies done during his neurological illness.

We realized our limitations, but we were encouraged that FDR, his wife Eleanor, and two of his physicians (Lovett and Draper) provided accounts of the symptoms, physical findings, and clinical course of the disease. Therefore, it seemed reasonable to use those accounts to reappraise the cause of FDR's neurological illness.

The classical approach used in medical diagnosis involves interactions between the art and the science of medicine. Once all of the clinical data are obtained, the most suitable medical hypothesis is constructed. Then, appropriate laboratory tests are selected to verify or refute the hypothesis.

Art and Science of Medical Diagnosis

There are several important aspects to the art of medical diagnosis that applied to our analysis of FDR's 1921 neurological illness.

1. *Skepticism*. Be skeptical of previous diagnoses (even those made by authorities), unless they are proved definitively.

2. *Primary History*. Obtain a detailed account of the illness, including the duration, intensity, and temporal occurrence of the symptoms. This is necessary, because patients often only reveal symptoms that seem most important to them, and may fail to state other symptoms that might be major clues to the diagnosis.

3. *Other Parts of the History*. Ascertain the past illnesses, current and past medical treatments, pertinent environmental exposures, and the family medical history.

4. *Physical Examination*. Conduct a thorough physical examination that includes not only parts of the body that would be predicted to be involved from the medical history, but other sites as well. That is important because the physical examination may reveal critical information not suggested by the history. Those findings may lead to a diagnosis. In fact, some findings are "pathognomonic", that is they are diagnostic of a particular disease. Therefore, a complete physical examination is usually warranted, particularly when the diagnosis is difficult.

5. *Crosschecking*. Crosscheck the findings from the medical history and the physical examination for possible interrelationships. For example, abnormal physical signs should be further explored by further inquiries into the medical history. Alternatively, symptoms and other information related by the patient should lead to a more detailed physical examination of certain parts of the body.

6. *Assemble and Correlate the Clinical Findings*. The findings from the medical history and the physical examination are assembled and correlated to establish the most likely diagnostic hypothesis.

7. *Establish the Hypothesis*. The most likely hypothesis concerning the cause of an illness is usually generated by comparing a patient's clinical findings with the

features of the suspected diseases. That process is called "pattern recognition". However, a probabilistic analysis (a method that deals with likelihoods – with the odds of an occurrence) of the clinical manifestations in suspected diseases may also be performed. Often, this is done informally. In some cases, a formal statistical analysis may be needed. Finally, the best diagnostic possibilities are established by reconstructing the pathogenesis of the suspected disease (the steps in the generation of the pathology of the disease).

8. *Select the Appropriate Diagnostic Tests*. Once the most likely diagnostic hypothesis is established, as needed, appropriate laboratory diagnostic tests are selected to verify or refute the diagnosis.

9. *Interpret the Results of Diagnostic Tests*. When the results of the laboratory tests are known, they should be interpreted in the context of the rest of the clinical findings. Most of the time a laboratory test is accurate, but sometimes there may be technical or clerical errors. Furthermore, low normal or high normal values may be falsely interpreted as being abnormal. When the results of laboratory tests do not correlate with the findings from the medical history or the physical examination, the clinical data should be reviewed and the laboratory tests in question should be repeated. If the first hypothesis is rejected, then a new hypothesis is devised and tested along the lines that have been previously recounted.

The science of medicine is intertwined with each of the steps used in the diagnosis. The more one knows about the proven mechanisms and presentations of diseases, the more one is able to interpret clinical findings, formulate a hypothesis, and determine how to test it.

In concert with the principles described above, we used three diagnostic strategies in the analysis of FDR's case: pattern recognition, Bayesian analysis, and reconstructing the pathogenesis. Those strategies will be further discussed, because of their importance in understanding the cause of FDR's 1921 illness.

Pattern Recognition

The first method we used was pattern recognition, the most commonly used strategy in medical diagnosis. In pattern recognition, the symptoms, physical findings, and other clinical data are compared with the clinical features found in the diseases that most closely fit the patient's illness. The diseases that best match the patient's clinical findings are then selected as the main diagnostic hypotheses. Physicians usually use pattern recognition, because the method is straightforward, rapid, and sufficient for the diagnosis of most illnesses.

The pattern recognition method is further discussed in Chapters 12-14.

Bayesian Analysis

The second approach we used, Bayesian analysis, is a probabilistic analysis described by the English clergyman and mathematician Reverend Thomas Bayes (1702-1761) (Portrait 17) and modified by the French scientist-mathematician Pierre-Simon Laplace (1749–1827) who introduced a general version of the theorem.[83,84]

In Bayesian analysis, clinical data are analyzed to determine the probabilities that specific clinical features in the patient are consistent with those in a suspected disease.[85] For example, fever may occur in disease "A" frequently, say in 80 percent of the cases, but less commonly in disease "B", say in 20 percent of cases. In pattern recognition, fever may be given a similar weighting in both diseases, but in probabilistic analysis fever would favor disease "A". In probabilistic analysis, the frequency of occurrence of each suspected disease is also considered. For instance, if disease "A" occurs twice as frequently as disease

"B", disease "A" will be twice as likely to be the correct diagnosis, all other things being equal. It is always best to use the frequencies of the diseases in the age group of the patient in question. For example, poliomyelitis occurs much more frequently in children than adults. When symptom probabilities and frequencies of occurrence greatly favor one particular disease, that disease is usually the cause of the patient's illness. However, a rare disease may be most likely when the symptom probabilities favor it far more than commoner diseases. Since even rare diseases may occur, if the symptoms closely match, a rare disease may be the correct diagnosis.

Portrait 17.

Reverend Thomas Bayes.

This eighteenth century clergyman (1702-1761) developed the basis of the statistical method used to analyze the clinical data from FDR's 1921 neurological illness.

Bayesian analysis is straightforward and uses simple mathematics (see Chapter 15 and Appendix A for an explanation of the mathematics of the method). It is particularly useful when the manifestations of two or more diseases overlap considerably with those found in the patient's illness. Although the method was not the primary way we arrived at the diagnosis in FDR's case, it confirmed the conclusion obtained from pattern recognition, and allowed us to assign probabilities that paralytic polio or an alternative diagnosis may have caused FDR's illness.[2]

Reconstruction of the Pathogenesis

The third method we used, reconstruction of the pathogenesis, starts with the presenting features of the illness and works backwards in a step-wise fashion, until the initiating cause is discovered. In a sense, it is like retrospective chess, in that one is presented with the end game (in medicine, the clinical manifestations of the illness) and is asked to recreate the positions of the chess pieces one, two, three, or more moves beforehand (in medicine, the sequences of the pathological process, from the end to the beginning). This retrospective medical diagnostic analysis requires an in-depth knowledge of potential diseases, normal and abnormal physiology, and the molecular mechanisms of diseases, along with deductive reasoning. It is the most rigorous scientific approach to diagnosis. Reconstructing the pathogenesis is particularly illuminating when the cause of a disease is difficult to discover because of its complexity, rarity, or controversial nature.

For readers wanting to more fully understand the method, an extended example of reconstructing the pathogenesis, using a case I observed years ago, is in Appendix C. Also, how reconstructing the pathogenesis was used in the diagnostic reassessment of FDR's illness is detailed in Chapter 16.

Chapter 12. Unlikely Causes of FDR's Illness

"It is a capital mistake to theorize before you have all the evidence." ~ Sherlock Holmes, *A Scandal in Bohemia*

The diseases that my colleagues and I considered in the diagnostic analysis of FDR's case were those that present with a non-traumatic flaccid paralysis. Using pattern recognition, most were quickly ruled out because their most prominent clinical features were absent in FDR's illness. They were as follows.

Coxsackie Infection

Coxsackie virus infections were ruled out because they occur principally in children, do not produce an ascending paralysis, and commonly have rigidity of the neck.[86] They principally produce mild, flu-like symptoms. Less commonly, far more serious problems may occur, including a flaccid or spastic paralysis. Affected individuals usually recover from those neuromuscular complications. Thus, the symptoms did not fit the pattern of FDR's illness.

Rabies

Rabies was not the cause, because its main features are an animal bite, severe muscle spasms, and death when not promptly treated after the bite.[87]

Viral Encephalitis

Since an encephalitis virus infection causes prominent, protracted cerebral symptoms, it is not a possible cause.[88]

Botulism

Botulism was ruled out, because the typical clinical symptoms in that disease, such as difficulty swallowing, facial weakness, drooping eyelids, blurred vision, dry mouth, and difficulty breathing, were not found in FDR's case. Also, the paralysis in botulism is descending, not ascending.[89]

Tetanus

Tetanus ("lockjaw") was not considered, because it presents with prominent muscular spasms (especially in the jaw, neck, and back muscles), which were absent in FDR's case.[90]

Other Toxins

Plant toxins were inconsistent with FDR's clinical presentation.[2] The possible exception was the fruit of the coyotillo, a shrub-like tree (*Karwinskia humboldtiana*). Ingestion of the fruit causes an ascending, symmetric flaccid paralysis that is similar to the pattern of FDR's paralysis.[91] However, exposure to the coyotillo toxin was ruled out, because the coyotillo tree is restricted to arid regions of Baja California, New Mexico, and South Texas, and because neurosensory symptoms do not occur after exposure to the toxin. In addition, permanent paralysis from coyotillo toxin is uncommon.

Other external toxins were very unlikely, since no other member of the Roosevelt household displayed neurological or other serious systemic problems during FDR's 1921 illness.

Other Neurological Diseases

An additional neurological disease we considered was transverse myelitis, an inflammatory lesion of a single segment of the spinal cord.[92] Although the disease has some clinical features that are similar to those displayed by FDR, and some cases may be due to immunological events, the disease was ruled out because an ascending paralysis, facial paralysis, and a descending pattern of recovery (such as occurred in FDR's case) do not occur in transverse myelitis.

The most common motor neuron disease, amyotrophic lateral sclerosis (ALS), was also considered. ALS causes a slowly progressive generalized muscle weakness and atrophy due to the degeneration of upper and lower motor neurons. ALS is characterized by stiff muscles, muscle twitching, and gradually worsening weakness. Moreover, difficulties in speaking, swallowing, and breathing occur. Most affected individuals die within a decade after the onset of the disease. Moreover, FDR's most prominent symptoms (dysesthesia and ascending, symmetric paralysis) do not occur in ALS.[93]

Another possible cause of bilateral flaccid paralysis of the lower extremities is Froin's syndrome, first described in 1903 by a French physician, Georges Froin (1874-1932).[94] Froin found that the paralysis was due to meningeal irritation. In this rare disease, the CSF is yellowish (xanthochromic) because of an exceptionally high concentration of protein in the CSF, and coagulates shortly after its removal because of the high protein concentration. The disease is usually due to a localized spinal meningitis or an epidural abscess.[95-97] In some ways, the neurological findings were perhaps similar to the disease that Keen assigned to FDR (a localized hematoma). However, it is unclear whether Keen was familiar with Froin's report. FDR's symmetric, ascending paralysis and partial clinical recovery ruled out Froin's syndrome.

Finally, porphyria polyneuropathy, a rare autosomal recessive genetic disease due to a deficiency in the enzyme porphobilinogen deaminase, presents as a peripheral neuropathy, and therefore was considered.[98] However, since abdominal symptoms, protracted mental disturbances, recurrences of those symptoms, and external activating agents such as medications were absent in

FDR's case, this type of porphyria was ruled out. Other diseases that somewhat mimic FDR's illness were not considered because of their low likelihood.[99]

Poliomyelitis and Guillain-Barré Syndrome Most Likely

Thus, because the other alternatives were so inconsistent with FDR's clinical presentation, the diagnostic possibilities narrowed down to two diseases. The first was paralytic polio, because it was the universally accepted diagnosis in FDR's case, and because a few features of his illness were in keeping with paralytic polio.[51,56,92,99] The second potential cause of his permanent paralysis was Guillain-Barré syndrome (GBS), an autoimmune, demyelinating neuropathy that damages peripheral motor and sensory nerves.[40,41,92,99,100]

Chapter 13. Was It Paralytic Polio?

"A man should look for what is, and not for what he thinks should be." ~ Albert Einstein

My colleagues and I considered paralytic polio in the differential diagnosis of FDR's 1921 illness, because it was the universally accepted cause, and because of his permanent paralysis and fever, which are both frequent in paralytic polio.

In dealing with this and other diagnostic possibilities, we realized that there is a range in the intensity of the pathology and hence in the clinical manifestations of many diseases. When a disease is being considered as a diagnosis, it is necessary to keep in mind the typical signs and symptoms and their frequencies, as reported in peer-reviewed articles in medical science journals. However, to take biological variability and the variable expression of disease signs and symptoms into account, and to "give poliomyelitis the best chance", we purposely over-estimated the probabilities that certain symptoms found in FDR's case occur in paralytic polio.

Five features of FDR's life and illness have been thought by many physicians and historians to favor a diagnosis of paralytic polio. They are 1) his sheltered childhood, 2) his vigorous exercise immediately preceding the illness,[101-103] 3) his prior tonsillectomy,[104,105] 4) fever at the onset of the paralysis,[92,106-109] and 5) his extensive permanent flaccid paralysis.[92,106-109] In this chapter, each feature is discussed and shown not to favor polio as strongly as commonly supposed.

Prior Exposure to Poliomyelitis

Many historians felt that FDR's late onset of paralytic polio was due to his sheltered early life and the resultant paucity of exposure to polioviruses during that period. However, the issue is more complicated, because after his early childhood at Hyde Park, FDR was exposed to many people of various ages. It is unclear whether he ever contacted someone with poliomyelitis, but it should be kept in mind that less than one percent of individuals infected with polioviruses develop the paralytic form of the disease. Many more develop an asymptomatic or mild illness that is not recognized as a poliovirus infection. Yet those asymptomatic individuals are able to transmit the viral infection. Thus, it is likely that FDR was exposed to polioviruses long before his 1921 neurological illness. However, that cannot be proven, since the methods used to demonstrate a prior infection were not available in 1921.

Many historians believe that FDR became infected with the poliovirus when he visited the Boy Scout Jamboree at Bear Mountain in July 1921. There was no evidence that any of the scouts or personnel at that gathering were infected with the virus. But since most infected individuals have the non-paralytic form of the infection, the possibility cannot be ruled out. However, it seems just as likely that FDR could have contracted a different infection at Bear Mountain, leading to a different cause of his paralytic illness. So the visit is not used as a factor in our diagnostic analyses.

Vigorous Exercise and Paralytic Polio

Around 1950, it was reported that vigorous exercise during the pre-paralytic phase of the disease predisposed stressed muscles to become paralyzed in poliomyelitis.[101-103] However, that contention was based upon testimonials, not upon controlled observations that quantitatively documented the degree of physical exertion in muscles that became paralyzed. Furthermore, poliovirus infections occur almost exclusively in children during the summer months, when children usually are more physically active. Therefore, the association of paralytic polio with exercise may be an example of "correlation is not causation".

For those reasons, the alleged association between exercise and paralytic polio was not used in our analyses.

Prior Tonsillectomy and Bulbar Poliomyelitis

Another clinical feature that supposedly favored the diagnosis of paralytic polio in FDR's case was prior tonsillectomy. It was found in the mid-twentieth century that tonsillectomy predisposes children to a rare form of poliomyelitis, bulbar poliomyelitis.[104,105] Bulbar poliomyelitis involves motor neurons of cranial nerves in the medulla oblongata (the brainstem). Apparently, components of the lymphoid tissue of the pharynx protect cranial motor nerves against invasion by polioviruses. Those cranial nerves, including the glossopharyngeal nerve (cranial nerve IX) and the vagus nerve (cranial nerve X), innervate muscles that control swallowing and speech. Because FDR did not have bulbar poliomyelitis, prior tonsillectomy was not included as a factor in our diagnostic analysis.

Fever and Permanent Paralysis in Paralytic Polio

Fever and permanent paralysis are major features of paralytic polio. Permanent paralysis is frequent in paralytic polio, and fever usually occurs at the onset of the paralysis.[92,106-109] Those two features were therefore used in our diagnostic analysis.

It is important to understand that there are four types of poliomyelitis.

1. *Asymptomatic Infections.* Between 90 and 95 percent of individuals infected with polioviruses are asymptomatic (Table 3, page 111).

2. *Mild Febrile Illness.* In about four to eight percent of poliovirus infections, a mild illness develops characterized by a few days (less than a week) of fever, malaise, a sore throat, mild gastrointestinal symptoms, and influenza-like symptoms.[92,106-109]

Table 3. Clinical Types of Poliomyelitis.

Severity of Polio Infection	Percent of Cases
Asymptomatic	90 - 95 %
Minor febrile illness	4 - 8 %
Non-paralytic aseptic meningitis	1 - 2 %
Paralytic polio	0.1 - 0.5 %

Table 4. Types of Paralytic Polio.

Type of Paralysis	Percent of Paralytic Cases
Spinal	80 %
Bulbospinal	18 %
Bulbar	2 %

3. *Aseptic Meningitis.* In one to two percent of poliovirus infections, a non-paralytic, aseptic meningitis characterized by headaches, stiffness and pain in the neck and back, myalgia, irritability, nausea, and vomiting occurs a few days after a mild febrile illness. This form of poliomyelitis lasts two to ten days and leaves no residual effects.

4. *Paralytic polio.* Paralytic polio occurs in less than one percent of poliovirus infections (Table 3). The paralysis usually involves muscles innervated by spinal motor nerves, in other words, muscles of the arms or legs. The paralysis is characteristically preceded by a febrile period that is like the illness found in

mild, non-paralytic polio. Additional symptoms that occur during the prodromal phase (before the paralytic phase) may include temporary severe muscle aches and spasms in the limbs or back, probably due to meningeal inflammation. Once the paralytic phase begins, the paralysis progresses for two to three days. Half of such affected individuals are permanently paralyzed. Furthermore, since polio is an anterior horn cell (motor neuron) disease, the muscles affected are usually represented segmentally and often in one limb. Paralytic polio only involves motor neurons. In about 80 percent of cases, the involvement is limited to spinal cord motor neurons (Table 4). If FDR had paralytic polio, it was the spinal form.

During the paralytic stage, there are no sensory abnormalities in the spinal form of paralytic polio.

Improbability of Paralytic Polio

When FDR's case was subjected to pattern recognition (a comparison of a patient's signs and symptoms with known diseases), paralytic polio was found to be improbable for the following reasons.

Paralytic polio is uncommon to rare in adults of FDR's age (39 years).[51,52,54,56,60,92,106-109]

Permanent paralysis and fever favored paralytic polio. However, the other features of FDR's illness, including the symmetric, ascending paralysis, the autonomic dysfunctions, and the remarkable sensory symptoms, were inconsistent with paralytic polio (Table 5, page 114).

Although fever was used as a diagnostic criterion in FDR's case, the pattern of the fever that FDR experienced was atypical of paralytic polio. As already mentioned, the pre-paralytic phase consists of a few days of fever and mild systemic symptoms.[92,106-109] After a brief respite (usually only a few days), the febrile paralytic phase begins.[92,106-109] Since a pre-paralytic phase (a prodrome) was absent in FDR's illness, the pattern was not consistent with paralytic polio. However, in the interests of "giving poliomyelitis the benefit of the doubt", we included fever as a criterion, and counted it as strongly favoring the diagnosis of paralytic polio, perhaps more than it deserved.

Roosevelt's paralysis was symmetric and ascending, and progressed more than four days, whereas the paralysis in poliomyelitis is typically asymmetric, variable in its ascent or descent, and usually progresses for only two to four days.[92,106-109] Indeed, our review of the medical research literature revealed only one report of paralytic polio with a symmetric, ascending paralysis.[110] Even in that report, the authors suggested that the neuropathology might have been due to an immune reaction against peripheral nerves, rather than a direct effect of polioviruses upon motor neurons.

Facial nerve paralysis, which FDR experienced during his illness, is rare in poliovirus infections except in the bulbar form, where polioviruses invade cranial motor neurons in the medulla oblongata. In bulbar poliomyelitis, several cranial nerve nuclei are likely to be damaged.[92,106-109] However, except for the facial nerve, there was no evidence that cranial nerves were involved in FDR's case. Therefore, FDR did not have bulbar polio, and so his facial paralysis is not consistent with a polio diagnosis.

FDR had prolonged decreased motility of the smooth muscles of the bladder and of the lower intestinal tract. Such protracted autonomic nervous system abnormalities are rare in paralytic polio.[92,106-109]

FDR experienced a brief loss of pain and touch (partial anesthesia) in his lower extremities. Immediately after, he endured severe, protracted pain to the slightest touch (hyperesthesia) in his lower extremities. Sensory abnormalities rarely if ever occur in paralytic polio.[92,106-109] Furthermore, one characteristic feature of paralytic polio, meningismus (neck stiffness), was absent in FDR's case.[92,106-109]

Thus, the clinical picture in FDR's neurological illness was mostly inconsistent with paralytic polio, but was mostly consistent with GBS, a disease that strikes sensory as well as spinal motor nerves, involves the facial nerves, and temporarily disables parts of the autonomic nervous system that are essential for motility of smooth muscles of the urinary bladder and lower intestinal tract.

Table 5. Comparison of FDR's Illness to GBS and Paralytic Polio. **Highlighting** shows whether a clinical finding favors GBS or paralytic polio.

	Age of Occurrence	*Fever*	*Permanent Paralysis*
FDR	39 Years	Present	Present
GBS	**Mainly adults**	Rare	15% of cases
Polio	Mainly children	**Common**	**50% of cases**

	Pattern of Paralysis	*Recovery from Paralysis*
FDR	Symmetric, ascending	Symmetric, descending
GBS	**Symmetric, ascending**	**Symmetric, descending**
Polio	Asymmetric	Asymmetric

	Numbness	*Meningismus*	*Hyperesthesia*
FDR	Transient	Absent	Prominent
GBS	**Common**	**Absent**	**Common**
Polio	Absent	Common	Absent

	Facial Paralysis	*Bladder / Bowel Paralysis*
FDR	Present	About 14 days
GBS	**Common, bilateral**	**Common: For 7-14 days**
Polio	Rare in non-bulbar form	Uncommon

Chapter 14. Was It Guillain-Barré Syndrome?

"The upper parts of the body, the last to be affected, are the first to recover their mobility which then returns from above downwards." ~ Octave Landry

Given that FDR's age and many features of his illness were inconsistent with poliomyelitis, my colleagues and I proceeded to investigate the possibility that FDR's paralytic illness was due to GBS. The reasons why GBS was considered can be best understood by reviewing how the clinical, histopathological, and immunological features of the disease were discovered.

Discovery of Guillain-Barré Syndrome

An account of the discovery of GBS gives context, and helps to understand why it was the most likely cause of FDR's 1921 neurological illness and why it took so long for GBS to be considered in FDR's case. Let us start with the physicians who first recognized the major clinical features of GBS.

Portrait 18.

Dr. Octave Landry.

In 1859, Landry (1826-1865) described what would later be known as Guillain-Barré syndrome.

Octave Landry (1859)

The French physician Dr. Auguste-François Chomel and the Irish physician Dr. Robert J. Graves (famous for his discovery of Graves' disease, the most common cause of hyperthyroidism) recognized some of the basic clinical features of GBS during a brief epidemic that occurred in 1828 in Paris, France.[111,112]

The first thorough report of the neuropathy appeared two decades later in 1859, when a French physician, Dr. Jean Baptiste Octave Landry de Thézillat (1826-1865) (Portrait 18), described ten previously healthy adults who developed a sudden, symmetric, ascending, flaccid paralysis, sometimes with dysesthesia (abnormal sensation).[113] His description was as follows:

"The sensory and motor systems may be equally affected. However the main problem is usually a motor disorder characterised by a gradual diminution of muscular strength with flaccid limbs and without contractures, convulsions or reflex movements of any kind. In almost all cases micturition and defaecation remain normal. One does not observe any symptoms referable to the central nervous system, spinal pain or tenderness, headache or delirium. The intellectual faculties are preserved until the end. The onset of the paralysis can be preceded by a general feeling of weakness, pins and needles and even slight cramps. Alternatively the illness may begin suddenly and end unexpectedly. In both cases the weakness spreads rapidly from the lower to the upper parts of the body with a universal tendency to become generalised.

The first symptoms always affect the extremities of the limbs and the lower limbs particularly. When the whole body becomes affected the order of progression is more or less constant: (1) toe and foot muscles, then the hamstrings and glutei, and finally the anterior and adductor muscles of the thigh; (2) finger and hand, arm and then shoulder muscles; (3) trunk muscles; (4) respiratory muscles, tongue, pharynx, oesophagus, etc. The paralysis then becomes generalised but more severe in the distal parts of the extremities. The progression can be more or less rapid. It was eight days in one and fifteen days in another case which I believe can be classified as acute. More often it is scarcely two or three days and sometimes only a few hours.

When the paralysis reaches its maximum intensity the danger of asphyxia is always imminent. However in eight out of ten cases death was avoided either by skillful professional intervention or a spontaneous remission of this phase of the illness. In two cases death occurred at this stage . . . When the paralysis recedes it demonstrates the reverse of the phenomenon which signaled its development. The upper parts of the body, the last to be affected, are the first to recover their mobility which then returns from above downwards."[113]

Landry cared for five of the patients and read about five others with similar findings. Two of Landry's patients died. The spinal cords and brains from the two deceased patients were microscopically normal. The peripheral nerves were not examined microscopically. In the survivors, recovery from the paralysis was in the reverse direction – from the upper to the lower part of the body.

Louis Duménil (1864)

In 1864, five years after Landry's report, a French surgeon, Dr. Louis Stanislas Duménil (1823-1890), *Médecin des Hospices,* demonstrated (by postmortem microscopic examinations) areas of segmental demyelination in atrophic peripheral nerves.[114] He did not refer to Landry's report, although the clinical features of the patients were probably similar to those reported by Landry. The more decisive relationship between Landry's ascending paralysis and peripheral nerve damage was demonstrated a decade later (see next section).

Portrait 19.

Dr. Ernst Viktor von Leyden.

In 1879, von Leyden (1832-1910) found that Landry's ascending paralysis was a peripheral neuritis, and that paralytic polio was due to spinal motor neuron lesions.

Ernst von Leyden (1879)

In 1879, twenty years after Landry's report, Dr. Ernst Viktor von Leyden (1832-1920) (Portrait 19), a German physician-neurologist from Danzig, found a peripheral neuritis characterized by fatty replacement of peripheral nerve tissue.[115] Long before that time, it was known that peripheral nerves serve as communication lines between the central nervous system and the rest of the body.

The patients reported by von Leyden most likely had GBS. Remarkably, in that same investigation, von Leyden discovered that paralytic polio was due to damaged motor neurons in the spinal cord.[115] That established a fundamental difference between the two diseases.

Thus, because of discoveries in France and Germany, the clinical and pathological distinctions between paralytic polio and Landry's ascending paralysis were essentially established by 1880. Some European physicians, such as the famed German neurologist Herman Oppenheim, were familiar with the findings.[116] Karl Landsteiner, who first experimentally transmitted the poliovirus, was aware of the clinical differences between paralytic polio and Landry's ascending paralysis.[47] However, the findings received much less attention in the United States and elsewhere until the second half of the twentieth century.

Portrait 20.

Dr. Georges Guillain.

In 1916, Guillain (1876-1961) and his colleagues found the cerebrospinal fluid abnormalities in Landry's ascending paralysis.

Georges Guillain, Jean Alexandre Barré, André Strohl (1916)

The next major advance in understanding the abnormalities in Landry's ascending paralysis occurred in 1916, when two French neurologists, Dr. Georges Guillain (1876-1961) (Portrait 20) and Dr. Jean Alexandre Barré (1880-1967) were serving in the *Centre Neurologique de l'Armée VI Française* during World War I. Along with a neurophysiologist, Dr. André Strohl (1887-1977), they made two important discoveries (CSF characteristics and nerve conduction abnormalities) in two French soldiers (25 and 35 years of age) with ascending, symmetrical paralysis.[117]

Although the soldiers were in a combat zone, their neurological problems were not caused by trauma. Their presenting clinical abnormalities were an ascending, symmetrical paralysis; loss of deep tendon reflexes; paresthesia (unusual cutaneous sensations); and pain on deep palpation of large muscles. The findings were in keeping with the abnormalities that Landry had described in 1859.

Cerebrospinal fluid (CSF) was collected from both patients during the first few days after the onset of the paralysis. The reason why the spinal taps were done was not stated, but the findings were important. The CSF in each patient contained a normal number of leukocytes and a high concentration of protein. This was the opposite of the CSF abnormalities in paralytic polio.

Strohl performed nerve conduction and electromyographic studies on the patients. Diminished nerve and muscle function were found in the lower limbs of both patients. This was in keeping with a peripheral neuropathy.

After World War I, physicians dealt with three somewhat similar neurological disorders: 1) Landry's ascending paralysis, 2) the peripheral neuritis described by Guillain, Barré, and Strohl, and 3) acute febrile neuropathies due to diphtheria or perhaps other infections. In 1927, the eponym Guillain-Barré syndrome was first used at a presentation by two French neurologists, Dr. Dragonescu and Dr. Claudian, at a meeting of *Société de Neurologie de Paris*. Perhaps unfairly, none of the names "Landry", "Duménil", "von Leyden", and "Strohl" became part of the eponym. On the other hand, the eponym "Landry-Duménil-Guillain-Barré-Strohl syndrome", or some other combination of names, would be very unwieldy.

In an extensive 1949 report, Dr. Web E. Haymaker and Dr. James W. Kernohan suggested a wider definition of the illness, and put forth the idea that Landry's ascending paralysis and Guillain-Barré syndrome (GBS) were indistin-guishable.[40] Guillain was outraged. He continued to insist until he died in 1961 that the disease that he and his colleagues described was different from the one that Landry reported in 1859. Guillain was incorrect. GBS was the same disease that Landry had reported,[113] and that Duménil[114] and von Leyden[115] had found to be a peripheral neuritis. Unfortunately, the failure of each physician to acknowledge the contributions of preceding ones hindered the recognition of GBS.

Pattern Recognition Favors Guillain-Barré Syndrome

FDR's neurological abnormalities were classical for the acute motor and sensory axonal neuropathy type of GBS (see Table 5, page 114). They were 1) an ascending, symmetric paralysis that progressed more than four days;[99,100,109,117-129] 2) facial paralysis in the absence of other cranial nerve abnormalities;[109,117-129] 3) prolonged, decreased motility of the bladder and large intestines;[109,117-130] 4) temporary numbness and protracted hyperesthesia;[109,117-129,131] 5) slow, symmetric, partial resolution of the paralysis in a descending fashion;[109,117-129] and 6) permanent, nearly symmetrical paralysis of the lower extremities.[109,117-129] Furthermore, stiffness of the neck (meningismus), commonly found in paralytic polio,[92,106-109] but not in GBS,[92,109,118-130] was absent in FDR's case.[1,14] Therefore, pattern recognition indicates that FDR most likely had GBS.

Chapter 15. Bayesian Analysis of Clinical Data

"Statistics is the grammar of science." ~ Karl Pearson

The first way that we arrived at the diagnosis of GBS in FDR's case was by pattern recognition. However, to test the hypothesis more objectively, we used Bayesian analysis, a simple yet powerful statistical method (see page 101) to quantitate the pattern recognition findings. To prepare for the analysis, the incidences ("prior probabilities") of paralytic polio and GBS in adults in the United States were estimated from past epidemiological reports in peer-reviewed journals.

This first part of Bayesian analysis is straightforward. All other things being equal, if disease "A" is twice as common as disease "B", disease "A" is twice as likely to be the correct diagnosis. A clinician first rules out common conditions before considering rarer diseases (but keeps the mind open to all possibilities).

Prior Probability of Guillain-Barré Syndrome

The incidence of GBS during the first half of the twentieth century was poorly understood, because the disease was not well appreciated at that time. Therefore, data from reports in peer-reviewed journals from the last half of the twentieth century had to be used to estimate the incidence of GBS.[121-127]

GBS is the most common type of non-traumatic, acute flaccid paralysis in adults. Approximately one in every thousand individuals in the United States will contract GBS sometime during their lifetime.[127] Current estimates of the overall incidence of GBS in the United States range from 1.1 to 1.8 new cases per 100,000 per year. In the United States, the incidence of GBS is highest in individuals 50 years or older (1.7 to 2.3 per 100,000 per year) and lowest in children from birth to 15 years (0.34 to 1.34 per 100,000 per year).[121-127] The incidence of GBS in individuals 30 to 40 years is closer to the rate in older than in younger people. After examining the data concerning the incidence of GBS from many reports, we estimated the incidence in adults around age 39 to be 1.3 new cases per 100,000 per year.[2]

Prior Probability of Paralytic Polio

In contrast to GBS, there are considerable data concerning the incidence of paralytic polio during the early part of the twentieth century. For paralytic polio, an incidence rate of 2.3 new cases per 100,000 adults aged 34-45 years was used as a starting point. This rate was selected from data obtained from the exceptionally severe poliomyelitis epidemic that struck New York City in 1916.[54] The prior probability of paralytic polio in FDR's age group in the United States in 1921 was likely much lower, because paralytic polio was at one of its lowest ebbs in the Northeastern region of the country at that time.[51,132] Thus, we gave paralytic polio an elevated prior probability to "give it the best chance to succeed".

Next, we corrected the reported incidence rate of paralytic polio to take into account unrecognized (in 1921) causes of non-traumatic flaccid paralysis. These other causes, such as GBS, did not suddenly spring into existence in subsequent decades. They had been occurring all along, but were misdiagnosed as polio. Therefore, the real incidence of paralytic polio in adults in 1921 was most likely lower because of an over-diagnosis of paralytic polio and a concurrent under-diagnosis of GBS. That was because Landry's ascending paralysis, or what is now called Guillain-Barré syndrome, was rarely recognized as a separate entity in the United States in 1921. To account for this, we subtracted from the paralytic polio rate in adults (2.3 per 100,000) those cases that were likely due to GBS (1.3 per 100,000), leaving a rate of 1.0 per 100,000. Overall, the prior probabilities in adults for GBS (1.3) and paralytic polio (1.0) for the year 1921 were not that different.

During the first part of the twentieth century, the diagnosis of paralytic polio was often accepted solely on clinical grounds, without measuring the concentrations of leukocytes or protein in cerebrospinal fluid. That was unwise. In the first few days of the paralytic phase of poliomyelitis, the CSF concentration of leukocytes is increased but the concentration of proteins is normal. The converse occurs in the first few days after the onset of GBS. To confuse matters, certain authoritative medical textbooks published around 1921 stated that elevated levels of protein in cerebrospinal fluid occurred in paralytic polio.[133] Thus, in 1921, examination of CSF might not have helped distinguish between paralytic polio and GBS in the first few days of a neurological illness.

Given the state of medical knowledge at the time, it is understandable why cases of GBS, particularly in adults in the United States, were falsely attributed to paralytic polio at the time of FDR's neurological illness. It was not until several decades later that the distinction between paralytic polio and GBS was commonly made in the United States, based on the history, a detailed neurological examination, studies of cerebrospinal fluid collected early in the illness, nerve conduction studies, viral cultures, and magnetic imaging of nerve roots in the spinal cord.

In the late 1950s and 1960s, poliovirus vaccines were widely and successfully applied.[51,52,60,68,69,132] As the number of new cases of paralytic polio dwindled, other non-traumatic causes of flaccid paralysis became more evident in all age groups. Thus, GBS, as well as other causes of non-traumatic flaccid paralysis, became better appreciated after paralytic polio declined and then disappeared in the United States and other countries in the latter part of the twentieth century.

Bayesian Analysis Greatly Favors GBS

Once we had the prior probabilities, step 1 of the Bayesian analysis was complete. Given that the prior probabilities for middle-aged Americans in 1921 were 1.3 for GBS and 1.0 for paralytic polio, and assuming that FDR's paralysis was caused by either GBS or paralytic polio, GBS would be the slightly more likely diagnosis if we had no other information (57% probability for GBS, 43% for paralytic polio).

Table 6. Bayesian Analysis of FDR's Illness. Posterior probabilities of GBS and paralytic polio (PP) in FDR's case were estimated by Bayesian analysis, based on prior probabilities (57% for GBS, 43% for paralytic polio) and symptom probabilities. Greater probabilities are in **bold**. The table is a modification of one found in reference 2.

FDR's Case	Probabilities	
	Symptom GBS / PP	Posterior GBS / PP
Hyperesthesia / numbness	**0.50** / 0.01	**0.98** / 0.02
Ascending, symmetric paralysis	**0.70** / 0.02	**0.98** / 0.02
Descending pattern of recovery	**0.70** / 0.02	**0.98** / 0.02
Facial paralysis	**0.50** / 0.02	**0.97** / 0.03
Bladder / bowel paralysis ~14 days	**0.50** / 0.05	**0.93** / 0.07
No meningismus	**0.99** / 0.10	**0.93** / 0.07
Permanent paralysis	0.15 / **0.50**	0.28 / **0.72**
Fever	0.01 / **0.90**	0.01 / **0.99**

But we do have other information. Step 2 of the Bayesian analysis takes a "symptom probability" into account, using a simple equation, to produce a "posterior probability". A symptom probability is the percent of cases of a disease that have the symptom at some point. For example, from the peer-reviewed literature, hyperesthesia and numbness are seen in only about 1% of paralytic polio (solely affects motor nerves) cases, but in about 50% of GBS (also affects sensory nerves) cases. The resulting "posterior probability" is the bottom line, the best estimate of how likely the diagnosis is correct. For example, after adjusting for the "hyperesthesia / numbness" symptom, GBS is the much more likely diagnosis (98% posterior probability).

Figure 12. Posterior Probabilities for GBS and Paralytic Polio. For each clinical finding in FDR's case, the likelihood the correct diagnosis was GBS or paralytic polio was determined.

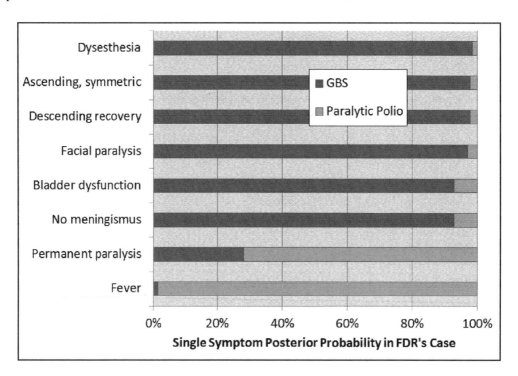

Bayesian analysis (Table 6) verified that GBS was the most likely cause of FDR's illness. Each Bayesian analysis focused on one symptom in FDR's case. For that symptom, the symptom probabilities were combined with the prior probabilities in a simple equation to produce the posterior probability. Six of eight Bayesian analyses favored GBS as the correct diagnosis over paralytic polio (Figure 12).

Table 7: Testing Sturdiness of the Bayesian Analysis. Adjustments in symptom probabilities in paralytic polio and GBS needed to equalize posterior probabilities (PostProb). Each number before the arrow ($\rightarrow$) is the actual symptom probability. Each number after the arrow is the adjusted symptom probability required to equalize the posterior probabilities.

Clinical Features	Adjustment to Equalize PostProb	
	GBS	Paralytic Polio
Hyperesthesia / numbness	-	$0.01 \rightarrow 0.65$
Ascending, symmetric paralysis	-	$0.02 \rightarrow 0.92$
Descending pattern of recovery	-	$0.02 \rightarrow 0.92$
Facial paralysis	-	$0.02 \rightarrow 0.65$
Bladder / bowel paralysis ~14 days	-	$0.05 \rightarrow 0.65$
No meningismus	-	$0.10 \rightarrow 1.00$
Permanent paralysis	$0.15 \rightarrow 0.38$	-
Fever	$0.01 \rightarrow 0.68$	-

We considered whether we were underestimating the chance of paralytic polio, because of the possibility that we had become too focused upon the diagnosis of GBS. To further ensure that we were being objective, we determined what adjustments in the symptom probabilities for paralytic polio were required to equalize the six posterior probabilities that favored GBS. Vast adjustments were required (Table 7). This test helped ensure that we were not experiencing confirmation bias, and showed the Bayesian analyses were generally robust (gave the same results even when input parameters were significantly changed).

Interestingly, looking at the two symptoms that favored paralytic polio, for one of them (permanent paralysis), a more modest change in the symptom probability (0.15 to 0.38) could equalize the posterior probabilities (make GBS equally likely). This further reinforces the likelihood that FDR had GBS.

Another way we tested the sturdiness of the Bayesian analysis was to arbitrarily lower the prior probability of GBS (originally 0.57) and correspondingly increase the prior probability of paralytic polio (originally 0.43). Changing prior probabilities to values that were still somewhat realistic did not change the result. Even at a prior probability of 0.1 for GBS (0.9 for paralytic polio), a huge change from the best estimates based on peer-reviewed articles, six of eight posterior probabilities still favored GBS.

Further Bayesian analyses taking all of FDR's symptoms into account to produce an overall probability (paralytic polio vs GBS) are presented in Appendix B. The result of the overall analysis is that FDR's 1921 illness was almost certainly (greater than 99.9% probability) caused by GBS.

So far, we have examined the diagnosis of FDR's illness from the clinical viewpoint and by applying Bayesian analysis. In the next chapter, we will look at the diagnosis using a third method, by comparing the pathogenesis of GBS and paralytic polio.

Chapter 16. Pathogenesis of FDR's Illness

"In solving a problem of this sort, the grand thing is to be able to reason backwards." ~ Sherlock Holmes, *A Study in Scarlet*

The cause of FDR's 1921 illness was further examined by determining whether the abnormalities and clinical course were more consistent with the pathogenesis of paralytic polio or GBS. Consequently, the pathogenesis of each disease is reviewed.

Poliomyelitis

The steps in the pathogenesis of poliovirus infections (Figure 13, below) are as follows:

Initial Infection and Multiplication

There are three serotypes of polioviruses, all of which are pathogenic.[51] Serotype 1 is the dominant cause of poliovirus epidemics. Serotype 2 was eradicated in 1999, while the other two serotypes (1 and 3) still occur in certain third world countries.[132]

Only humans are naturally infected with polioviruses. Polioviruses infect by binding to a specific receptor on the surface of epithelial cells lining the pharynx (throat) and intestines. The receptor is an immunoglobulin-like molecule called CD155.[134] The binding of the poliovirus to CD155 and the survival of the virus appear to be enhanced by a prior interaction of the virus with lipopolysaccharides, large molecules consisting of a lipid and a polysaccharide on outer membranes of Gram-negative bacteria.[135] Once poliovirus binds to its receptor, the poliovirus RNA (its genome) enters the host cell. Once inside, the

RNA binds to ribosomes (complex translational apparatus that produces proteins). At that point, viral peptides required for viral multiplication are made.

Pre-Paralytic Phase

Polioviruses are ingested

Polioviruses bind to CD155 receptors on intestinal epithelium

Viruses uncoat and then replicate in intestinal epithelium

↓

Newly generated polioviruses enter the blood

Paralytic Phase

Some polioviruses bind to CD155 on axons of motor neurons

Microtubules transport polioviruses to anterior horn cells

Anterior horn motor neurons are damaged or die

Skeletal muscle becomes weak or paralyzed

Figure 13. Pathogenesis of Paralytic Polio.

Systemic Spread of Polioviruses

Several days after the infection begins, polioviruses invade two additional cell types: 1) dendritic cells (specialized cells that take up, process and present antigens) in lymphoid tissues of the oropharynx (such as the tonsils and adenoids), and 2) microfold cells (specialized antigen-uptake cells) in the epithelium of Peyer's patches in the lower small intestine. Polioviruses then spread to lymph nodes in the neck and abdomen, where they multiply. A systemic immune response to the virus is initiated. At the same time, polioviruses spread to the blood (Figure 13) and to other non-neural sites such as lymphatics and lymph nodes. All of these events occur during the pre-paralytic phase of the disease.

Uptake and Transport by Motor Nerve Axons

Polioviruses spread to the central nervous system by attaching to the CD155 receptor on axons of motor neurons (Figure 13).[136] Each motor neuron has one axon, a slender projection that conducts nerve impulses to a muscle.

In 1950, it was found that the intramuscular site of common immunizations correlated with the development of paralysis in that same limb.[137] In 1985, a similar finding was reported to occur in certain tropical countries.[138] Provocation of paralytic polio in specific sites by intramuscular injections of the pertussis vaccine or the diphtheria / pertussis / tetanus (DPT) vaccine was found in an outbreak in Oman in 1992.[139]

It was likely that the injections predisposed motor nerves closest to the injection site to transmit the polioviruses up the motor axons. The transmission of polioviruses by intramuscular poliovirus injections has been replicated in experimental animals.[140] In those experimental animals, transection of the affected motor nerve prevented the polioviruses from reaching anterior horn cells in the spinal cord.

The poliovirus receptor CD155 spans the cell membrane of intestinal epithelial cells and motor nerve axons. On the outside of the membrane, the poliovirus attaches to part of CD155. Polioviruses attached to CD155 are taken into the cell. Inside the axon of the motor neuron, part of CD155 strongly associates with light chains of dynein, an intracellular motor transport protein.[141] At that point, the dynein starts "walking" along a microtubule (long tubular polymer in the cytoplasm), carrying its deadly cargo with it. Polioviruses are thus transported up the motor axon to the body of the motor neuron in the spinal cord.

Polioviruses then shed their coats and replicate in the bodies of motor neurons. Finally, the permeability of mitochondria (membrane bound organelles that generate most of the cell's chemical energy) is increased, and apoptosis (programmed cell death) occurs.[142] As a result, motor neurons invaded by polioviruses are destroyed. In contrast, sensory neurons are not invaded or affected by polioviruses, because they lack the CD155 receptor or any other mechanism that permits polioviruses to invade them. In experimental bonnet monkeys (Macaca radiata), some longitudinal spread of the virus occurs up and down the spinal cord,[143] but that has not been demonstrated in humans.

During paralytic polio, some inflammation develops in the spinal cord, as lymphocytes and some neutrophils invade the meninges and spaces around tissue blood vessels. But the major mechanism of motor neuronal injury and death appears to be apoptosis (non-inflammatory, programmed cell death).[144]

Why only a small percentage of infants and children with polio contract the paralytic form is undetermined. A genetic predisposition has been postulated, but never demonstrated.[145]

Paralytic Polio Inconsistent with FDR's Illness

FDR's illness is not consistent with the pathogenesis of paralytic polio because: 1) FDR did not experience the fever and mild systemic symptoms that characterize the pre-paralytic phase of poliomyelitis, 2) FDR had prominent sensory symptoms, but sensory neurons, which lack CD155, are not attacked by polioviruses. 3) FDR had autonomic nervous system involvement, but that is rare in paralytic polio, since polioviruses do not attack autonomic nerves.

Poliomyelitis	Guillain-Barré Syndrome
Antibodies are formed against polioviruses	Antibodies are formed against *C. jejuni* LPS
↓	↓
Antibodies prevent attachment of poliovirus to CD155 receptor	Antibodies cross-react with GM1 on peripheral nerve axons
↓	↓
So, antibodies **prevent** polio	So, antibodies **cause** GBS

Figure 14. Contrasting Antibody Effects. Antibodies protect against polio, but produce neuropathies in GBS.

Guillain-Barré Syndrome

To further determine whether FDR's illness was in keeping with GBS, the pathogenesis of GBS was reviewed. In contrast to poliomyelitis, where antibodies protect against the infection, in GBS autoantibodies that arise in response to certain infections are responsible for the neuropathy (Figure 14).

Role of Prior Infections in GBS

Landry remarked in his original report that some of the patients with ascending paralysis had been ill for some weeks before their paralysis began. The nature of their preceding illnesses is not known. In the 1980s and 1990s, it was found that most patients with Guillain-Barré syndrome experienced some type of infection four to six weeks before the onset of the neuropathy. In order of their frequencies, the predisposing agents were *Campylobacter jejuni (C. jejuni)*, *Cytomegalovirus*, Epstein–Barr virus and *Mycoplasma pneumoniae*.[146] By the time the clinical features of GBS appeared, the preceding infections had resolved.

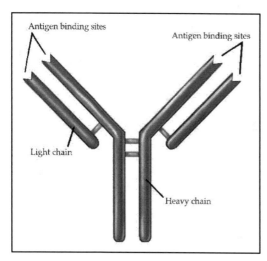

Figure 15.

Structure of an IgG antibody.

Each antibody has two identical antigen binding sites, located at the variable regions of the heavy and light chains.

The temporal relationship between an antecedent infection and the onset of neurological abnormalities led to the idea that the neuropathies in GBS were due to immunological events generated by the prior infections. It was hypothesized that some weeks after an infection, high serum concentrations of antibodies to the infecting agents were somehow involved in the pathogenesis of the disease. It was later found that IgG antibodies (Figure 15) against the infecting agents also recognized a key chemical structure on peripheral nerves. The lag between the inciting infection and the clinical onset of the neurological manifestations in GBS is due to the time it takes to produce sufficient concentrations of pathogenic IgG autoantibodies (Figure 16).

Autoantibodies to GM1

Soon after it was recognized that the neurological features of GBS were preceded by certain infections, supporting evidence for an immune-mediated mechanism for the pathogenesis of GBS emerged. This discussion is limited to the type of GBS that affects motor and sensory nerves, and to the most common types of autoantibodies.

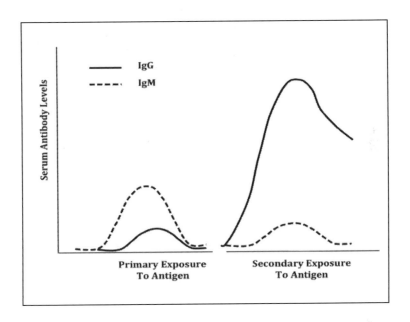

Figure 16. Primary and Secondary Antibody Responses. Temporal patterns of IgM and IgG serum antibody responses following the first and subsequent exposures to an immunogen (immunizing antigen).

Serum antibodies to gangliosides (molecules composed of a glycosphingolipid with one or more sialic acids) were first found in GBS in 1988,[147] and in the axonal form of the disease in 1990.[148] In 1994, cross-reactions of serum antibodies between certain *Campylobacter* lipopolysaccharide antigens and human GM1 gangliosides were demonstrated in patients with chronic neuropathies.[149] Subsequently, many patients with GBS were discovered to have serum IgG antibodies directed against both *C. jejuni* antigens and GM1 gangliosides on axons of motor and sensory nerves.[150] This is referred to as "molecular mimicry", where an external antigen fools the immune system into producing autoantibodies. The GM1 gangliosides on the nerve axons stabilize paranodal junctions (highly specialized cell-to-cell junctions) and ion channel clusters in myelinated peripheral nerves. The autoantibodies damage axons of nerves by disrupting lipids in their cell membranes.[150] When the myelin (an insulating sheath) is damaged, nerve signal conduction is impaired.

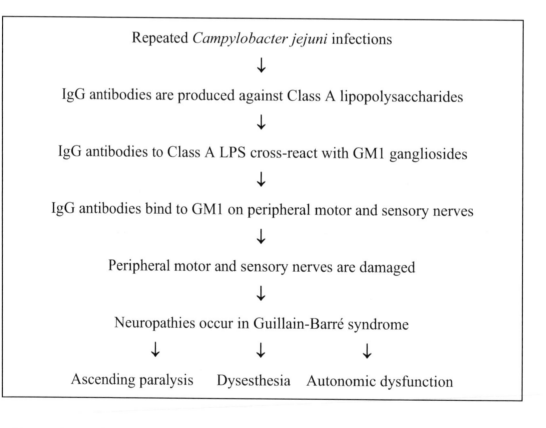

Figure 17. Pathogenesis of GBS due to Campylobacter jejuni.

Because of the damage caused by the autoantibodies, the nerves become dysfunctional or are destroyed (Figure 17). Activated T cells, activated components of complement, inflammatory cytokines and macrophages also participate in the inflammatory process initiated by autoantibodies.

Experimental Animal Model of Guillain-Barré Syndrome

An experimental animal study published in 2001 provided further evidence for the immunological pathogenesis of GBS.[151] When a mixture of human gangliosides was injected into rabbits, each animal developed high serum titers of IgG antibodies against GM1 gangliosides, and also developed an acute flaccid paralysis of the limbs. Histological examinations of the injected rabbits revealed degeneration of peripheral motor nerves. IgG antibodies to GM1 gangliosides were present on the axons of the peripheral nerves. Thus, exposure to human gangliosides induced an axonal neuropathy that coincided with the appearance of high serum titers of IgG antibodies to GM1 gangliosides. That confirmed the role of IgG autoantibodies in the pathogenesis of GBS.

Inadvertent Creation of GBS by Treatment with Gangliosides

Even earlier, in 1995, there was an unfortunate and unintended verification of the immunological basis of GBS in humans.[152] Fifteen adult patients with non-specific pain syndromes were experimentally treated with injections of human gangliosides. Eight of the adults had no obvious untoward reactions and no detectable serum IgG antibodies against GM1 gangliosides. However, the remaining seven individuals developed a severe axonal degeneration, characterized by muscular paralysis that did not entirely remit, and by high serum titers of IgG antibodies to GM1 gangliosides.

Normally, the body's immune system distinguishes between self and non-self. A healthy immune system quickly and efficiently attacks non-self antigens, such as surface proteins on invading bacteria. In contrast, the immune system (except for "natural" antibodies that arise without antigenic stimulation) normally leaves self-antigens alone.[153]

In the 1995 study just described, the immune system malfunctioned in about half of the individuals injected with human gangliosides. For some reason, the immune system considered the injected gangliosides to be "non-self", and produced antibodies against them. Unfortunately, the antibodies also reacted with the naturally occurring gangliosides on nerve cells, leading to an autoimmune neuropathy very similar to GBS. Thus, any doubt concerning the role of IgG antibodies to human GM1 gangliosides in the pathogenesis of GBS was laid to rest.

Significantly, only about half of the individuals were adversely affected by the injected gangliosides, even though the same doses of the self-antigens were given. A likely explanation is that the individuals had different degrees of prior exposure to cross-reactive *Campylobacter* lipopolysaccharides or to other microbial agents that immunologically trigger GBS. However, a genetic predisposition to produce autoantibodies against gangliosides cannot be ruled out.

Swine Flu Vaccine Triggers Guillain-Barré Syndrome

Much less is known about the autoimmune responses that occur when microorganisms other than *Campylobacter* trigger GBS. However, a frightening but instructive outbreak of GBS in 1978 and 1979 confirmed that GBS was an immunologically mediated disease.

In the United States, over 500 people developed GBS soon after receiving a vaccine against a strain of the influenza virus that was in part derived from a porcine influenza virus ("swine flu").[154] It is not known how many affected individuals became permanently paralyzed, but five percent of those vaccinated who developed GBS died of respiratory failure (due to paralysis of the muscles of respiration).

At the time, it was not established which viral antigens were involved in the pathogenesis of the vaccine-induced GBS. However, recent investigations in experimental mice suggest that the influenza virus hemagglutinin (a glycoprotein on the surface of the virus) from the 1978 influenza virus vaccine induces the formation of antibodies to GM1 gangliosides that are responsible for GBS.[155]

The epidemic of GBS triggered by the swine flu vaccine increased the awareness of GBS in the medical profession and in the general public. Consequently, persons seeking an influenza vaccination are now asked whether they had GBS before receiving the vaccine. Thus, many primary care physicians, nurses, pharmacists, and the general public began to be educated about GBS.

Possible Association of GBS with Zika Virus

Recently, Zika virus infection has been noted to be associated with GBS in Polynesia, Brazil, and other tropical countries. At the time of this publication, relatively little information on this possible association has appeared in the scientific literature. A GBS outbreak possibly associated with Zika virus infection was reported in French Polynesia.[156] Forty-two patients were diagnosed with the acute motor axonal type of GBS between October 2013 and April 2014. Thirty-seven experienced a transient illness about 6 days before neurological symptoms appeared. Forty-one had IgM or IgG antibodies against Zika virus. Their clinical and electrophysiological findings were compatible with the acute motor axonal type of GBS. All were treated with intravenous infusions of human immunoglobulins. One was treated with plasmapheresis. All rapidly improved. Anti-glycolipid antibodies were found in 19 patients, but anti-ganglioside antibodies associated with GBS were uncommon.

At the time of this publication, an immunological pathogenesis of GBS due to Zika virus is not proven. However, if Zika virus is shown to cause GBS, the discovery might lead to new insights concerning that autoimmune neuropathy.

Autoantibodies Interfere with Nerve Function and Repair

Antibodies against human GM1 gangliosides not only injure peripheral nerves, but also interfere with their function and repair.[157] The disruption of nerve repair appears to be due to autoantibodies with a particularly strong binding to GM1 gangliosides. In contrast, autoantibodies that bind weakly to GM1 gangliosides may still disrupt the function of peripheral nerves without permanently damaging them. Different antibody affinities help to explain why some patients with GBS recover quickly, others recover more slowly, others are permanently paralyzed, and some die.

Features of Most Common Inciting Agent – *C. jejuni*

To further understand the pathogenesis of GBS, the characteristics of the most common inciting microbial agent, *C. jejuni*, are considered. The bacteria are common in many wild and domesticated animals including poultry, goats, and cattle.[158,159] They commonly colonize the intestines, but usually do not cause disease. *C. jejuni* spreads to humans by consumption of contaminated water, unpasteurized milk, improperly prepared beef, or contaminated poultry. In humans, *C. jejuni* produces an inflammation of the lower intestines. The most prominent symptoms are fever, abdominal cramps, and diarrhea.

C. jejuni is one of the main causes of foodborne bacterial disease in many countries. At least a dozen species of *Campylobacter* have been implicated in human disease. *C. jejuni* and *C. coli* are the most common ones that cause human enteric infections. *Campylobacter* infections spread by the fecal-oral route and by ingestion of contaminated food or water. Direct human-to-human spread is far less common. *Campylobacter* enteritis in humans usually lasts two to ten days. Few deaths result from the infection.

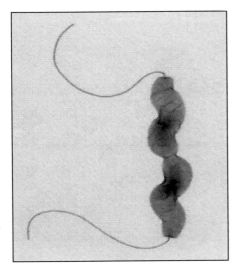

Figure 18.

Campylobacter jejuni at the end of a division cycle.

Antibodies to *C. jejuni* can cross-react with human gangliosides, leading to Guillain-Barré syndrome.

Many humans with *C. jejuni* infections are asymptomatic. Nevertheless, asymptomatic infections can boost the immunological response to the pathogen. When enough antigenic stimulation occurs in a susceptible individual, immunological tolerance is broken. At that point, pathogenic IgG antibodies to peripheral nerve gangliosides are produced, leading to the neuropathy called GBS.

Epidemics of Guillain-Barré Syndrome in Children

There probably was an outbreak of GBS in Paris, France in the spring of 1828, but details were meager.[111,112,160]

Although the majority of cases of GBS in industrialized countries occur sporadically in adults, epidemics of the axonal neuropathy type of GBS in children have occurred in Mexico and Northern China, and an outbreak occurred at the border between Mexico and Arizona. These epidemics have provided further insights into the role of *C. jejuni* infections in the production of GBS.

Summer epidemics of GBS have struck rural Northern China since the early 1990s. In contrast to Westernized countries, children and young adults have principally been affected. The clinical course of GBS in Northern China was first reported in 1993 to be marked by a rapidly progressive ascending paralysis.[161] Respiratory failure was frequent. Sensory involvement was absent. In this "axonal" type of GBS, motor nerve conduction was reduced, whereas sensory nerve functions were normal. Afflicted children usually recovered motor function. The disease recurred in about five percent of the cases. The mortality rate was between three and five percent.

In a study of GBS in Northeast China involving 129 children, published in 1995,[162] 65 percent had the motor axonal form. Serum antibodies to *C. jejuni* and glycolipids were elevated in 66 percent of thirty-eight children who were tested. The motor axonal form of GBS in those children was due to infection-induced antibodies against four key gangliosides GM1, GD1a, GT1a, and GQ1b.

More recently, clinical features of GBS in 293 affected Chinese children were found to be more variable.[163] Most were one to four years of age. About 46 percent experienced an infection one to four weeks before the neurological symptoms appeared. About 36 percent of the patients had sensory and motor nerve involvement. Cerebrospinal fluid findings typical of GBS occurred in 88 percent of tested patients.

In a study published in 2007, it was found that similar summer outbreaks of GBS occurred in young children from Mexico City.[164] Of 121 affected children, 46 had acute motor axonal neuropathy and 32 had the acute inflammatory demyelinating form. Twenty patients had positive stool cultures for *C. jejuni*. Serum IgG antibodies to *Campylobacter* were detected in about 44 percent of those with acute motor axonal neuropathy and in about 37 percent of those with the acute inflammatory demyelinating form. Thus, IgG antibodies to peripheral nerve gangliosides triggered by *C. jejuni* infections are the principal cause of GBS in Mexico, as well as in China.

In June 2011, an outbreak of GBS occurred in the southwestern Arizona border cities of San Luis and Yuma and across the border in Sonora, Mexico.[165] Twenty-six adults (18 from Sonora, eight from Arizona) were involved. Twenty-one patients had an antecedent diarrhea. Eighteen patients were tested for serum antibodies to *C. jejuni*, and all 18 tested positive. The outbreak may have been due to tap water contaminated with *C. jejuni*.

Why do epidemics of GBS commonly occur in children in China and Mexico but not in North America and Europe? That is probably because children in third world countries have earlier and more intense exposures to *C. jejuni* from contaminated water or foods. A second, closely related possibility is that pathogenic serotypes of *C. jejuni* are more prevalent in those regions. However, it does not appear that the affected populations are genetically more susceptible to the disease, because individuals from the affected areas who immigrate to the United States do not seem to have an increased susceptibility to GBS. However, a genetic determinant cannot be ruled out, since many thousands of children in the regions of China and Mexico with epidemics did not develop GBS.

In Westernized countries, because of better public health practices, there is less exposure to contaminated foods. But over many years, the exposures may mount until sufficient antigenic exposure produces enough pathogenic antibodies to trigger GBS.

Principal Immunogens in Pathogenic *Campylobacter*

Campylobacter lipopolysaccharides are key antigens in the pathogenesis of most cases of Guillain-Barré syndrome. The *Campylobacter* lipopolysaccharides that induce GBS are class A lipopolysaccharides that cross-react with GM1 gangliosides. Furthermore, monoclonal antibodies, developed *in vitro* to GM1 and GD1a, bind to class A *C. jejuni* lipopolysaccharides, but not to other lipopolysaccharides. Finally, 68 percent of *C. jejuni* strains isolated from patients with GBS have lipopolysaccharide class A, but only 17 percent of strains isolated from infected patients who do not develop GBS.

Low affinity IgM antibodies to *Campylobacter* lipopolysaccharides are common in normal children and adults. In the few cases where large amounts of IgG antibodies to *Campylobacter* class A lipopolysaccharides are produced, GBS often results.

The degree and frequency of exposure to *Campylobacter* lipopolysaccharides is important in the production of GBS.[166-168] About ninety-nine percent of humans infected with ganglioside-mimicking strains of *C. jejuni* do not develop significant amounts of antibodies to *Campylobacter* lipopolysaccharides or to GM1 gangliosides. And GBS does not develop in previously infected individuals with very low serum concentrations of antibodies to *Campylobacter* lipopolysaccharides. This suggests that repeated sensitizations are required to produce the autoimmune neuropathy.

Possible Past *Campylobacter jejuni* Infections in FDR

Could FDR have had symptomatic *C. jejuni* infections many years before his 1921 illness? Such an enteric infection might have occurred in 1912 when he was age 30. The infection was thought to be typhoid fever due to *Salmonella typhi*. However, the illness lasted only a few days, whereas typhoid fever is a serious protracted disease marked by many different symptoms.[169] In the first week of typhoid fever, progressive fever, malaise, anorexia, and abdominal pain typically occur. In the second week, high fever, prostration, anorexia, abdominal distention, diarrhea or constipation, loss of weight, "rose spots" (a skin eruption seen in about one-third of cases), and enlargement of the liver and spleen are commonly seen. In non-fatal cases, the fever declines and there is a slow recovery.

Thus, FDR's enteritis nine years before his neurological illness did not fit typhoid fever. The illness was more likely due to the Norwalk virus,[170] a less virulent *Salmonella* species,[169] or *C. jejuni*.

A *C. jejuni* infection might also have occurred in 1915, when FDR was briefly hospitalized with abdominal pain for suspected appendicitis. Since his symptoms disappeared in a few days, it was probably not appendicitis. A viral or bacterial enteritis, such as *C. jejuni,* was a likely cause.

Thus, it is plausible that FDR had a *Campylobacter* infection in 1912 and/or 1915. If he was exposed to *C. jejuni* again in 1921, his immune system could have produced autoantibodies leading to an autoimmune neuropathy.

Other Autoimmune Neuropathies

Once we determined that GBS was a likely cause of FDR's 1921 neurological illness, we considered whether any of the less common autoimmune neuropathies were diagnostic possibilities:

1. *Miller Fisher Syndrome.* The Miller Fisher syndrome occurs in about one out of a million people each year.[171,172] The disease is triggered by autoantibodies not to GM1 as occurs in GBS, but instead against ganglioside GQ1b.[173] The disease is characterized by acute paralysis of external eye muscles, descending paralysis, and poor voluntary control of muscle movement (ataxia). Facial nerve palsy and a drooping eyelid (ptosis) may also occur. Dysesthesia is unusual. The prognosis is usually very good. Residual effects of the disease are uncommon.[172]

2. *Bickerstaff's Brainstem Encephalitis.* This rare autoimmune neuropathy is characterized by progressive ophthalmoplegia (weakness of external eye muscles), ataxia, disturbed consciousness, and overactive reflexes.[174] Autoantibodies to GQ1b often occur.[173]

3. *Acute Autonomic Neuropathy.* Because FDR had dysfunction of his urinary bladder and lower bowel, an acute autonomic neuropathy was considered.[175,176] Patients with an acute autonomic neuropathy may present with orthostatic hypotension (low blood pressure on standing), dryness of the eyes and mouth, excessive or decreased sweating, difficult urination, and peripheral vasoconstriction (cold, pale hands and feet). FDR had none of those dysautonomic symptoms except difficulty in urination.

4. *Chronic inflammatory demyelinating polyneuropathy* (CIDP) is a rare acquired immune-mediated inflammatory disorder of the peripheral nervous system that is considered the chronic counterpart of GBS.[177] In contrast to GBS, the paralysis in CIDP progresses for at least two months and the neurological symptoms are frequently recurrent. CIDP was therefore not the cause of FDR's illness.

In summary, most of FDR's clinical features, including his ascending paralysis, facial paralysis, and hyperesthesia, were inconsistent with the less common autoimmune disorders listed above. Therefore, none of them caused FDR's neurological illness.

FDR's Illness Most Consistent with GBS

Although FDR did not have a symptomatic illness during the several weeks preceding the onset of his neurological problems, an asymptomatic infection with *C. jejuni* could have triggered his autoimmune neuropathy. Of more importance, the motor, sensory, and autonomic nerve involvements that FDR displayed were typical of the pathophysiology of GBS triggered by IgG antibodies to class A

Campylobacter lipopolysaccharides. The antibodies cross-react with GM1 gangliosides on motor, sensory, and autonomic nerves.

Thus, reconstruction of the pathogenesis of FDR's illness (as well as the other diagnostic strategies previously discussed) indicates that paralytic polio was improbable, and that GBS was the most likely cause of his disease.

Chapter 17. Was FDR Close to Death in 1921?

"the only thing we have to fear is fear itself." ~ FDR, First Inaugural Address, 1933

It has not been widely appreciated how close to death FDR came in 1921. FDR faced a number of life-threatening medical problems including the possibility of respiratory failure, urinary tract infection, injury to the urethra or bladder, bacterial infections secondary to decubitus ulcers, clots in the leg veins, and malnutrition. This chapter addresses each of these serious threats.

Potential Respiratory Failure

FDR's peripheral neuropathy steadily progressed from the most distal motor nerves (in his feet and legs) to the lower cervical motor nerves. The intercostals (the muscles between the ribs) that assist with voluntary respiration were affected when the thoracic nerves were damaged. Thus, for some weeks, FDR's respiratory function might have depended principally upon the phrenic nerves, comprised of motor axons from the third, fourth and fifth cervical nerves. The phrenic nerves are involved in voluntary respirations, but they are solely responsible for involuntary respirations. When the phrenic nerves are activated, the thoracic diaphragm, which separates the chest from the abdomen, contracts and therefore descends. The descent creates a negative pressure in the thorax. Consequently, air that contains vital oxygen flows into the air sacs (alveoli) of the lungs.

When the phrenic nerves are damaged, the thoracic diaphragm cannot descend. Therefore, the pressure in the thorax is not reduced and little or no air is inhaled. Consequently, oxygen concentrations in the arterial blood quickly fall (hypoxia).

When both voluntary and involuntary respirations fail, brain cells are damaged and death comes soon thereafter due to hypoxia.

At the peak of FDR's 1921 neurological illness, the muscles of his hands innervated by cervical nerves number seven and eight were very weak to paralyzed.[1,2] An additional ascension of the peripheral neuropathy to the fifth cervical motor nerve or beyond could have impaired the phrenic nerves. Oxygen deprivation would have occurred. That would have been fatal because few artificial means of supporting respiration were available in 1921. It was a close call.

Lack of Artificial Respiratory Assistance

The treatment of respiratory failure requires tracheal intubation, supplemental oxygen, and assisted mechanical ventilation of the lungs. At the time of FDR's illness, a tracheotomy could be performed in major hospitals and sometimes by general practitioners in homes or clinics. Performing and maintaining a tracheotomy on Campobello Island in 1921 would have been difficult.

Furthermore, positive pressure ventilation to support respiration was unavailable in 1921. The first practical mechanical ventilator (Figure 19), constructed from an iron box and two vacuum cleaners, was invented in 1928 by Phillip Drinker, an industrial hygienist, and Dr. Louis Agassiz Shaw, a Harvard physician.[178,179] The respirator was used in 1928 to treat an eight-year-old girl with respiratory failure due to paralytic polio.[180] Her dramatic recovery popularized the use of the device in polio patients with respiratory failure.

Three years later, in 1931, John Haven Emerson, an American inventor, introduced the "iron lung", an improved, less expensive negative pressure regulator. It had portal windows and a bed that slid in and out of the cylinder, allowing attendants to adjust the patient's body and place bed coverings, clothing, or medical devices such as thermometers, stethoscopes, and blood pressure cuffs in the cylinder.[181] Emerson's invention was a lifesaver for patients with bulbospinal or bulbar poliomyelitis, and later was used to treat patients with other causes of respiratory failure, including GBS.

Figure 19. Iron Lung. The iron lung saved the lives of many patients with respiratory failure due to paralytic polio or GBS.

Lack of Other Supportive Measures

Other medical therapies, including suction devices, oxygen tanks, and a host of medications, which are the mainstays of emergency rooms and intensive care units in modern hospitals, were not commonplace until the last half of the twentieth century.[182] But even if they had been available in major hospitals in 1921, they would have been to no avail to FDR, because of the remoteness of the site where he became ill.

Other Potential Health Threats

Franklin Delano Roosevelt faced other life-threatening problems during his 1921 neurological illness. One of the most serious was a prolonged inability to urinate. When that occurs, urine backs up from the bladder into the ureters. If the backup continues, then urine accumulates in the pelvises of the kidneys. If the pelvises become distended, the kidneys may become compressed and injured. Furthermore, stasis of urine increases the likelihood of a kidney infection by bacteria in the urine that ascend to the kidneys.

Eleanor Saved FDR's Life

To deal with FDR's inability to urinate, Eleanor was instructed how to empty his bladder by inserting thin glass catheters into the bladder via the urethra. It is remarkable that the catheterizations did not cause a urinary tract infection, since bacterial contaminants could have been introduced. Such a bacterial infection of the urinary tract could have been fatal, since antibiotics to treat such infections had not yet been developed. Also, as previously mentioned, thin, fragile glass catheters are prone to break when they are inserted into or removed from the bladder.[22,23] If that occurred, injury to the bladder or urethra might have led to bleeding, a severe urinary tract infection, perforation, or a fatal peritonitis.

In addition, FDR could have easily developed pressure sores because of excess stress on vulnerable bony prominences, such as the heels, ankles, coccyx, sacrum, hips, and elbows. Secondary bacterial infections at such sites, which might lead to an underlying osteomyelitis, are common. A septicemia could have subsequently developed.

Moreover, by feeding him, nutrient deficiencies were prevented. In essence, Eleanor's nursing care was responsible for FDR's survival.

Chapter 18. Could FDR's Outcome Have Been Improved?

"The good physician treats the disease; the great physician treats the patient who has the disease" ~ William Osler

If FDR had been diagnosed in 1921 with GBS, could the extent of his permanent paralysis have been reduced? No, it could not have. Aside from the use of physical therapy, there were no ways of improving the recovery of muscular function in patients with GBS until the end of the twentieth century. A brief review of the current medical management of patients with GBS highlights that few if any measures were available for the management of a GBS case in 1921.

Current Medical Management of GBS

Currently, when a sudden non-traumatic flaccid paralysis develops, the patient is taken as soon as possible to a medical center. There, a physician (preferably a neurologist) quickly obtains the history of the present illness and performs an extensive physical examination that includes the nervous system.

If the presumptive diagnosis is GBS, cerebrospinal fluid is collected as soon as possible to help confirm or refute the diagnosis. As previously recounted, at the clinical onset of GBS, the protein concentration in the CSF is usually increased (100 to 1000 mg/dL; normal is 15 to 45 mg/dL), whereas the number of leukocytes in the CSF is normal (10 cells or less per mL). Electromyography and nerve conduction studies also help to confirm whether a neuropathy is present. Serum antibodies to GM1 gangliosides or to other gangliosides may also be measured, not only to verify the autoimmune process, but also to gauge the height of serum IgG antibody titers to GM1 gangliosides. The latter is important, because very high serum IgG antibody titers to GM1 in GBS suggest a poor prognosis. Other diagnostic procedures, such as neuroimaging, might be warranted if the diagnosis is uncertain.

If the diagnosis is GBS, the patient is hospitalized immediately to monitor the progress of the paralysis, the vital signs, and arterial blood gases. If respiratory failure is imminent, tracheal intubation and assisted ventilation are required to raise arterial blood oxygen levels, and to decrease arterial blood levels of the waste gas carbon dioxide.

Two-thirds of patients with GBS experience abnormalities in the autonomic nervous system such as severe fluctuation of the arterial blood pressure and irregularity in the cardiac rate.[183] These abnormalities are usually readily treated medically.

Immunotherapy of Guillain-Barré Syndrome

Once the diagnosis of GBS is established, immunotherapy is started as soon as possible to lower serum levels of pathogenic IgG autoantibodies to GM1 gangliosides. The first antibody-lowering method is plasmapheresis (literally "taking away plasma").[183-185]

An average adult has about 5 liters (1 liter ≈ 1 quart) of blood. Plasma, the fluid part of blood, comprises about 55 percent of the blood volume, or about 2.75 liters in an average adult. In addition, an average adult has about 10 liters of interstitial fluid (the fluid surrounding the cells). About the same concentrations of IgG are in plasma and interstitial fluid.

In plasmapheresis for GBS, about 300 mL of the patient's blood (about six percent of the total blood volume) is withdrawn, the plasma (which contains pathogenic IgG antibodies) is separated from the red blood cells, the removed plasma is discarded, and the red blood cells are re-infused into the patient. When blood is withdrawn, interstitial fluids flow into the blood stream to maintain the blood volume and replenish plasma proteins that have been removed.

Withdrawing 300 ml of blood removes about 165 ml of plasma, only about 1.3 percent of the circulating pathogenic antibodies in the body (0.165 liters / 12.75 liters). Four to five plasmaphereses are carried out over five to seven days to lower the serum and interstitial fluid concentrations of the pathogenic IgG antibodies.

Serum levels of pathogenic IgG autoantibodies to GM1 gangliosides can also be lowered by intravenous infusions of normal human IgG (400 mg/kg of body weight/day) for five consecutive days.[183,185,186] One reason that the treatment works is as follows. When the serum concentration of total IgG rises, the catabolism (breakdown) of all IgG molecules accelerates. In patients with GBS treated with human IgG infusions, the concentrations of the pathogenic IgG antibodies in the serum and interstitial fluids decrease, as the body increases the catabolism of total IgG. Lowering the serum concentration of pathogenic antibodies to GM1 gangliosides by either method (plasmapheresis or human IgG infusions) shortens the duration of GBS, and lessens the chance of residual motor paralysis.[183-186]

Usually, human IgG infusions are used rather than plasmapheresis, because infusions are simpler, quicker, and less risky.[183]

Despite these improvements in clinical care, many patients have residual effects.[183] Furthermore, even in advanced intensive care units, two to three percent of patients with severe GBS die because of medical complications, including respiratory failure and secondary infections due to antibiotic-resistant microbial pathogens.

Rehabilitation of Patients with GBS

Once the neuropathy begins to recede and the patient can cooperate, rehabilitation is begun. The initial degree and rate of progression of the motor disability, the presence or absence of respiratory failure, and the rate and extent of recovery of motor function are important prognostic indicators. A rapid progression of the neurological abnormalities and a slow rate of recovery indicate a poor prognosis and a high probability of permanent paralysis, as occurred in FDR's case.

A training program is initiated to help the patient regain skills for self-care. A progressive physical therapy program aids to rebuild strength in skeletal muscles innervated by healthy motor nerves, but that have become atrophied because of disuse.[187,188] The therapy also helps prevent motor movements that would place undue strain upon muscles being used to compensate for weakened ones. Passive movement of weakened extremities is also helpful to prevent contractures until voluntary motion is regained.

Physical therapy also speeds recovery from nerve damage. In the modern era of immunotherapy, the rate of nerve regeneration is faster, so muscles (which have not been allowed to atrophy) regain their function more rapidly. Moreover, intense physical therapy not only decreases residual motor disability in patients recovering from GBS,[188] but also enhances the regeneration of sensory nerves.[189]

There are two other important reasons to institute physical therapy as soon as possible. The first is to prevent thrombosis (clot formation) in veins of the lower extremities. If a clot dislodges, it becomes an embolus that travels via the veins to the right side of the heart and then to the pulmonary arteries. Once emboli lodge in the lungs, they cause pulmonary infarctions (tissue death due to vascular occlusion).[190] Such infarctions are potentially fatal, because they block blood flow to the lungs, may cause bleeding into the lower respiratory tract, and may lead to secondary bacterial pulmonary infections.

The second reason for the early institution of physical therapy is to encourage patients to believe that they will get well. A physical therapist who understands the psychological as well as the physical needs of the patient can enhance the patient's recovery.

Nutrition is also important during the first several weeks of the illness, since deficiencies of certain micronutrients, including essential vitamins and minerals, may occur because of poor oral intake. Strict vegetarians are at greater risk for vitamin B12 deficiency,[191] and therefore may need B12 supplementation over that found in the usual multi-vitamin preparations. That is particularly important, since vitamin B12 deficiency causes a neuropathy that could worsen the autoimmune neuropathy.[192]

The patient should be educated concerning the illness. This may require repeated explanations, for a patient may be in pain, sleep-deprived, anxious about the disease, worried about the extent of the paralysis, or otherwise distracted.

It is important to establish how much the patient knows about the disease and to correct any misconceptions. When the physician does not have the time or the ability to explain the nature of the disease and the rationale of the treatment, another health care professional should do so. The patient and family members must be given opportunities to ask questions – to seek clarifications of medical matters, including the terminology.

In addition, many individuals affected by GBS have to deal with the plight of their families, the status of their occupation or profession, the exorbitant expense of prolonged hospitalization, and the cost of rehabilitation. Because of such distractions, the patient may not be listening or comprehending what is being said.

Even with the best of care, some 15 to 20 percent of patients with GBS become permanently disabled. The risk of permanent paralysis is even higher (about 35 percent) in those patients who develop the most severe manifestations of GBS in the first few weeks of the disease,[193] as occurred in FDR's case.

Since virtually all of the measures that are currently standard practice for the medical management of GBS were not developed until decades after FDR's 1921 illness, his prognosis would not have improved even if the correct diagnosis had been made.

Chapter 19. Other Famous People with GBS

"I was appalled by the extent that I had withered." ~ Joseph Heller

Two other famous persons with autoimmune neuropathies provide important insights regarding the diagnostic dilemma in FDR's 1921 illness, and illustrate the advances that have happened in the diagnosis and medical management of GBS.

Portrait 21.

Dr. Harvey Williams Cushing.

While serving in the United States military during the First World War, Cushing (1869-1939) developed a neuropathy that resembled Guillain-Barré syndrome.

The first case was the famous neurosurgeon Dr. Harvey Williams Cushing (1869-1939), who sustained a severe neurological illness in 1918. His illness exemplifies the lack of appreciation of Landry's ascending paralysis and other autoimmune neuropathies during the early twentieth century, even among the best clinical neurologists in the United States. Furthermore, his case is presented because of the potential impact it could have had on the diagnosis of FDR's neurological illness.

The second case was the famous author Joseph Heller (1923-1999), who became ill in 1981. A study of his case reveals how, in the modern era, a GBS diagnosis can quickly be made and the patient effectively managed by a team of health care experts.

Dr. Harvey Williams Cushing

Dr. Harvey Williams Cushing (Portrait 21) was one of the most famous neurosurgeons of his time.[194] He studied neurosurgery in Bern, Switzerland and Liverpool, England. In 1901, Cushing became Associate Professor of Surgery and the Head of Neurosurgery at Johns Hopkins School of Medicine in Baltimore. In 1911, he became Surgeon-in-Chief at the Peter Bent Brigham Hospital in Boston. The next year, Cushing was appointed Professor of Surgery at Harvard University Medical School in Boston, where he had trained as a medical student.

During his academic career, Cushing made important new contributions to the field of neurosurgery and wrote about his discoveries and innovations in numerous monographs. Cushing was innovative, industrious, and dedicated. He developed an understanding of the dynamics of intracranial pressure, a pathological classification of gliomas (a type of brain cancer), and many of the neurosurgical techniques that would be used for the rest of the twentieth century. He also discovered a disease due to an increased secretion of adrenocorticotropic hormone (the pituitary hormone that stimulates the adrenal cortex to produce the hormone cortisol). The disease is still known as Cushing's disease.

Dr. Cushing was also awarded the Pulitzer Prize for his book *The Life of William Osler*. In addition, Cushing wrote an authoritative book concerning the famous Belgian pioneer in anatomical studies, Andreas Vesalius (1514-1564), who wrote the influential *De Humani Corporis Fabrica*. Thus, Cushing was a first-rate physician, surgeon, researcher, and medical historian.[194]

Military Service in World War I

Before the United States entered World War I, the Surgeon-General of the United States, Dr. William Crawford Gorgas (1854-1918), asked the medical leaders of certain universities, including Harvard, to form a base hospital that could be deployed rapidly in Europe, if the United States entered the war. In September 1915, Cushing accepted the responsibility to form such a front-line base hospital.

On April 6, 1917, the United States declared war on Germany. The United States Base Hospital was mobilized in April, sent to France in May, and attached to the British Expeditionary Force in France. Cushing directed the activities of the physicians and other personnel, and performed many surgical procedures, despite being at the front lines and sometimes under attack by German bombers. During the conflict, he also experimented with magnets to remove metal fragments from the brains of wounded soldiers.

Cushing's Neurological Illness (1918)

During the last months of World War I, Cushing was promoted to the rank of Colonel and became the Senior Consultant in Neurological Surgery for the American Expeditionary Forces in France. As he recounted in his war diary, at age 48 (August 6, 1918) he developed a febrile illness, which he thought was viral influenza.[195] That was likely because of the influenza pandemic that also involved the military in France where Cushing worked. By August 11, Cushing felt *"feeble"*. Five days later, he was bed-ridden because of general profound weakness. Then, he began to recover and felt well enough to return to work.

Two months later, he again became ill. On October 8, he was febrile and *"wobbling like a 'tabetic' "* (high stepping gait, with feet slapping the ground, seen in syphilis patients with lesions in the dorsal spinal column). As we will see, Cushing did not have syphilis but a very different disease.

Cushing acted as his own physician, probably because a neurologist was not present in the military hospital and no one else had his knowledge of neurological disorders. He recorded the course of his protracted neurological illness. The deep tendon reflexes in his legs were absent. His legs were numb up to his knees. By October 14 (the sixth day of the illness), he experienced diplopia (double vision, usually due to paralysis of muscles that control the external movements of the eye). By October 18 (the tenth day of the illness), he was bedridden, and his leg muscles were atrophic. By the next day, there was a bilateral facial paralysis, uvular paralysis (the uvula is the tip of the soft palate that goes up when the doctor has you say "ah"), and transient irregularities in the size of the pupils of his eyes. Moreover, his total white blood cell count was low (2,000 leukocytes / mm^3; normal range is 4,500 to 10,000 / mm^3).

On October 13, a fellow medical officer named Dr. Schwab took Cushing to a hospital in Priez-la-Fauche located in Northeastern France. There, Cushing continued to experience the previously described neurological symptoms. His neurological deficits peaked on November 3 (the 26th day of the illness), when his hands became numb and dysfunctional. He then slowly recovered.

In summary, Cushing's protracted illness was characterized by a preceding illness that could have been influenza or some other viral infection, an ascending symmetric flaccid paralysis, numbness and paresthesias of hands and feet, areflexia in the upper and lower extremities, irregularities in the size of the pupils of the eyes, bilateral facial paralysis, diplopia, uvular weakness, ataxia, and fever.

Cushing thought that he had developed a neuropathy, but he did not understand its cause. After a slow recovery, his physical stamina was quite limited for some months. Indeed, some weakness of his hands and legs persisted for the rest of his life.

Analysis of Cushing's Illness

In 1987, the American neurologist Dr. Stephen Reich analyzed Cushing's neurological illness.[196] Reich concluded that Cushing had GBS. Reich was essentially correct. However, Cushing's illness was more complex than classical GBS. The diplopia, uvular weakness, and ataxia were in keeping with a variant of GBS, the Miller Fisher syndrome (see page 145).[171,172]

Also, leukopenia (low white blood cell count) is not a feature of GBS or other autoimmune neuropathies. Since gangliosides are on human neutrophils and lymphocytes,[197] Cushing's leukopenia may have been due to autoantibodies against GM1 as well as other gangliosides.

Thus, it is possible that Dr. Cushing had a unique autoimmune neuropathy similar to GBS and Miller Fisher syndrome, but also affecting blood leukocytes. To prove that contention, an extensive study of the antigen-binding specificities of his serum autoantibodies, including those against GM1 gangliosides, GQ1b, GQ1b-GM1 complexes, and GQ1b-GD1a complexes, would have been required.[166,167,173] Furthermore, it would have been necessary to determine whether he had antibodies directed against blood leukocytes. But those types of investigations were not possible until the latter part of the twentieth century.

Attendance at Meeting With Georges Guillain (11-11-1918)

Cushing developed his neuropathy just two years after Guillain, Barré, and Strohl discovered the CSF abnormalities and nerve conduction defects in what would later be known as Guillain-Barré syndrome, and just three years before FDR's illness. In a curious turn of fate, on November 11, 1918, the day of the Armistice ending World War I, Cushing and Guillain attended a conference of the *Chirurgicale Interaliée* in Paris, France. This was confirmed by Cushing's diary and Guillain's signature on the guest list and his picture with the group. Did Cushing and Guillain discuss Cushing's recent neurological illness or Guillain's 1916 report? It is unlikely, because Cushing was still recovering from his neurological illness. Indeed, eight days before then, his illness had peaked. Therefore, Cushing probably did not have enough stamina to hold a prolonged discussion with any physician at the conference. Furthermore, the event was a social gathering where many physicians bid a farewell to their military service in France. Moreover, if such a discussion had occurred, Cushing would probably have made some note of it in his war diary or in other writings after he returned to the United States.

What Might Have Been

Cushing's case illustrates that what we now know as GBS was poorly appreciated or unknown in the United States in 1921, because Cushing did not mention it in his diary.

Would history have changed if Guillain had met Cushing during the military medical conference held in Paris at the time of the Armistice? If the two had met, Guillain might have obtained many clues concerning Cushing's health even within a few moments of time. The clues could have included: 1) his body habitus and general demeanor (sluggish, apprehensive), 2) the color of his skin and mucous membranes (pallor or jaundice) 3) skin lesions (erythema, macules, papules, vesicles), 4) his eye movements, including ptosis (drooping) of the upper eyelids, nystagmus (involuntary eye movements), or strabismus ("crossed" eyes), 5) his gait (unsteady, uncoordinated, asymmetrical), 6) his speech (halting, slurred, aphasic), 7) the clarity of his response to simple questions (name, time of day, location, profession, work during the war), 8) the strength of his handshake (forceful or weak), 9 the tone of his deltoid muscle (palpated by some during a greeting), and 10) the rate and volume of his radial pulse (checked during the handshake).

If Guillain had met Cushing, he could well have noticed Cushing's uncertain gait, the flaccidity of some of his muscles, and weakness in his extremities. Such observations could have led Guillain to ask Cushing about his neurological problems. If Cushing had responded in detail about his recent illness, then Guillain could have discussed the peripheral neuropathy that he and his colleagues discovered in 1916 and the similarities of that disease to Cushing's case. In that scenario, after Cushing returned to the United States, he probably would have shared the information with his colleagues at Harvard, including Dr. Robert Lovett who would be FDR's physician in 1921. That could have possibly led to a diagnosis of GBS in FDR's case.

However, Cushing apparently never considered whether Landry's ascending paralysis, or what we now call GBS, caused his neurological illness. Indeed, he died (1939) before GBS became widely appreciated in the United States.

Portrait 22.

Joseph Heller.

Heller (1923-1999), a famous American novelist, wrote a telling tale of his bout of GBS.

Joseph Heller

The potential complications of GBS, as well as the measures that may be life-saving and reduce the permanent effects of the neuropathy, are vividly depicted in the story of the famous American novelist Joseph Heller (Portrait 22), who developed his neuropathy six decades after FDR's illness.

Joseph Heller's 1981 encounter with GBS (at age 58) is germane because the disease was severe, the recovery was very slow, many modalities used in the current medical management of GBS were in place, and Heller recounted the illness in a gripping, yet humorous way.

Many years before his illness, Heller served as a bombardier during the Second World War, and attained fame for his 1961 fictional satire about that conflict, *Catch-22*.[198] Indeed, the expression *Catch-22* came to denote a problematic situation for which the only solution is denied by a circumstance inherent in the problem itself, or by a rule concerning the problem.

Heller's Neuropathy

Twenty-five years after *Catch-22* was published, Heller and his friend Speed Vogel wrote the novel *No Laughing Matter*.[199] It is a blow-by-blow account of Heller's prolonged struggle with an autoimmune neuropathy that had many clinical features of GBS. His story illustrates many aspects of GBS, as well as the impact of a severe autoimmune neuropathy from the patient's point of view.

In 1981, at age 58, Heller was in excellent health when he suddenly experienced moderate difficulty in swallowing, a metallic taste when drinking water, and weakness of the arms and shoulders. Since he was usually very physically active, he was somewhat concerned when he became fatigued while running and could not perform his usual number of push-ups that same day. But he did not think that it was a major problem, and thought that he would be normal after a good night's rest.

The next morning, he was no better. Although it was Sunday, he related his symptoms over the telephone to an internist in New York City, Dr. Mortimer Bader. Dr. Bader told Heller that he had GBS. Dr. Bader then called his twin, Richard, who was also an internist. Richard Bader concurred with the diagnosis and agreed that Heller needed to be hospitalized as soon as possible.

As he was leaving with Mortimer Bader, Heller found that it was difficult to open the car door. They stopped at a restaurant for lunch before proceeding to the hospital. Much to Heller's surprise and distress, he could not chew his food. Later that day, when he was admitted to the Intensive Care Unit of Mount Sinai Medical Hospital in New York City, he could not walk unaided.

That same day Dr. Walter Sencer, an excellent neurologist-psychiatrist at the Mount Sinai School of Medicine, performed a thorough neurological examination. Sencer told Heller, "*You're going to have a mild case, probably. And you're going to get almost everything back.*" But as Heller later wrote in his typical ironic fashion, "*I forgot to ask him what I was going to lose.*" Sencer noted weakness of the tongue muscles (needed to articulate constants), masseter muscles (needed for chewing), sternocleidomastoid muscles (rotate and flex the neck), and the muscles of his arms and hips.

A lumbar puncture and nerve conduction studies were performed. Heller's neurological status, respiratory function, and nutritional state were closely monitored. His neurological functions quickly deteriorated. Sencer patiently explained to him that four cranial nerves were involved. They were as follows. 1) Cranial nerve V, the trigeminal nerve, controls muscle of mastication (chewing) and receives sensations from the face; 2) Cranial nerve VII, the facial nerve, controls facial, digastric, stylohyoid, and stapedius muscles. The facial nerve also provides the sense of taste for most of the tongue. 3) Cranial nerve XI, the spinal accessory nerve, controls the sternocleidomastoid and trapezius muscles required to shrug the shoulders and move the head. 4) Cranial nerve XII, the hypoglossal nerve, controls muscles of the tongue and other glossal muscles needed for speech and swallowing.

The story also revealed an unexpected insight into a close friend who was as famous as Joseph Heller. The friend, the highly successful actor and comic movie producer Mel Brooks, perhaps knew about as much about GBS as many doctors then or now. Indeed, when Brooks visited Heller during the early phase of his hospitalization, he questioned him closely whether he had neurosensory symptoms – numbness, tingling, or unusual pains – that are typically found in GBS. Brooks then explained about the disease and its prognosis to Heller. He told Heller a great deal about Landry's ascending paralysis, when Landry reported his findings, the incidence of GBS, and that an infection often precedes the paralysis. When Heller asked him how he knew so much about GBS, Brooks commented in an offhanded way that he regularly read *Harrison's Principles of Internal Medicine, Dorland's Medical Dictionary, The Merck Manual*, and the weekly issues of one of the best medical journals, *The Lancet*.

Brooks was better informed about GBS than I or probably most other physicians were in the 1980s. I marvel that one of the most famous entertainers of his day could accumulate so much information on a subject so far removed from his field.

Very soon, Heller experienced considerable difficulty expelling secretions from the lower respiratory tract. The pooled secretions threatened to obstruct the lower airway. If you have ever started choking because of food stuck in your throat, you know the agony of the experience and the relief once the food is dislodged or passed into the stomach. Heller's problem was protracted and necessitated frequent suctioning to clear the airway.

As a result of the pooled secretions, Heller's respiratory functions diminished. Drs. Mortimer and Richard Bader accordingly advised an immediate tracheotomy (a surgical procedure to create an opening through the neck into the trachea) and artificial ventilation. However, at the proverbial last moment, the internist in the intensive care unit, Dr. Alvin Teirstein, and Heller's neurologist, Dr. Sencer, vetoed the procedure. In the next few days, his pulmonary function improved and the tracheotomy was cancelled.

However, just when Heller's clinical course was on the upswing, his sputum became more copious, thicker, and yellow to rusty brown in color. A chest X-ray revealed pneumonia in his lower lungs. Intravenous penicillin was started promptly because of a suspected bacterial infection, probably due to *Streptococcus pneumoniae*, the most common cause of bacterial pneumonia. Heller responded rapidly to the antibiotic. The pneumonia completely resolved during the next several days.

Heller was losing weight during that time despite frequent nasogastric tube feedings. Furthermore, his muscles were progressively atrophying. Heller wrote, "*I was appalled by the extent that I had withered.*" During those depressing times, Heller feared that he would continue to deteriorate and might die. He was afraid to sleep, for he imagined that he would never wake up. The insomnia further wore him down.

Heller's speech became slurred because of involvement of certain cranial nerves. The speech impairment was vexing for one so verbally adept as Joseph Heller. For a few weeks, it became difficult to communicate with his caregivers and to make his wishes known. The problem was compounded by difficulty in writing due to weakness of the muscles of his hands.

Life in Intensive Care

Heller expressively described how the atmosphere in the intensive care unit often swung abruptly from an oppressive calmness to a fearsome tempest. Ordinarily, time in the intensive care unit crept by – replete with sameness of sounds and sights of monitoring devices, feeding tubes, urinary catheters, sickening sounds of suction machines, fluids dripping silently and relentlessly into intravenous lines, and moans and groans from sick patients in nearby beds. And in stark contrast were cheerful nurses checking vital signs frequently throughout the day and night, and the repetitive chartings and conversations in the nursing station that could not be heard, but were evidenced by moving lips, laughter, furrowed brows and hand gestures. To top it off, there were the daily physician rounds involving many specialists, who used a language that was difficult if not impossible to comprehend, even though it was supposedly in your native tongue.

A steady stream of medical and nursing activities by specialized personnel gently swirls about you in an intensive care unit. It is rather like being adrift alone in an open sea. Although the temperatures in intensive care units are mild, nutrition is ample, specialized care is the name of the game, and the personnel are cheerful, something is amiss. You cannot strive for yourself. You have lost most of your independence. The world is confined to your bed and the small space surrounding it. You are essentially in the power of others, benign as they may be. Days and nights run together. Your biological clock is on the blink. You long for the out-of-doors, for a release from this medical enclave.

Then, unexpectedly, the boredom may be interrupted by a storm, hopefully not involving yourself. Abruptly, the alarms on monitors shrilly sound. Visitors are removed, as specialized physicians, nurses and other health care personnel stream in with therapeutic devices and medications to rescue the dying patient. Curtains are drawn to block out the feverish activities by the medical-nursing staff. Family members and visitors wait anxiously for the verdict. You lie helpless on the edge of this flurry of restorative activity, and wonder what the outcome might be. And if all efforts fail, as happened to some of Heller's fellow patients, the thought might arise that you may be the next to bite the dust.

Heller remarked that his doctors and nurses repeatedly reassured him that he would get completely well, or close to completely well. But he asked himself, could they be sure? Were they simply trying to buoy up his spirits, and not admitting to the depressing facts of his illness? And at times in the intensive care unit, it seemed there were elements of Catch-22 for which Heller was famous.

If you (the patient) have difficulty speaking, as in Heller's case, it is difficult to make your wishes known. The Catch-22 is that Heller had weakness in his hand muscles and difficulty writing, so this alternative way for him to communicate also did not work well. In cases like this, unless the medical staff or visitors take extra time and effort, you become only vaguely aware or oblivious to the happenings in the world around you.

Additionally, Heller dealt with a host of personal problems during his hospitalization. He was in the middle of a divorce. His publisher had to be reassured that he would meet his next deadline, in the literary sense of the word. The usual bills, as well as hospital expenses, had to be paid. Letters had to be answered. Heller had to reassure his family that he would get well. And unexpectedly, he found love and would later marry one of his nurses.

Rehabilitation

After six weeks in intensive care, Joseph Heller was transferred to Rusk Institute of Rehabilitation Medicine where he was treated for six weeks. After he returned home, he was far from fully recovered. He could walk with aids, dress and feed himself, negotiate with his publisher, reassure his family and friends, deal with his finances, divorce, remarry and start writing again.

Heller's outpatient physical rehabilitation program was intense and prolonged. Improvement was slow, probably because of the time it takes for peripheral nerves to regenerate. He gradually learned to walk by using a cane, handrail, or wall to steady himself. After some months, he was walking more normally and driving his car. A year after the onset of his illness, he had regained most of his motor functions. Three years after the onset, he was learning how to run again.

Insights from the Cushing and Heller Cases

Several insights are gained from reviewing the Cushing and Heller cases. As previously noted, even though Cushing was exceptionally knowledgeable about neurology, he was unaware that the neuropathy that struck him in 1918 had been previously described by European physicians. As was the case with FDR's illness, GBS (Landry's ascending paralysis) was not considered as a possible diagnosis, because of an understandable lack of knowledge.

FDR developed GBS before many of the diagnostic and virtually all of the therapeutic measures used to manage GBS patients were discovered. The contrasts between the medical managements of Heller's and FDR's cases are remarkable. In 1982, Heller was diagnosed immediately with GBS, whereas FDR was not diagnosed correctly during his illness and for many decades to come. Heller's case was painstakingly documented. The documentation for FDR's case provides enough information to show the diagnosis was most likely GBS, but overall FDR's medical record is much less complete. Heller's illness gives us an idea of some painful and difficult things FDR may have experienced, suggests how close FDR may have come to death, and indicates that FDR was probably fortunate to have survived and recovered the motor functions of his upper body.

Heller's case clearly shows the great strides that have been made in the recognition, management, and outcome of autoimmune neuropathies during the latter part of the twentieth century. As previously discussed, the care of affected patients improved greatly by the time Heller developed GBS. By 1982, it was suspected that GBS was an immunologically mediated disease. But a fundamental advance in treatment of the disease, reducing the concentrations of pathogenic autoantibodies by plasmapheresis or intravenous infusions of human IgG, did not emerge until the 1990s.

In contrast to Heller's case, little was done during the first, crucial months of FDR's recovery to prevent permanent paralysis. Yet, despite his severe motor handicaps, he continued to have high aspirations. Precisely how Roosevelt accomplished his lofty goals is difficult to know. Perhaps it was a combination of his advantageous upbringing, the support from his wife and close colleagues, his prior accomplishments in government, and his particular genetic endowments.[200] One other factor may have played a role. FDR may have appreciated that after his close call with death, he was given a second chance to live out his dream of becoming President of the United States.

Chapter 20. Responses to Critics
of GBS Diagnosis

"Colonies of the poliovirus were now creeping upward through the spinal cord."
~ James Tobin

In 2003, we demonstrated that the cause of FDR's 1921 neurologic illness was most likely GBS.[2] Yet most recent FDR biographies,[5,201-204] histories of poliomyelitis,[205-207] a recent book on GBS prepared for the general public,[208] a published peer-reviewed article written by an orthopedist,[209] a book concerning a child with polio,[210] an online commentary by a neurologist,[211] and a published invited article written by three rehabilitative medicine physicians,[212] all still state unequivocally that FDR had paralytic polio.

It is a normal part of the scientific process to receive criticisms. For example, peer-reviewed articles are only published after the author responds to criticisms from anonymous expert reviewers. Our 2003 and 2016 papers went through that process.

It is important to pay close attention to critiques. We accordingly sought out any recent sources that mention FDR's 1921 illness. In this chapter, we will objectively respond to all the criticisms of which we are aware. The critiques will be discussed in chronological order.

Most historians failed to mention our 2003 article. Every year, new biographies of FDR are written, ranging from simplistic children's books to scholarly treatises hundreds of pages long. Most books we have examined, with the exception of those histories mentioned below, flatly assert that FDR had polio and make no mention of the possibility that he had GBS. It is not practical for us to read all the new books concerning FDR that come out every year, although we have scanned many of them. The most prominent ones mentioning GBS as an alternative diagnosis, along with relevant scientific articles that have been published, are as follows.

Historian David Oshinsky (2005)

Soon after our 2003 article was published,[2] I sent a reprint to Dr. David M. Oshinsky, Professor of History at the University of Texas at Austin, because I had become aware that he was writing a book concerning poliomyelitis in which FDR's illness might be discussed. Oshinsky's book, *Polio, an American Story*,[205] published in 2005, mainly covered the effort to find a polio vaccine. However, Oshinsky also described FDR's illness in the space of a few pages, though mostly not from a clinical point of view. He briefly mentioned our 2003 article and acknowledged the possibility that FDR had GBS. But in the remainder of the book he repeatedly stated that FDR had paralytic polio.

Oshinsky chose not to describe and critique our findings, and not to counter the evidence we presented, namely that FDR's symptoms were much more consistent with GBS. Instead, he put forth other arguments in an attempt to defend the long-standing belief that FDR had paralytic polio.

For example, he indicated that FDR's brief immersion in the cold water of the Bay of Fundy the day before the symptoms of his neurological illness began was deleterious to his immune system, and thus increased his susceptibility to poliovirus infection. In fact, the opposite mostly occurs. Following brief immersion in cold water, certain immune system responses are temporarily enhanced,[213] and others are unchanged.[214] The status of FDR's immune system at that time is unknown. Therefore, the immersion in cold water cannot be used as evidence for or against a polio diagnosis.

Next, Oshinsky argued that FDR developed paralytic polio at age 39 because he was shielded from polioviruses during his protected childhood. There is no question that FDR had a protected childhood. However, FDR had many possible exposures to polioviruses after his early childhood. He could have had an asymptomatic polio infection. We simply do not know.

For the sake of argument, suppose that FDR was particularly susceptible to develop polio later in life because of a protected childhood. Then why did his 1921 illness not resemble polio, and instead closely resemble GBS? Oshinsky is silent on this key question. Any serious discussion of the cause of FDR's illness must focus on whether his symptoms are more compatible with GBS or with paralytic polio. Oshinsky's analysis does not take the symptoms into account, and offers nothing else to make up for the omission.

More fundamentally, Oshinsky relied upon the diagnosis made by FDR's physicians, whom he portrayed as basically infallible. For example, Oshinsky claimed that Dr. Lovett's 1917 book, *The Treatment of Infantile Paralysis*, *"remains today one of the classics in the field"* (where "today" may be interpreted to mean "2005", the year Oshinsky's book was published). Lovett's book was indeed a classic in the field when it was published and for some years afterwards. But today, Lovett's book provides a historical insight into what was known (and not known) about paralytic polio in 1917, but not much more. Lovett's book even fails in some ways to serve as an accurate guide to the clinical features of paralytic polio. For example, Lovett believed that Landry's ascending paralysis, now termed GBS, was one of the clinical presentations of paralytic polio.[20] Today, GBS is known to be a totally different illness.

Given such basic misunderstandings and knowledge gaps, it is understandable why Lovett made an incorrect diagnosis in 1921. What is less understandable is the reluctance of modern-day historians to reconsider long-held beliefs in the light of new information. To Oshinsky's credit, his book granted the possibility that FDR had GBS. But he avoided any substantive presentation of the evidence in favor of GBS, and mischaracterized our article by saying *"The authors note that there is a strong case to be made for polio"*. That statement was taken out of context and gave a false impression. To the contrary, we clearly spelled out the inconsistencies of FDR's case with paralytic polio. And our overall conclusion was that GBS was the most credible cause of FDR's 1921 illness, based on his symptoms, the pathogenesis of paralytic polio and GBS, and the confirmatory Bayesian analyses we carried out. In that respect, *"Six of eight posterior probabilities strongly favoured Guillain-Barré syndrome"*.[2]

Oshinsky received the 2006 Pulitzer Prize for History for writing *Polio, an American Story*. Therefore, the book is considered to be an authoritative source on polio. The result is that future historians may possibly reference *Polio, an American Story* as "evidence" that FDR had polio. But it is not evidence. The book covers little of the medical aspects of FDR's case, and gives only a passing mention to our findings.

Tellingly, Oshinsky says in his book, *"What is certain, however, is that FDR believed he had polio, as did his family, his doctors, other polio victims, and the American public. Without him, the great polio crusade would never have been launched"*. Since Oshinsky's main purpose was to tell the story of *"the great polio crusade"*, perhaps determining the true cause of FDR's illness mattered little to him. Since the crusade happened in the past, all that mattered was what people at that time believed.

In contrast, for the purposes of our investigations of the cause of FDR's 1921 paralytic illness, it little matters what the people of that time believed. Instead, what matters is the evidence, and what it tells us. Our objective analysis of all the available evidence reveals that the long-standing diagnosis of paralytic polio was likely incorrect and that GBS was the most likely cause of FDR's 1921 illness.

Historian Susan Richards Shreve (2007)

It is worth mentioning that, even beyond the insistence that FDR had polio, writers who venture into the scientific aspects of polio often get the facts mixed up. For example, the book *Warm Springs: Traces of a Childhood at FDR's Polio Haven*, written by Susan Richards Shreve in 2007, is a touching story of her experiences as an eleven-year-old girl with polio.[210] Unfortunately, the book pulls "facts" concerning polio out of thin air, as in the following passage:

"By the middle of the twentieth century, three separate polio viruses had been identified by scientists. The most common of these had the symptoms of influenza, with high fever and muscle aches, and disappears after a couple of weeks with no residual damage. Many people, including children, had this strain without ever knowing they'd contracted anything more serious than the flu. The least frequent and most damaging of the viruses is that of bulbar polio, which attacks the medulla oblongata, the part of the brain that controls autonomic functions such as breathing and relays signals between the brain and the spinal cord. We are most familiar with this crippling strain of the virus, which affects the limbs – usually, as in the case of Roosevelt, the legs. During the active phase of the virus, the limbs are so painful that a patient cannot bear to be touched, even by sheets."

Shreve strung together a series of errors, and thus arrived at the wrong conclusions. First, over 90% of poliovirus infections are asymptomatic, so the most common course is different from what she presents. Second, influenza-like polio infections are mild and do not typically produce high fever. Third, the notion that one type of poliovirus causes an influenza-like outcome and a different type causes paralytic polio is not supported by scientific research. All three serotypes are capable of damaging motor neurons. Finally, hyperesthesia (extreme sensitivity to touch) only rarely occurs in paralytic polio, but is common in GBS.

The point is not to single out *Warm Springs* for special criticism. As we will see throughout this chapter, Shreve is far from the only historian writing about FDR's illness who got the facts wrong and failed to understand some basic concepts. Also, Shreve was not the only writer who veered off track by using fallacious circular reasoning, by basing an understanding of polio on FDR's symptoms.

Historian Jean Edward Smith (2007)

The book *FDR*, published in 2007,[7] described FDR's 1921 illness. The author, Jean Edward Smith, a biographer and professor of political science at Marshall University, mentioned our 2003 article, but neither accepted nor rejected our findings. However, he consistently referred to FDR's illness as polio.

Physicians Gareth Parry and Joel Steinberg (2008)

A paradoxical criticism of our 2003 article[2] appeared in a 2008 book, *Guillain-Barré Syndrome: From Diagnosis to Recovery*,[208] written for the lay public. The authors were Dr. Gareth B. Parry, Professor of Neurology at the University of Minnesota Medical School, and Dr. Joel S. Steinberg, who specializes in evaluating patients with physical disabilities and impairments.

Parry and Steinberg rejected the diagnosis of GBS in FDR's case with the statement that *"most people familiar with GBS feel his [Roosevelt's] illness was much more typical of polio than GBS."* It is hard to take this "argument from unnamed authorities" seriously, because which people and what was more typical of polio were not mentioned. Argument from authority is a common logical fallacy. The famous astronomer Carl Sagan summed it up well when he wrote, *"One of the great commandments of science is, 'Mistrust arguments from authority.' . . . Too many such arguments have proved too painfully wrong. Authorities must prove their contentions like everybody else."*

Parry and Steinberg also asserted that sensory symptoms occur in paralytic polio, but they did not specify the symptoms and they gave no references to support that contention. Moreover, their assertion runs counter to reports of paralytic polio in previously mentioned peer-reviewed journal articles.

Despite Parry and Steinberg's insistence that FDR had polio, mostly based on their argument from authority, they contradicted themselves when they presented factual clinical information concerning GBS. In the book they say, 1) *"By the time the average [Guillain-Barré syndrome] patient goes to the doctor, there will be some combination of symmetric weakness, usually in an ascending pattern, and abnormal sensation."* and 2) *"Polio differs from GBS in that the weakness of polio is usually asymmetrical."* Those very features – abnormal sensation and symmetric, ascending paralysis – were prominent in FDR's case and are typical of GBS and not of paralytic polio. Yet the authors do not believe that FDR had GBS. The most likely explanation for the paradox is the difficulty most people have accepting new information that overturns long-standing beliefs, as discussed later in this book.

Physician Zachary Friedenberg (2009)

FDR's 1921 neurological illness was discussed in a detailed peer-reviewed article published in 2009, *"Franklin D. Roosevelt: his poliomyelitis and orthopaedics"*, by an American orthopedist, Dr. Zachary Friedenberg.[209] A great deal of his article concerned FDR's role in developing the rehabilitation facility at Warm Springs and FDR's professional relationships with certain orthopedists. FDR's 1921 illness was presented, but mostly concerning fever and paralysis. Because of FDR's fever and the expertise of his physicians, Friedenberg concluded that FDR's 1921 illness was paralytic polio. As we indicated, fever favored the diagnosis of paralytic polio.[2] However, the temporal pattern of the fever was atypical of paralytic polio, since FDR did not have the prodromal febrile period typically found in paralytic polio. In addition, FDR's fever lasted significantly longer than the fever that usually occurs during the paralytic phase of poliomyelitis. Of greater importance, Friedenberg did not address the other features of FDR's neurological illness that were far more in keeping with GBS. Consequently, his conclusion is not warranted. Taking all of FDR's symptoms into account, and the prevalence of GBS and paralytic polio in adults, it is much more likely that FDR had GBS.

Physician Stephen Lomazow (2010)

In an online commentary that appeared seven years after our 2003 article,[2] Dr. Stephen M. Lomazow, an American neurologist and Assistant Professor of Neurology at Mount Sinai School of Medicine, indicated that my colleagues and I omitted an important finding that proved FDR contracted paralytic polio in 1921.[211] He largely based his opinion upon a telegram that Dr. Lovett sent to Dr. Keen shortly before Lovett was to see FDR at Campobello Island. Lomazow's online commentary was as follows.

"I had the opportunity to get into the Robert Lovett papers at Harvard . . . there is a note from Lovett that reveals that FDR probably had a spinal tap at the outset of his 1921 illness . . .

GBS was described in 1916 and Lovett (as many of FDR's later physicians) being the world's leading expert on Polio would surely have known how to differentiate the two. Unfortunately he died unexpectedly in 1924, leaving FDR to find another guru who eventually turned out to be Dr. McDonald. As I have stated at other times, the world's leading expert on polio in the late 1920's was none other than "Doctor" Franklin Delano Roosevelt . . .

The bottom line here, is that Lovett would surely have known that a spinal tap would unequivocally differentiate between the two diseases (polio has white cells, GBS high protein) and most probably knew the results (as undoubtedly did

FDR himself). It can therefore safely be inferred that FDR's 1921 neurological illness was indeed polio.

Despite Goldman's sound academic treatise, based largely on a statistical analysis, he was not privy to the fact of the spinal tap (at least, he didn't cite it in his references). This, aside from the facts that the degree of atrophy, the muscle tenderness at the outset of the disease and the perfect timing for the incubation period between FDR's well known visit to the Boy Scout camp and onset of his illness are all most compatible with polio, all lead to the inevitable conclusion that FDR's 1921 illness was poliomyelitis."

Lomazow's main point is that a spinal tap was done, as supposedly proved by Lovett's note (actually a telegram), which we were supposedly not aware of. However, my colleagues and I had examined Lovett's correspondence,[21] and were aware of the note. Lovett's telegram was as follows.

"Leave Boston tonight Tuesday – proceed to Eastport and patients house – desirous to return Wednesday night. Have telegraphed wife of patient – unless already done spinal tapping, cell count, & globular reaction‡ would be useful. This I cannot do personally. Shall arrive at Harvard Club Boston tonight."

After reading the second article we published concerning FDR's 1921 illness, Dr. Lomazow emailed me in October 2016 some additional arguments in favor of his belief that FDR had paralytic polio. His email was as follows.

"I read that you continue to defend your thesis that FDR did not have polio. The spinal tap is referred to in the Lovett papers and James Tobin's new book reveals additional solid evidence that it was performed in 1921.

I need not tell you that GBS had been described by the time of FDR's illness. Lovett and Draper were the world authorities at the time and were surely aware of the difference. There is also other clinical evidence. The incubation period

---

‡ "Globular reaction" means protein measurement.

traces back to FDR's visit to a Boy Scout camp.

Also, on April 12 1945, Howard Bruenn documented an active triceps reflex. It is doubtful it would have been present with the history of GBS.

In my 40 years of practice, neither me nor any of my esteemed neurological colleagues have even seen anywhere near the degree of atrophy exhibited by FDR. His case undoubtedly involved a profound amount of anterior horn cell disease, unlikely to be produced by an acute (or chronic) inflammatory demyelination neuropathy. Do you know of such a case? If so I'd love to see it. While I appreciate your statistical analysis I respectfully disagree with your conclusion that FDR had GBS."

I replied and asked him to clarify certain points. Lomazow replied in November 2016. His email message was as follows.

"Basically I have faith in Dr Lovett, Levine and Draper who were the world's experts at the time and would clearly have been cognizant of the differential diagnosis including GBS. My opinion is based on the information uncovered by Jim Tobin and also the reference to the test in the Lovett papers at Harvard. I wish that I had the actual report of the spinal fluid analysis but it has not surfaced.

Also, decades of clinical neurological practice reinforces my thesis. I have yet to come across a GBS patient with such profound atrophy and would be most interested if you could produce one.

Also, perhaps the greatest authority on the disease after Lovett was FDR himself, who obviously felt that he had polio and treated hundreds of polios at Warm Springs."

My responses to Lomazow's criticisms are as follows.

1. *Claim that a spinal tap was performed.* As has been indicated previously in this book, Dr. Lovett requested a spinal tap in a telegram sent to Dr. Keen.

However, he also indicated in that message that he would not be able to do the procedure. A search of all of the correspondence by FDR's physicians reveals no evidence that a spinal tap was performed. In addition, the remoteness of Campobello makes it even less likely that a spinal tap was done, and the lack of any mention by Bennet, Keen, or Lovett that it was done strongly indicates that the procedure was not performed. Thus, for Lomazow to assert *"the fact of the spinal tap"* is an incredible leap of logic. The issue of whether FDR had a spinal tap is discussed in further detail in the analysis of the critique by the journalist / historian James Tobin (see page 183).

2. *Claim that FDR's physicians were surely aware of the differences between paralytic polio and GBS.* The evidence is to the contrary. In his book published in 1917, *The Treatment of Infantile Paralysis*,[20] Lovett mistakenly indicated that Landry's paralysis was a manifestation of paralytic polio. Lovett's incorrect understanding is further discussed in the section concerning Ditunno and his colleagues (see page 203). Furthermore, FDR's physicians never mentioned GBS in their communications concerning FDR's case, strongly suggesting that they were not aware of it as a diagnostic possibility.

3. *Claim that FDR was "the world's leading expert on polio".* Lomazow's repeated assertion is incredible, even bizarre. FDR played an important role in developing programs to rehabilitate victims of paralytic polio, but he never developed an understanding of the pathogenesis or diagnosis of polio or of other neuromuscular diseases. It is revealing that (in a letter to Dr. Ober dated May 9, 1925) FDR repeatedly referred to *"polyo"* and *"polyomielitis"* instead of the correct spellings.[21] So much for his expertise in polio.

4. *The interval after visiting the Boy Scout Camp.* The time that elapsed between FDR's visit to the Boy Scout Jamboree and the onset of his neurological illness (about 2 weeks) was in keeping with the incubation period of poliomyelitis, but there was no evidence that FDR was exposed to polioviruses during his visit.

Also, FDR could just as easily have been exposed at the Jamboree to *C. jejuni*, the most common microbial agent that leads to GBS.

5. *Assertion that active triceps reflex makes GBS doubtful.* Lomazow's assertion is without foundation. Most patients with GBS have a descending pattern of recovery from their paralysis. FDR completely recovered motor function in his upper extremities, including the triceps brachii muscles. The presence of a triceps reflex 24 years after a neurological illness is therefore in keeping with a GBS patient who had recovered the function of the triceps muscles.

6. *Claim that degree of atrophy not consistent with GBS.* That claim is incorrect. A number of experts on GBS have reported that many patients with severe GBS continue to have paralysis of the lower extremities. This will be discussed in more detail in the section concerning Ditunno and his colleagues (see page 206).

7. *Muscle tenderness supposedly argues against GBS.* Protracted pain in involved muscles is unusual in the paralytic phase of paralytic polio. However, FDR experienced severe pain to the slightest touch for several weeks after the onset of his illness. Hyperesthesia is common in GBS, but rarely if ever occurs in polio because sensory nerves are not involved in polio. This striking finding in favor of GBS is further discussed in the section concerning Ditunno and his colleagues (see page 207).

In summary, all of Lomazow's objections are without foundation. Also, Lomazow failed to address FDR's other symptoms (e.g., facial paralysis, ascending paralysis, bladder and bowel paralysis) that favor GBS. The most likely cause of FDR's 1921 neurological illness remains GBS.

Historian James Tobin (2013)

An extended criticism of our assertion that FDR had GBS was made by Dr. James Tobin, Professor of Media, Journalism and Film at Miami University in Ohio. In 2013, Tobin published the book *The Man He Became: How FDR Defied*

Polio to Win the Presidency.[204] In a lengthy footnote, Tobin mentioned our 2003 article. However, he did not present or discuss our analyses showing that FDR likely had GBS. Instead, he advanced what at first glance might seem a convincing counter-argument, namely that FDR's cerebrospinal fluid (CSF) was known to have been examined by his physicians, and that therefore their diagnosis of polio is to be trusted.

Tobin based his counter-argument largely on an "unpublished note" by Dr. Samuel A. Levine, the Boston cardiologist who first declared that FDR had infantile paralysis. I was previously unaware of the "unpublished note". Because Tobin quoted just a few sentences from the note, it was initially impossible to assess the strength of Tobin's claim. I was thus eager to see the entire note. If it demonstrated that a spinal tap had been done for diagnostic purposes within the appropriate time frame, and if the CSF findings were consistent with polio, that would be solid evidence for poliomyelitis.

I learned that Dr. Samuel Levine's son, Herbert Levine, was like his father a noted cardiologist. It therefore seemed likely that Herbert Levine was the holder of the "unpublished note". But I was saddened to learn that Herbert Levine had passed away in 2014.

I consequently contacted Tobin, relayed the news about Herbert Levine's death, requested background information about the "unpublished note", and asked if I could gain access to the full text. He responded promptly and graciously.

Tobin related that he first became aware of Levine's "unpublished note" when he read the 1984 book *The Making of Franklin D. Roosevelt: Triumph Over Disability*, by Richard Thayer Goldberg.[215] This additional information, that there had been a previous citation, made the story even more intriguing. It showed that a first-hand account by the doctor who first diagnosed FDR to have polio had remained unpublished for more than three decades, despite being cited in two books.

In his response to me, Tobin indicated that he had obtained a copy of the note from Herbert Levine, but that he was unable to share it with me, because he had obtained the copy with the understanding that he (Tobin) would only use it for his particular research. Apparently, Herbert Levine had shared a copy of his father's "unpublished note" at least twice (first with Goldberg, then with Tobin), both times with the stipulation that the note would only be used for a particular research purpose, and not shared with others.

At this point, I feared that the "unpublished note" might be unavailable to me. If the document had not been preserved after Herbert Levine's death, I would have been unable to respond to Tobin's declaration that *"a lumbar puncture was indeed done"*. Also, it would have been regrettable that a potentially important historical document would remain "unpublished", and would not be preserved for future study.

Tobin further related that the "unpublished note" was a double-spaced typescript, six and a half pages long. He did not know where the original copy of the note was, but assumed it was still in the possession of Herbert Levine's family. Tobin suggested I contact the family, through the Tufts New England Medical Center, and ask for a copy of the note.

I was somewhat hesitant to proceed, since it was so soon after Herbert Levine's death. I knew from personal experience how long the grieving process can take. Also, I knew little about Levine's family. Therefore, I chose to ask the Director of Media Relations and Publications at Tufts Medical Center, Ms. Julie Jette, for advice concerning how to obtain the document. She referred me to the widow of Dr. Herbert Levine, Mrs. Sandra Levine.

I contacted Mrs. Levine. Her cooperation and understanding were greatly appreciated. She found the "unpublished note", agreed to send me a copy, and subsequently gave the document to The Francis A. Countway Library of Medicine in Boston, where it now resides.[216] For the convenience of the reader, an exact copy of Samuel Levine's "unpublished note" is reproduced in Appendix E. The text of the note, with Levine's handwritten ~~strikeouts~~ and *(additions)* indicated, is as follows:

The Early Days of President Franklin D. Roosevelt's
Attack of Poliomyelitis

One Saturday morning in late August of 1921 while I was at the Peter Bent Brigham Hospital, I received a telephone call from a Mr. Frederick A. Delano from Washington, D.C. He said he wanted to see me on a very important matter concerning his nephew, Franklin D. Roosevelt. Although I had planned to work at the hospital that day, the problem seemed quite serious, and I therefore arranged to confer with him in my office, which at that time was at 21 Bay State Road.

*I quickly learned from Mr. Delano that FDR was critically ill at Eastport, Maine. He had been well and had come up from Baltimore or Washington to his summer house. Soon after arriving on August 10, he developed pains in his back and limbs on returning from a swim. Fever and chills ensued, and the next day he lost the use of both arms. Mr. Delano began to receive letters and telegrams about ~~the President's~~ **(his nephew's)** sudden illness. At first, no doctors could be reached, but soon Dr. W.W. Keene, a well-known elderly retired surgeon from Philadelphia who was relatively close by, was called to examine the patient. He attributed the symptoms to a "clot on the brain," i.e., a cerebral stroke. Later reports sent to Mr. Delano alluded to the possibility of poliomyelitis, since at that time a severe epidemic of infantile paralysis had become prevalent in the northeastern part of the country.*

Realizing that the diagnosis remained puzzling, Mr. Delano quickly left Washington and on reaching Boston contacted the Harvard Infantile Paralysis Commission Office. This commission consisted of Dr. Francis W. Peabody, who was in charge of the medical or clinical aspects of the problem, Dr. Robert Lovett, in charge of surgical or orthopedic aspects, and Dr. Milton J. Rosenarr, in charge of the public health and epidemiologic problems involved. The commission had been formed when cases of poliomyelitis became widespread in Massachusetts in the summer and fall of 1916. During this devastating epidemic, a call was made for two young medical volunteers to see patients on an emergency basis in any part of the state. Dr. John Wentworth and I, who were both working at the Brigham at that time – he as an assistant resident and I as a medical intern – volunteered to do this work. For about two months, day and night, we were both busily engaged in answering frantic calls and seeing many children and some young adults who had contracted or were suspected of having poliomyelitis. As a result, I had the opportunity to see about 300 cases of infantile paralysis. I tell this long introductory tale to explain how a student of cardiology came to be involved in a celebrated case of acute poliomyelitis.

On inquiring at the Commission Office, Mr. Delano learned that Dr. Lovett was in Newport, Rhode Island, and that Dr. Peabody and Dr. Rosenarr were also out of town for the summer. He was told that Dr. Samuel A. Levine had done a good deal of the field work and had examined many polio patients, providing medical care for those with acute cases during the epidemic of 1916 (five years before). In fact, I was the only one involved in the work of the commission who was in town at that time to offer Mr. Delano any advice.

On reading through the letters and telegrams that Mr. Delano had received and hearing the content of the various telephone conversations that had taken place between Eastport and Washington, it seemed clear to me that Mr. Roosevelt was suffering from acute poliomyelitis. I explained to Mr. Delano that the initial general malaise and limb pains followed by weakness and then paralysis of the limbs, the low-grade fever that subsided in a few days, and the fact that an epidemic of poliomyelitis was still raging made this diagnosis quite certain. The possibility of a cerebral stroke suggested by Dr. Keene could definitely be dismissed. (This was no reflection on the retired professor of surgery, who was then over 80 years old and probably had had little if any experience with acute poliomyelitis.)

At this point, Mr. Delano asked me if there would be any point in my traveling to Campobello immediately. Had this question been put to me differently or had I answered it more wisely, FDR's health might not have suffered so severely. Transportation by airplane had not yet become available, and it would have taken at least 24 to 36 hours to get there by train, boat, and motor car. Since the advice I intended to give could be transmitted by telephone, I replied that my presence was not really essential and urged that a physician be called from Bangor to perform a lumbar puncture. This procedure could be carried out that very day (Saturday), thereby saving at least 24 hours.

One might ask why I regarded the lumbar puncture to be so important under the circumstances. I had performed this procedure many times during the polio epidemic of 1916. Often I found that the cerebrospinal pressure was markedly elevated, and the fluid sample spurted out, quickly filling the test tube. More importantly, removal of some of the fluid relieved the intense pressure and in some cases resulted in an immediate improvement in the patient's clinical condition. In one patient a severe headache might suddenly be dispelled, another might show a prompt reduction in fever, and still another might regain lost motor function. I recall seeing one young girl begin to wiggle her toes as I finished the procedure although they had been completely immobile just before the puncture. It appeared that the relief of pressure alone permitted some local nerve fibers to function. In fact, a good many of the patients my colleagues and I had seen were definitely in the pre-paralytic stage, and after the lumbar puncture had been performed to confirmed [sic] the diagnosis, paralysis never developed.

Thus, there ~~was~~ *(were) two reasons for recommending that* ~~the President~~ *(FDR), who was still in the acute stage of the illness, undergo a lumbar puncture. First, if the pressure was found to be elevated, the relief might actually mitigate the paralysis that had already occurred or prevent further paralysis. Second, it would establish the diagnosis, which until now had remained questionable. Therefore, rather than delaying the procedure for two days while I traveled to Campobello, I urged that the puncture be performed by a physician in the vicinity. Little did I anticipate what would actually take place. If Mr. Delano had insisted that I go up there immediately, naturally I would have gone, but time was precious and I did not want to appear to be better equipped to perform the puncture than some other physician close by.*

Thus ended the conference with Mr. Delano but not the particular episode in which I was engaged. Two days later, I received a telephone call from Dr. Robert Lovett, who was anxious to have a conference with me. Arrangements were made for him to have dinner with me at the Harvard Club. He had finally been reached by telephone in Newport and was on his way up to see ~~the President~~ **(Mr. Roosevelt)***. I told him all that I **(had)** learned from Mr. Delano concerning FDR's condition and expressed no doubt about the diagnosis of poliomyelitis. To my surprise he asked me how one could distinguish the paralysis associated with cerebral thrombosis or hemorrhage (Dr. Keene's presumptive diagnosis) from that of poliomyelitis. Inasmuch as Dr. Lovett had been my teacher in an undergraduate course on orthopedic surgery, I wondered whether he was now testing me about the neurologic findings in these two types of paralysis. I replied that in poliomyelitis (in which peripheral motor neurons are involved) motor reflexes are decreased or absent, whereas in a cerebral lesion (with upper motor neuron involvement) reflexes are exaggerated, and one might elicit a positive Babinski sign or an ankle clonus. Since Dr. Lovett's practice was concerned mainly with orthopedic reconstruction, which is generally begun some weeks after the onset of an illness, he had had little opportunity to study or care for patients during the early stage of acute poliomyelitis. Most likely he wanted to be apprised of some of the features characterizing the acute phase of this disease. In* *any event, I added that I had urged that a lumbar puncture be performed but had not been informed of the result.*

Some days later I received a letter from Mr. Delano dated September 1, 1921, with the following note: "Referring to my visit and my consultation with you in regard to Franklin Roosevelt, Dr. Keene of Philadelphia adhered very strenuously to his diagnosis of blood clot or congestion of the spinal cord, but finally said that he would be glad to call in Dr. Lovett in consultation. He personally sent for Dr. Lovett to come to Eastport, and the two doctors met there and, as you may suppose, Dr. Lovett not only convinced himself, but convinced Dr. Keene (I think) that the case was really infantile paralysis. Although Mr. Roosevelt is getting along as well as could be expected and will probably be moved to New York about the middle of this month, we all realize that it is a very serious matter…."

By the time Dr. Lovett saw the patient, the lumbar puncture had still not been done. At last, on Wednesday the procedure was carried out – four days after I **(had)** *advised it. It was never made clear to me whether my suggestion was not relayed by Mr. Delano, whether no one was available to* ~~do it~~ **(carry out my instructions)**, *or possibly whether the local physicians believed this maneuver to be inadvisable. During those several days of delay, however, further paralysis had taken place, and it never will be known whether more prompt removal of the spinal fluid would have altered the course of the disease.*

As I mentioned earlier, if the spinal fluid was under increased pressure, clinical experience warrants the opinion that progress of the disease might well have been influenced favorably and that the final outcome might have been less disabling.

A practical lesson may be learned from this experience. My advice was not followed. Realizing the gravity of the situation, I should have been less timid and self-effacing and should have replied to Mr. Delano that I would telephone directly myself, giving the orders to the household to call in a physician (possibly from Bangor) to perform the puncture. Furthermore, I should have resolved to leave immediately to go and see the patient, even though I could not have reached him in less than 24 hours. On the other hand, at that time I was inexperienced and had not been practicing medicine for very long. This difficulty would have been solved if Mr. Delano had stated that he wanted me to up there as soon as possible rather than leaving the decision up to me and asking whether I should go. (Such ~~things~~ (difficulties) were ~~not~~ (never) mentioned in William Osler's Textbook of Medicine.) Perhaps the President's tragic illness could be considered a blessing in disguise, ~~acting as~~ (in that it may have been) the stimulus for the wonderful accomplishments of Franklin Roosevelt and his wife Eleanor.

When was Levine's note written? Given the many references to FDR as President, the note was certainly written no earlier than 1933, and most likely after FDR died (1945). The note could well have been written in the 1950's, more than 30 years after the events it describes. The strikeouts and handwritten changes to the note appear to be in Samuel Levine's handwriting.

There are significant factual errors in Levine's note.

1. Levine confused Eastport, Maine with Campobello Island. FDR was only briefly in Eastport, when he was being transported to New York City. Up until then, he was at Campobello Island, a part of Canada.

2. The *"well-known elderly retired surgeon"* was "Keen", not "Keene".

3. The note states that in the summer of 1921, *"a severe epidemic of infantile paralysis had become prevalent in the northeastern part of the country"*, and that *"an epidemic of poliomyelitis was still raging"*. Neither assertion is true. No epidemic of poliomyelitis was reported in the Northeast United States at the time of FDR's illness.

4. The note states that FDR *"lost the use of both arms"* one day after the onset of his illness. That was incorrect. All other accounts say that the paralysis began in the legs, gradually ascended to involve the muscles of the abdomen and thorax, and only later reached the upper extremities (see Figure 4, on page 22).

5. Dr. Keen did not suggest that FDR had a *"clot on the brain"*. Instead, Keen's diagnosis was *"a clot of blood from a sudden congestion --- settled in the lower spinal cord"*.

6. In the note, Levine stated that the main purpose of a lumbar puncture would have been to improve the outcome of FDR's illness by lowering the elevated CSF pressure. Levine based his incorrect notion on his experiences when he was an intern treating children with poliomyelitis during the severe 1916 epidemic in the Northeast United States. However, the CSF pressure is normal or only slightly increased in paralytic polio.[217] To our best knowledge, and contrary to Levine's belief, polio does not cause damage by increasing CSF pressure. Instead, polioviruses selectively damage and kill anterior horn motor neurons. Furthermore, there is no objective evidence that a spinal tap relieves any of the symptoms or lessens the possibility of paralysis in polio.

The significant errors of fact put the reliability of Levine's note in doubt. Conceivably, if Levine had been directly involved with FDR's case, he would not have made so many factual errors. In that respect, Levine never saw FDR during his 1921 illness and to our knowledge was never contacted again about his illness.

Perhaps the facts gleaned from the note can best be summarized as follows: 1) Levine had seen some 300 children and some young adults with paralytic polio in the 1916 epidemic. 2) Frederic Delano traveled to Boston to consult with someone on the Harvard Infantile Paralysis Commission Office concerning FDR's serious illness. 3) Since the three commissioners were out of town, Delano instead spoke with Levine, an internist-cardiologist in Boston. 4) Levine quickly concluded that FDR had paralytic polio, and recommended that a spinal tap be done to relieve elevated CSF pressure. 5) Before traveling to see FDR, Lovett met and spoke with Levine at the Harvard Club.

An additional important point was the title of Levine's note, *The Early Days of President Franklin D. Roosevelt's Attack of Poliomyelitis*. That indicated that Levine wrote the note at least 12 years after the onset of FDR's illness. For most people, it is difficult to recall details of events that happened even a few months ago. Unless Levine kept a diary, his recall should be suspect. But so far, no diary has been reported.

Independent of the other errors and inconsistencies, Levine's belief that a spinal tap was performed on FDR (*"At last, on Wednesday the procedure was carried out"*) is highly questionable, for several reasons: 1) Who performed the spinal tap? Levine makes no mention. If a spinal tap had been done, Levine would probably have mentioned who did it. The most likely reason for the omission is that it was not done. Lovett made it clear that he would not do the procedure. So it is hard to imagine who else might have done it, since Bennet was not equipped to do the procedure, and neither was Keen since he was vacationing. 2) Who told Levine that a spinal tap had been done? There is no mention, casting further doubt on the account. By his own admission, Levine was unclear what happened at Campobello. After Lovett left for Campobello, Levine did not take care of FDR, and was not consulted about his case. 3) What were the findings from the alleged procedure? Levine makes no mention of the results of a lumbar puncture. If he considered the procedure to be so important, it seems he would have mentioned something about what happened. Neither did FDR's physicians, FDR himself, or FDR's associates indicate that the procedure was done, or what the results were. For example, in a letter from Frederic Delano to Dr. Samuel Levine dated September 1, 1921, a spinal tap was not mentioned.[218] Other letters from Eleanor and FDR's physicians were written (See Appendix D). None of the letters mentioned a spinal tap.[21,264] Given the invasive nature of a spinal tap, and the difficulty that would have occurred doing the procedure on a patient in FDR's condition, it seems highly unlikely that a direct observer would have failed to mention anything about it.

According to Levine's note, during the dinner at the Harvard Club, Levine and Lovett discussed a patient that neither had seen. They therefore had few of the facts that could be gleaned from the physical examination and FDR's clinical course. Thus, it appears that the diagnosis of paralytic polio was established even before Lovett saw the patient.

Tobin asserted the following: *"Absolute certainty about the diagnosis is impossible without the laboratory tests later developed to distinguish between polio and GBS. But the existing evidence, taken together, indicates that poliomyelitis was by far the most likely cause of Roosevelt's illness and the resulting paralysis."* His arguments in favor of paralytic polio were as follows.

1. FDR was genetically predisposed to paralytic polio.

2. FDR's childhood was so protected that he was very susceptible to a poliovirus infection at age 39, or FDR had a "weakened immune system".

3. FDR's prior tonsillectomy and vigorous exercise before the illness predisposed him to paralytic polio.

4. His fever and permanent paralysis were common features of paralytic polio.

5. FDR's hyperesthesia was typical of paralytic polio.

6. FDR's ascending paralysis was due to polioviruses rising from lower to higher reaches of the spinal cord.

All of the above are either incorrect, neutral (do not favor either cause), or already taken into account in our analyses. My responses to his arguments reiterate earlier discussions of poliomyelitis in this book.

1. *Genetic Predisposition*. There is no basis to conclude that FDR was genetically predisposed to paralytic polio. No other members of FDR's family ever had paralytic polio. Furthermore, a genetic basis for paralytic polio has never been discovered. Thus, the statement that FDR was genetically predisposed to paralytic polio is unsubstantiated.

2. *Protected Childhood and "Weakened Immune System"*. Tobin as well as Oshinsky stressed that FDR was unusually susceptible to poliomyelitis because of his protected childhood. FDR did have a protected childhood. However, after his first several years at Hyde Park, FDR was exposed to many people who may have been infected with polioviruses. In particular, the epidemic of poliomyelitis that swept through New York City in 1916, causing 8,900 cases of paralytic polio and killing 1,922 people, occurred while FDR was living there. Thus, the chances were high that FDR may have experienced an asymptomatic or mild poliomyelitis infection long before 1921. There is no objective way to determine FDR's prior exposure to poliovirus. However, his clinical symptoms strongly indicate that he did not have paralytic polio in 1921, but GBS.

Concerning the idea that FDR had a *"weakened immune system"* due to stress, this is opposite to FDR's known resilience to stress throughout his lifetime. And FDR's pre-1921 illnesses were well within the range of normal for the time. Although FDR most likely had an autoimmune disorder (GBS), there is no evidence that he had an immune deficiency.

3. *Prior Tonsillectomy and Prior Exercise*. Prior tonsillectomy increases the susceptibility to bulbar poliomyelitis, but not to the spinal form of paralytic polio. Since FDR did not display clinical evidence of bulbar poliomyelitis, prior tonsillectomy was not factored into our diagnostic analysis.

As was previously discussed, prior exercise was thought to predispose poliovirus-infected people to paralysis in a limb that was exercised vigorously soon before the illness. The idea is plausible, but unproven. The studies that purported to show a correlation were uncontrolled and the degree of exercise was not quantified. So prior exercise is not established as a factor favoring a diagnosis of paralytic polio.

4. *Fever and Permanent Paralysis.* Fever is a standard feature of paralytic polio, but as previously discussed, fever typically occurs in both the pre-paralytic and paralytic phases of the disease. A pre-paralytic febrile phase was absent in FDR's illness. Nevertheless, since fever is rare in GBS, fever was used as a point in favor of paralytic polio even though its pattern was unusual (Table 6, page 125).

Permanent paralysis occurs more frequently in paralytic polio (about 50 percent of cases) than in GBS (about 15 percent of cases). In patients such as FDR who experience paralysis of all four limbs, the incidence of permanent paralysis in GBS rises to about 35 percent.[193] To give polio the benefit of the doubt, we used the lower incidence of permanent paralysis in GBS (15 percent). Thus, permanent paralysis favored paralytic polio.

We factored both fever and permanent paralysis into our analyses as favoring paralytic polio. However, taking all of FDR's symptoms into account, the overall clinical picture is overwhelmingly in favor of GBS. The problem is that Tobin failed to address or take into account FDR's other symptoms.

5. *Hyperesthesia.* FDR had protracted, prominent hyperesthesia (extreme sensitivity to touch). Transient hyperesthesia may occur in the aseptic meningitic form of poliomyelitis, but only rarely in paralytic polio. The reason why polioviruses do not cause hyperesthesia is because sensory nerves lack the receptor for polioviruses (CD155). In contrast, protracted hyperesthesia is common in GBS because of involvement of peripheral sensory nerves and sensory nerve roots. In addition, FDR had numbness in his legs, again indicating damage to sensory nerves, which is consistent with GBS.

It was disappointing that Tobin did not comment upon other features of FDR's illness that favored GBS, including the following:

1. A longer-term, ascending, symmetrical paralysis is characteristic of GBS but is rare in paralytic polio. Instead, in paralytic polio, the paralysis is asymmetric and intensifies for only a few days.

2. Facial paralysis does not occur in the spinal form of paralytic polio, but is common in GBS.

3. Protracted difficulties in defecation and urination (indicative of involvement of the autonomic nervous system) are rare in paralytic polio, but common in GBS.

4. A consistent descending pattern of recovery from paralysis is absent in paralytic polio, but common in GBS.

Tobin also had additional significant misconceptions concerning poliomyelitis.

He stated that the poliovirus was *"nothing more than a little sphere of fat enclosing a smaller strip of genetic material"*. That is incorrect. The outer covering of polioviruses is a capsid (a protein shell of a virus) composed of three major proteins.[219]

He showed no understanding that polioviruses invade the central nervous system by attaching to CD155 on the axons of motor neurons, and are transported up the involved motor nerves via a specific mechanism to the body of the motor neuron. Instead, Tobin stated the following:

"Colonies of the poliovirus were now creeping upward through the spinal cord. The ensuing war between these viral invaders and the body's immunological defenders resulted in severe inflammation inside the spinal cord. The roaring inflammation, in turn, aroused the sensory nerve cells."

Tobin wrongly believed that motor neurons infected with polioviruses die because of inflammation. There is some inflammation in the affected parts of the spinal cord, as lymphocytes migrate to the tissues surrounding blood vessels in the spinal cord. However, motor neurons infected by polioviruses die because of programmed cell death (apoptosis), not because of inflammation. Macrophages recruited to the site of injury remove the apoptotic cells and cellular debris caused by the infection but apparently do not participate in the death of the neurons.

Finally, the idea of *"colonies of the poliovirus . . . creeping upward through the spinal cord"*, though a dramatic image, is at odds with what happens. Polioviruses reach the bodies of motor neurons by being transported up the axons of motor nerves. Then apoptosis causes the death of the affected motor neurons. Further spread of the virus up the spinal cord, if it occurs, is quite limited.

I appreciated Tobin's discovery of Dr. Samuel Levine's "unpublished note" that stated that a lumbar puncture was performed on FDR. However, if a lumbar puncture was done, it is peculiar that Lovett never mentioned it in his letter to Draper. Furthermore, if it was done, why were the CSF findings never revealed?

Tobin emphasizes as evidence that Lovett wrote Draper on September 12, 1921, *"I thought that [the diagnosis] was perfectly clear as far as the physical findings were concerned."* But that statement is not evidence that a spinal tap was done. If Lovett had said *"CSF findings"* or *"laboratory findings"*, that would have indicated that a spinal tap was done. But *"physical findings"* means information gained from a physical examination of the patient. Lovett's three-page letter goes on at some length describing *"physical findings"*: hyperesthesia, facial paralysis, chills, fever, muscle weakness, bladder paralysis, and other findings. But a spinal tap is never mentioned. Thus, the composite evidence strongly indicates that a spinal tap was not done.

Even if a spinal tap had been performed, it would have been done at the earliest about 15 days after the onset of the neurological illness, around when Lovett first saw FDR. Ordinarily, lumbar punctures are performed at the onset of paralysis to sort out whether the diagnosis is paralytic polio or GBS.

One should keep in mind that the classical distinction between paralytic polio and GBS, the concentrations of leukocytes and total protein in CSF, blurs after the first several days of the onset of paralysis in both diseases. Several days after the onset of paralytic polio, the number of leukocytes in CSF often diminishes and the protein concentration rises.[220] The composition of CSF also changes in GBS several days to some weeks after the onset of the disease, in that the number of mononuclear leukocytes increases.[221] Hence, when CSF is collected two or four weeks after the onset of paralysis in either paralytic polio or GBS, examinations of CSF are not helpful in the diagnosis.

Therefore, if a lumbar puncture had been done on the fifteenth day of FDR's illness or thereafter, the results of the CSF examination would likely have been confusing. We are left with no evidence that a spinal tap was done, and the knowledge that it would not have been diagnostic in any case, because it would have been too late in the course of the illness. Thus, the diagnosis of the cause of FDR's neurological illness instead depends upon an analysis of the history, the physical findings, and the clinical course.

Tobin insisted in his book that *"If Howe had telephoned Draper immediately, it is highly likely that Draper would have dropped everything to locate the closest anti-poliomyelitis serum and have it rushed to FDR"*, with the implication that his paralysis would have been minimized, or even prevented. Indeed, Dr. Simon Flexner and other scientists recognized that antibodies formed after humans or monkeys were infected with poliovirus. Furthermore, they observed that naturally infected humans and experimentally infected animals were resistant to reinfections with polioviruses. The idea of passive immunotherapy with human serum collected from post-polio survivors therefore seemed plausible.

The idea was tested during the 1916 epidemic in New York City.[222] Human serum was collected months to years after an attack of polio. Because polioviruses were only known at that time to infect neural tissues, human serum was administered into the CSF by lumbar puncture in patients with early or late clinical features of poliomyelitis. In treated patients with pre-paralytic polio, meningeal symptoms including rigidity of the neck, severe arching of the back and neck (opisthotonus), hyperirritability, headaches, and vomiting developed and the fever intensified. In some cases, convulsive movements were seen. That might have been because of the formation of antigen-antibody complexes that induced inflammation of parts of the central nervous system.

It was not proven that immune serum treatments prevented paralysis, although the trend seemed to be in that direction. However, the alarming meningeal symptoms associated with the procedure discouraged further use of immune serum in the treatment of patients with early signs of poliomyelitis. Therefore, in 1921, FDR's physicians would not have tried human serum injections into CSF via a lumbar puncture. Furthermore, in a letter to Bennet dated September 20, 1921, Lovett said that he doubted that convalescent immune serum was useful in the treatment of polio, based upon a study conducted in 1916 by Dr. Peabody.[21]

Periodically, other physicians administered convalescent human serum into CSF of patients who supposedly were in the pre-paralytic stage of poliomyelitis. The results of those interventions were inconclusive.

Since some investigations suggested that injections into the CSF were risky, intramuscular injections of immune serum were considered. However, many years elapsed before controlled experiments could be performed to test whether intramuscular injections of human serum would be beneficial.[223,224] Although the injections had prophylactic effects, by then, polio vaccines were developed that were superior to passive immunotherapy afforded by injection of antibodies to polioviruses.

Tobin indicated that we had arrived at a diagnosis of GBS by a statistical analysis. However, he failed to mention that we first examined the cause of FDR's illness by using the most common diagnostic technique, pattern recognition. Pattern recognition indicated that paralytic polio was improbable, and that GBS was by far the most tenable diagnosis. We then tested the results of pattern recognition by Bayesian analysis, a simple, well-accepted statistical method. The statistical analysis confirmed the diagnosis of GBS. Furthermore, the reliability of the Bayesian analysis was examined by determining what enhanced symptom probabilities were needed to equalize the likelihood that the diagnosis was paralytic polio. The amounts of those artificial increases were unrealistic. Thus, the Bayesian analysis still favored GBS after the input factors were artificially adjusted to favor polio.

Finally, the reconstruction of the pathogenesis of FDR's illness independently indicated that paralytic polio was improbable and confirmed the diagnosis of GBS.

In summary, despite Tobin's certainty that FDR had paralytic polio, *The Man He Became* fails to make the case for that conclusion, as follows: 1) Samuel Levine's "unpublished note", which we obtained and had archived, provided no credible basis for the assertion that a spinal tap was done. 2) Even if a spinal tap had been done weeks into the illness, the results would likely have not been diagnostic. 3) The other arguments advanced by Tobin had either already been taken into account (e.g., fever), or did not support a polio diagnosis (e.g., tonsillectomy). 4) *The Man He Became* failed to address or take into account most of the arguments in favor of GBS. 5) The book had significant misconceptions concerning poliomyelitis.

Physicians Ditunno, Becker, and Herbison (2016)

In 2016, three physicians who specialize in physical medicine and rehabilitation, John F. Ditunno Jr, Bruce E. Becker and Gerald F. Herbison (who for brevity will be referred to as "DB&H"), published an extensive critique of our 2003 article.[212] In their article, DB&H totally discounted the possibility that FDR's

1921 illness was GBS. They concluded that the illness was without doubt paralytic polio. Their objections concerning the diagnosis of GBS and their arguments in favor of paralytic polio will be discussed in this section.

Before addressing the specific points, I note that DB&H unfortunately resorted to "attacking the messenger", by making personal references. First, they called our work an *"academic hobby"*. As applied to someone else's work, "academic hobby" is a pejorative, suggesting "less serious". The implication is unacceptable. Our analysis of the cause of FDR's 1921 illness was serious research based upon the available clinical evidence, well-accepted diagnostic methods, and a thorough study of the potential causes of the illness.

Second, they said that we *"selectively chose some of his* (FDR's) *reported symptoms"*. If we indeed *"selectively chose"*, that would be scientific misconduct. The charge is false. We bent over backwards to give polio the "best chance" as the diagnosis, as explained in our publications and other sections of this book. DB&H reinforced the message by mentioning *"missing critical pieces of information from the 2003 retrospective"*. Those *"missing pieces"* were never specified, and it is unclear what they might be.

Finally, they called questioning FDR's diagnosis a *"contrived controversy"*. Synonyms for "contrived" include "fake", "artificial" and "phony". They are saying that we intentionally stirred up a false controversy. As related earlier in this book, our discovery that FDR most likely had GBS was serendipitous, not something we were looking for.

Despite their unbecoming and unprofessional words, DB&H apparently exerted a great deal of effort, and produced an eleven-page article replete with many references. Therefore, I took their critique seriously and responded thoroughly to their claims.

The critique by DB&H was an invited article, apparently not peer-reviewed by outside reviewers, since it was accepted the same day it was submitted (May 10,

2016). The lack of peer review by neurologists cognizant of the clinical features, pathogenesis and diagnostic criteria for paralytic polio, GBS and other neurological diseases could explain the misconceptions in their article. Our analysis involved the participation of excellent neurologists, immunologists, and epidemiologists. In contrast, those types of scientists did not participate in the study by DB&H.

Their article contained some basic flaws. Twelve major ones are as follows.

1. DB&H insisted that FDR's physicians were fully aware of the distinctions between paralytic polio and GBS. That was not so. In Lovett's book published in 1917, *The Treatment of Infantile Paralysis*,[20] he mistakenly indicated that Landry's paralysis was a manifestation of paralytic polio.

Lovett differentiated between 1) progressive paralysis that appears in the legs and gradually ascends and 2) bulbar poliomyelitis. But he was convinced the ascending paralysis was paralytic polio. He wrote, "*It is probable that the great majority of the cases that have in the past been described under the term of "Landry's paralysis" really were examples of this type of infantile paralysis.*"

Lovett also stated, when speaking of paralytic polio, "*When the paralysis reaches the external muscles of respiration, as it very often does, death is likely and occurs early. The diaphragm is also sometimes involved.*" As we previously discussed in the 2003 article and in this book, an ascending paralysis that finally involves the thoracic muscles and the diaphragm is typical of severe GBS and not of paralytic polio. In that respect, in Chapter 33 of Adams and Victor's *Principles of Neurology*,[126] concerning polio, it was stated that "*rarely there may be an acute symmetrical paralysis of the muscles of the trunk and limbs as occurs in the Guillain Barré*". In keeping with that statement, I was able to find only one report of an ascending, symmetric paralysis in a patient with confirmed paralytic polio.[110] Even in that report, the authors suggested that the paralysis was due to immunological events as found in GBS rather than to the invasion of motor neurons by polioviruses.

Lovett did not reference Landry's 1859 report or other articles dealing with Landry's ascending paralysis, except the work of the Swedish physician – epidemiologist Ivar Wickman,[225] who mistakenly believed that Landry's paralysis was a variant of paralytic polio.

In 1879, Dr. Ernst Leyden found histological evidence that paralytic polio and Landry's ascending paralysis were separate diseases.[115] However, Lovett did not refer to that report in his book or other writings. Furthermore, DB&H failed to mention that all reports before 1921 of what we now call GBS were by European physicians, as far as can be determined from a review of the literature. The reality is that very few American physicians in 1921 knew that GBS was a separate disease, distinct from polio.

If FDR's physicians knew that GBS (Landry's ascending paralysis) was a separate disease that caused flaccid paralysis, and had considered GBS as a potential cause of FDR's illness, it stands to reason they would have mentioned it at least once in their letters and notes. That did not occur.

2. DB&H inferred that FDR experienced hyperesthesia before his illness. Their claim was based on a letter from Dr. Lovett to Dr. Draper dated September 12, 1921. In the letter, Lovett wrote *"he went down there very tired, took a bath, went swimming and stayed there a good while. He ran home in his wet bathing suit and subsequently had chills, high temperature and pain. Questioning however showed that there had been hyperesthesia of the legs preceding the bath (swim) for a day or two."*[21]

However, in a 1924 letter from FDR to Dr. William Egleston including a description of the onset of the illness,[14] and in other accounts, neither a prodromal hyperesthesia nor any indication of a pre-paralytic illness was mentioned. In addition, an isolated prodromal hyperesthesia is rare in paralytic polio. The lack of other prodromal symptoms argues against paralytic polio in FDR's case.

A mild febrile illness occurs before the paralytic phase in virtually all cases of paralytic polio.[51,92,106-109,217,226-228] The febrile pre-paralytic phase of paralytic polio usually lasts for 4 to 5 days but may persist for two weeks. Fever, malaise, gastrointestinal symptoms, sore throat, back and neck pain, and neck stiffness are common in the pre-paralytic phase of paralytic polio.[228] The absence of a pre-paralytic phase in FDR's case was therefore inconsistent with paralytic polio.

Back to the claim by DB&H that we *"selectively chose"* analysis factors that favored GBS, the opposite is the case, because the absence of a pre-paralytic phase was not included in our analysis, even though that would have favored GBS.

3. DB&H argued that the incidence of paralytic polio in adults was higher than previously appreciated and that the disease in adults was more severe than in children, based on an article published in 1952 by Louis Weinstein and his colleagues concerning patients admitted to a Boston hospital in 1949.[229] Of the 428 patients, fifty-two (12 percent) were between 31 to 50 years of age. In the study, symmetric paralysis of the arms and legs was more common in the adults than in the children. However, many of the cases between 31 to 50 years of age likely had GBS (not paralytic polio), for the following reasons:

3a. Weinstein stated that cerebrospinal fluid (CSF) was examined and was either normal or consistent with paralytic polio. However, no CSF findings were presented. Moreover, it was unclear when during the illnesses CSF was collected. As previously discussed, that is important because CSF findings that distinguish between paralytic polio and GBS hold for only the first few days following the onset of paralysis.

3b. At the time of the Weinstein study, *in vitro* cultivation of polioviruses had just been discovered,[62] and serological studies for detecting antibodies to polioviruses were not available for clinical diagnosis. Therefore, these definitive diagnostic tests were lacking in their investigation.

3c. Nerve conduction studies, which may have revealed evidence of a peripheral neuropathy, were not performed. In that respect, diminished nerve conduction would have been consistent with GBS and inconsistent with paralytic polio.

3d. The Weinstein study almost certainly had a mix of GBS and polio patients, but GBS was not considered. Therefore, the study cannot be used to describe the features of polio, any more than apples and oranges blended together could be used to describe apples.

For the above reasons, the Weinstein manuscript would not be accepted by current major peer-reviewed journals.

Concerning the suggestion by DB&H that the incidence of paralytic polio was increased in adults in the mid-twentieth century, in a 1951 article also by Weinstein,[230] it was reported that of 2,255 cases of paralytic polio occurring in Massachusetts in 1949 and 1950, only 89 (4 percent) were 35 years or older. This confirms that paralytic polio remained uncommon in adults.

Finally, we already took into account the possibility that the 1921 adult paralytic polio rate might be higher when we did the Bayesian analysis of FDR's symptoms (see page 123), by using the incidence of paralytic polio during the severe polio epidemic in New York City during 1916. Because FDR's symptoms strongly favor GBS, the most likely diagnosis remains GBS, regardless of the exact disease incidence rates.

4. DB&H claimed that virtually no patients with non-bulbar GBS are bound to a wheelchair. Their statement was incorrect. Even after the advent of immunotherapy, about 20% of patients with GBS were unable to walk for at least 6 months after the onset of the disease.[129] Moreover, in an article published in 2005 regarding the long-term outcome of patients with GBS,[231] it was stated that

"In 15.6% some form of aid like a cane, a crutch, or even a wheelchair was used." This is also borne out in a recent textbook on neurology,[126] where it was reported that 10 percent of patients with GBS had pronounced residual effects. They indicated that this occurs particularly in patients such as FDR who develop a severe, rapidly evolving form of the disease or in those who required respiratory assistance because of respiratory failure.[126]

It is important that these recent untoward outcomes of GBS occurred despite the use of immunotherapies that significantly decrease the morbidity and mortality of the disease. When FDR became ill in 1921, those immunotherapies had not been discovered. Therefore, the possibility of severe permanent paralysis in GBS would have been much greater in 1921 than in more recent times.

5. DB&H stated that FDR had *"severe leg and back pain = meningeal irritation"*. That was incorrect. Typically, the most prominent symptom due to meningeal irritation (meningismus) is stiffness of the neck – not leg or back pain. It is true that some muscle pains may occur briefly in acute paralytic polio. However, the prolonged pains in FDR's lower extremities to the slightest touch are atypical of polio and common in GBS. In the letter that FDR sent to Egleston in 1924 concerning his 1921 illness,[14] FDR wrote, *"There was no special pain along the spine and no rigidity of the neck."* Thus, another key feature of paralytic polio, meningismus, was absent in FDR's 1921 illness.

6. DB&H stated that FDR did not have dysesthesia (the term we used in our articles), but hyperesthesia that supposedly strongly favors polio. The original reports in the medical literature indicated that protracted muscle pain was uncommon in paralytic polio. Unfortunately, a simultaneous study of paralytic polio and GBS in a large group of patients with flaccid paralysis that utilized modern diagnostic methods was never done because of the virtual obliteration of polio at the same time GBS was being recognized by many physicians. Furthermore, DB&H are misusing standard medical terminology in an attempt to

support their argument. Severe pain to the slightest touch, i.e. hyperesthesia, is one of the principal manifestations of dysesthesia. *Stedman's Medical Dictionary* defines "dysesthesia" as *"A condition in which a disagreeable sensation is produced by ordinary stimuli"*. Therefore, our use of the term dysesthesia was correct.

It is clear that FDR had protracted hyperesthesia during his illness. *"His skin and muscles had developed a sensitivity to touch so painful that he could not stand the pressure of the bedclothes, and even the movement of the slightest breeze across his skin caused acute distress."* The quote is found in Hugh Gallagher's book *FDR's Splendid Deception* and subsequently in several other histories concerning FDR.[1] The extreme sensitivity to touch was confirmed by FDR in a letter to Dr. Egleston dated October 11, 1924.[14] In that letter he stated that *"all the muscles from the hips down were extremely sensitive to the touch and I had to have the knees supported by pillows. This condition of extreme discomfort lasted about three weeks."* Another primary source is the book *Affectionately, F.D.R.* by James Roosevelt (FDR's oldest son), published in 1959. The book says *"He barely could stand the pressure of the bed sheet on his body"*.[28]

The extreme skin sensitivity to touch is highly significant. Anyone can appreciate that pain caused by the slightest breeze is very unusual, and purely sensory. As previously described in this book and in our articles on this subject, FDR's pains in the lower extremities persisted for several weeks. Hyperesthesia is not typical of paralytic polio because sensory neurons are not infected by polioviruses. In contrast, sensory nerves are often damaged in GBS.[131] Thus, hyperesthesia is not a feature of paralytic polio, but is common in GBS.[232,233]

7. It was also peculiar that DB&H stated that there were no *"objective sensory symptoms"*. Part of the problem is their confusing terminology. They intermix, and fail to define, *"objective sensory loss"*, *"sensory loss"*, and *"sensory findings"*, so it is often difficult to tell what they mean. It is pertinent that

Eleanor Roosevelt reported in a letter to James R. Roosevelt (FDR's older half-brother) dated August 14, 1921 that FDR *"had so much pain in his back and legs"*.[15] Dr. Bennet reemphasized the hyperesthesia and tenderness in his letter to Dr. Lovett dated September 1, 1921. In any case, FDR's protracted hyperesthesia was certainly a sensory finding, arguing in favor of GBS. In addition, FDR had transient numbness in his legs, yet DB&H did not include that as a sensory finding. Numbness is a combination of anesthesia (sensory loss) and paresthesia (tingling). Sensory loss has been experienced by virtually everyone, when their foot has "fallen asleep" (foot numbness). The assertion by DB&H that FDR experienced *"no diminution of sensation in affected parts"* is therefore incorrect. FDR had temporary numbness of the lower extremities early in his illness.[15]

8. DB&H claimed that fasciculations (twitchings) of skeletal muscles, which occurred in FDR's forearms, are limited to motor neuron diseases including paralytic polio. This is another incorrect assertion. Fasciculations may occur in peripheral neuropathies.[234]

9. DB&H claimed that FDR's paralysis only progressed for 3 days, which would be consistent with polio. Most of the progression happened within the first few days of the illness, also consistent with GBS, but there was also some progression days later, which was not consistent with paralytic polio. It is unclear precisely how long the paralysis progressed, but it was beyond 3 days. As reported in his September 12 letter to Draper, on day 15 (August 24) of FDR's illness, Lovett found that FDR had facial paralysis, which was not noted on day 4 (August 13).[21] So sometime between day 4 and day 15, the paralysis progressed. It is hard to find symptom probabilities for "days paralysis progressed", and difficult to pin down exactly how long the paralysis progressed. Therefore, that was not included in the Bayesian analysis. However, the historical evidence indicates that the paralysis progressed beyond the two to four days typically found in paralytic polio, so this factor also favors GBS.

10. DB&H claimed that FDR's bladder paralysis is equally consistent with GBS and paralytic polio, directly opposite to our claim that bladder paralysis (along with bowel paralysis) occurs much more frequently in GBS.

By referencing Lovett's 1922 article concerning polio,[235] DB&H claimed that inability to void is common in paralytic polio because of weakness of abdominal, pelvic floor and girdle skeletal muscles. That is true for voluntary urination. Normal urination begins when the external urethral sphincter and levator ani muscles completely relax.[236,237] In the ninth edition of Adams and Victor's *Principles of Neurology*, with respect to paralytic polio, it is stated that "*Retention of urine is a common occurrence during the early phase in adult patients, rarely persisting.*"[126] The early phase of paralytic polio is the first two to four days while the muscular paralysis progresses. In contrast, FDR's failure to urinate lasted three weeks.

It is important to understand that emptying the bladder is both voluntary and involuntary. Difficulty in voluntary urination may occur in paralytic polio when key skeletal muscles are weakened, but involuntary urination persists.[106-109] In contrast, both voluntary and involuntary urination are frequently impaired in GBS.[130]

In normal adults, the bladder accommodates increasing volumes of urine with little change in the tension of its wall until the volume reaches 300-400 ml. When this threshold is reached, the individual experiences discomfort due to increased tension in the bladder wall. When abdominal, pelvic floor and girdle skeletal muscles are paralyzed, voluntary voiding is impossible.

Involuntary urination is triggered by autonomic nerves.[238] Detrusor muscles – smooth muscles of the bladder wall – together with urethral sphincter muscles located at the neck of the bladder are innervated by lumbar sympathetic nerves and by parasympathetic nerves from sacral segments 2 – 4 of the spinal cord.

Those smooth muscles are activated when the threshold pressure on the bladder wall is reached.

FDR was unable to urinate for at least three weeks according to a letter from Dr. Bennet to Dr. Lovett written on September 1, 1921.[21] The realization that FDR had a protracted paralysis of his bladder helps to understand the cause of his 1921 illness. Since polioviruses do not infect autonomic nerves, protracted inability to urinate does not occur in paralytic polio. In contrast, prolonged paralysis of the bladder is common[130] in GBS because of involvement of both motor and autonomic nerves.[239]

11. DB&H claimed that facial paralysis is not uncommon in paralytic polio, and thus not a factor in favor of GBS. That is incorrect. Facial paralysis in the spinal form of paralytic polio is rare.[92,106-109] See Table 6, page 125. Even the 2% symptom probability for facial paralysis that we assigned, to "give polio the best chance", is probably too generous.

12. Finally, DB&H failed to include bowel paralysis in their list of FDR's symptoms (Table 2 in their paper), or to discuss the symptom. There is no reason to exclude it. The exclusion is ironic given their claim that I *"selectively chose some of his (FDR's) reported symptoms"*. Prolonged paralysis of the bowel is consistent with the involvement of autonomic nerves seen in GBS, and is not consistent with paralytic polio.

Out of all the arguments in their paper, there is one that has validity, but it turns out to only weakly favor polio, and does not alter the overall conclusion that FDR had GBS. DB&H point out that patients with GBS typically have permanent *"objective sensory findings"* or permanent loss of sensation, in contrast to cases of paralytic polio. This is true.

In an article published in 2005 involving 90 patients with GBS,[240] 60 percent of them had noticeable *"disturbed sensation"* in their lower extremities one year after the onset of the disease. That seems to include dysesthesia (tingling and hyperesthesia), as well as anesthesia (loss of sensation).

The omission of this symptom was unintentional. We appreciate DB&H adding this additional factor that could be used in the analysis.

Sensory examinations were not mentioned in the reports by FDR's physicians. However, it seems reasonable to assume his physicians conducted a sensory exam on his lower extremities, and detected normal sensation. It is a simple and routine examination. Also, given that FDR was fitted with braces and wore shoes, it seems safe to assume that he would have noticed a total loss of sensation.

However, a lesser loss of sensation could have escaped notice. Or FDR could have detected sensory abnormalities, but kept them to himself. Nevertheless, assuming that FDR did not have permanent disturbed sensation, how does that affect the diagnostic probabilities?

Plugging the symptom probabilities for "no disturbed sensation at one year" into the Bayesian analysis, the results are nearly identical. The overall posterior probability remains greater than 99.99% in favor of GBS (see Appendix B), whether the new factor is included or not.

Why does adding the new factor not make more of a difference? The answer is easy to see. If 60% of GBS cases have permanent disturbed sensation, 40% do not. FDR could have easily fallen into the 40% category.

Focusing on the single symptom Bayesian analysis is helpful for better understanding why the new factor makes so little difference. "No disturbed sensation at one year" by itself indicates a 66% posterior probability that FDR had paralytic polio. This is weaker than any other "single symptom posterior probability" (see Table 6, page 125). Thus, the new factor has only a weak influence on the overall result. Seven of the eight other symptoms have posterior probabilities around 95%, and thus have a much stronger influence.

We are open to new information that would help better assess whether FDR had GBS or paralytic polio. Out of the many arguments advanced by DB&H, this one item was the only one that proved valid. If it had turned out to make a significant difference, that would have been fine with us. Our only interest is determining the likely cause of FDR's illness.

DB&H feared that correcting the historical record would somehow damage FDR's legacy, or somehow cause other harm. The bottom line from their point of view is that "It is time to put this controversy to rest". However, regardless of the cause of FDR's paralysis, his legacy is untarnished, including the establishment of the rehabilitation center at Warm Springs, and the creation of The National Foundation for Infantile Paralysis that funded the work that led to the first safe, effective poliovirus vaccine. Concerning his legacy, it makes no difference what disease FDR had, GBS or paralytic polio. What was important was his dedication to help victims of a crippling disease.

DB&H stated that they were absolutely certain that FDR had paralytic polio. Given the facts, that is an extreme position, and sets the bar very high for them. Their stated desire to *"put this debate to rest"* fails, because their claims fail. In contrast, our position is very moderate. We have shown that FDR's clinical course seems more consistent with GBS, but we acknowledge that one cannot be absolutely sure of the diagnosis, and that all should keep an open mind on the possibilities. We have been and are willing to modify our conclusions concerning the cause of FDR's 1921 neurological illness if new scientific information emerges that contradicts the diagnosis of GBS. So far that has not occurred.

DB&H acknowledged that *"only in the past decade have the features of his illness, and the historical impact of his illness on disability and health care, been scrutinized systematically."* Many others have written about FDR's illness, but always under the assumption that the diagnosis was paralytic polio. The 2003 JMB article was the first where *"the features of his illness"* were *"scrutinized systematically"*, because this was the first attempt to carry out a differential diagnosis and the first to note the many similarities between FDR's illness and GBS.[2] Previous authors, including DB&H, had been so conditioned by confirmation bias that they never questioned the diagnosis.

In retrospect, it was fortunate that DB&H published their article before this book was finished, because it served as an ultimate test for our analysis. First, DB&H are physicians, so they had the ability to launch a complete attempt at refutation. Second, DB&H apparently made a great effort attempting to prove that FDR had polio. It seems unlikely that anyone else will exceed their effort. Finally, in contrast with other critiques, for the most part DB&H (appropriately) approached the problem from the point of view of FDR's symptoms and clinical course. They argued that most of the factors favoring GBS (eg, dysesthesia, inability to urinate, facial paralysis) instead favored polio or were neutral. However, as detailed previously in this section, their arguments do not hold up to scrutiny. So FDR's symptoms and clinical course still strongly favor GBS as the cause of his 1921 paralytic illness.

In conclusion, all of the criticisms of our thesis (that FDR had GBS) from historians and physicians have been successfully answered. Some of the reasons for the persistence of the belief that FDR had polio will be discussed in the next section.

Chapter 21. Confirmation Bias

"I have said it thrice. What I tell you three times is true." Lewis Carroll ~ *Hunting of the Snark*

Portrait 23.

Francis Bacon.

Bacon (1561-1626) was the first to discuss confirmation bias.

Those who still contend that FDR had paralytic polio may hold to that belief because of confirmation bias, the tendency to selectively seek out or interpret information that confirms preconceptions, and ignore or not look for reasonable evidence to the contrary.[241]

Confirmation bias is common in medicine as well as in other disciplines. Preferential treatment of evidence that supports existing opinions or beliefs is difficult for many to avoid, particularly when the belief is widely held.[242]

Confirmation bias is one of the mechanisms by which we imprison ourselves in the past.

Recognition of Confirmation Bias

Confirmation bias was recognized some four hundred years ago by the English philosopher-scientist Francis Bacon (1561-1626) (Portrait 23). He made two salient observations concerning it.[243] One was, *"The first conclusion colours and brings into conformity with itself all that comes after"*. The second was, *"It is the peculiar and perpetual error of the human understanding to be more moved and excited by affirmatives than by negatives."* Thus, it is often difficult to refute a prior belief that has been widely held for many years. Indeed, the advancement of a new idea that potentially refutes a long-standing belief is often met with considerable skepticism. Such skepticism is necessary until the new idea has been verified independently or until no evidence to the contrary appears.

However, when challenged with convincing evidence contrary to their beliefs, many not only tend to reject the evidence, but adhere even more strongly to their initial notions. That seemingly closed loop pattern of thinking reinforces confirmation bias.

N-Rays

Confirmation bias may strike even famous scientists. An interesting example was the "discovery" of N-rays in 1903 by the French physicist Dr. Prosper-René Blondlot (1849-1930) (Portrait 24).[244] Blondlot (along with his colleague Dr. Ernest Bichat) established that the speed of electricity in a conductor is very close to the speed of light. He had also previously established the speed of radio waves.[245]

Portrait 24.

Prosper-René Blondlot.

Blondlot (1849-1930) mistakenly believed that he had discovered "N-rays".

In 1903, when Professor Blondlot was trying to polarize Röntgen rays (X-rays), he observed changes in the brightness of an electrical spark in a gap placed in the path of an X-ray beam.[244] He named the radiation "N-rays" after the university where he worked – *Nancy-Université*. Furthermore, he insisted that N-rays emanated from most substances.[246] Almost immediately, other physicists in France claimed that the radiation was real, and quickly published articles concerning N-rays in *Comptes Rendus de l'Académie des Sciences*. About three hundred articles investigating N-rays appeared in the next few years in science journals.

Very soon, biological effects of N-rays were reported. A French Professor of Medical Physics, Dr. Augustin Charpentier, reported in 1904 that N-rays were emitted from a stretched muscle. Charpentier then claimed that N-rays increased human sensitivity to sight, smell, taste, and hearing. Very soon thereafter, a psychiatrist, Dr. Gilbert Ballet at *Hôtel-Dieu de Paris* found that N-rays detected neurological diseases, such as spastic paraplegia.

A wave of enthusiasm for diagnostic and therapeutic uses of N-rays swept over the medical profession in France and certain other European countries. Indeed, N-rays seemed to be a combination of medical imaging and radiation therapy rolled into one.

And yet, there were many skeptics, including Lord Kelvin from England and Heinrich Rubens from Germany, both of whom failed to replicate Blondot's findings.[247] Some critics posited that Blondlot and others were detecting heat waves. To these doubters, Blondlot explained that their eyes had to be acclimated to the dark and had to be viewing an object at a particular oblique angle to detect the radiation.

An adventuresome American physicist, Dr. Robert W. Wood from Philadelphia, also failed to verify the presence of N-rays. Soon thereafter, Professor Heinrich Rubens and other physicists attending the British Association for the Advancement of Science held in Cambridge, England asked Wood to go to Nancy and help resolve the issue. Wood agreed and obtained an invitation from Blondlot to witness his experiments.

When he visited Blondlot, Wood struck the fatal blow to N-rays. While Blondlot was conducting an experiment in a darkened laboratory, Wood surreptitiously replaced a metal file, which was supposed to give off N-rays, with an inert piece of wood that should not have. N-rays were observed by Blondlot, but not by Wood. In the next experiment, Wood secretly removed an essential prism from the experimental apparatus. Yet, Blondlot insisted that he observed N-rays.

Wood reported his findings the next year in the journal *Nature*.[248] In his report, Wood did not identify where he had been or whom he had visited. However, most readers of Wood's brief article seemed to know that it was about Blondlot at the *Nancy-Université*.

Blondlot and certain other physicists continued to believe in N-rays for the next few decades. And the term "N-rays" continued to appear in some major dictionaries into the 1940s.[249] But the world of physicists and other enlightened scientists realized that N-rays did not exist.

The duration of confirmation bias concerning N-rays lasted just a few years, because carefully controlled experiments conclusively proved that the radiation did not exist. Overcoming confirmation bias in the case of FDR's illness has been more challenging, mostly because the confirmation bias lasted for many decades. If FDR's diagnosis had been questioned decades earlier, confirmation bias would not have built up so much. But it was not until 2003 that the diagnosis was questioned. By that time, the mantra *"FDR had polio"* had been repeated countless times. At this point, the amount of confirmation bias is perhaps overwhelming. Another factor allowing confirmation bias to persist is the lack of any laboratory experiment to definitively settle the issue. Even a sample of FDR's DNA would be of no help to establish the correct diagnosis. The original sources of information concerning FDR's illness strongly indicate that he had GBS. But confirmation bias, the belief in oft-told tales, can be stronger than reality.

Confirmation Bias in Medical Practice

Confirmation bias is widespread in many walks of life, including medicine. To illustrate confirmation bias in a practical way, I will describe two pre-school age children I cared for in the 1980s when I was the attending physician on an inpatient service at the University of Texas medical school in Galveston. Each child had been hospitalized repeatedly for poorly controlled "asthma". In each case, new doctors would read the medical chart, see the "asthma" diagnosis, and accept it. But because of certain aspects of the medical history and certain physical findings, in both cases I suspected that the diagnosis was incorrect.

Before proceeding, let me briefly review the occurrence, symptoms, signs, and diagnosis of asthma. In the 1950s and 1960s, it was uncommon to see children with asthma in the clinics and rare for them to be hospitalized. In contrast, by the 1980s many cases of asthma in children were occurring throughout the United States and in other industrialized countries. During that period, at least one child was hospitalized for asthma each week in our hospital.

Asthma is characterized by inflammation of the lower bronchi that leads to lower respiratory obstruction, more prominent in the expiratory phase of respiration. Wheezing, coughing, and dyspnea (shortness of breath) commonly occur. Physical examination reveals evidence of air trapped in the lungs (over-expansion of the chest seen on inspection and hyperresonance of the chest found by percussion). The expiratory phase of respiration is prolonged. High-pitched sibilant sounds, most commonly called wheezing, are heard principally in the expiratory phase of respiration. If a patient with an acute attack is seen soon enough, the expiratory obstruction is usually reversed within several minutes by injecting epinephrine or inhaling a beta-2 adrenergic agonist. Both treatments relax the smooth muscles that surround the terminal bronchi. Although the diagnostic criteria remain somewhat imprecise, the diagnosis of asthma is commonly made by demonstrating bronchospasm reversed after treatment with a beta-2 agonist.

Because the incidence of asthma in children was high, and other causes of repeated obstruction of the lower airways were much less common, usually the diagnosis of asthma was correct. However, after I reviewed the medical charts of both children, I was struck that their physical findings were poorly described. It was unclear what was meant by "wheezing" and what phase of respiration was impaired. Also, although heights and weights of both children had been recorded for each hospitalization, the data had not been used to construct growth charts.

It did not take long for the mother of the first child to tell me that she was concerned that her six-year-old son was not growing well despite having an excellent appetite. She also described the "wheezing" to be more a rattling than a whistling sound, and that the wheezing happened during inspiration as well as expiration, was present most days, seemed worse early in the morning, and seemed to improve after coughing.

Physical examination revealed a cooperative, but underweight child. His height and weight were below the third percentile (3% level) for his age. His growth chart revealed that his growth had been progressively slowing for at least the past three years. Coarse breath sounds were detected throughout all lung fields in both phases of respiration, and partially cleared after postural drainage and coughing. I reviewed the current and past chest X-rays. The lungs were hyperinflated. The bronchi were thickened and dilated throughout the lung fields.

Because of his unresponsiveness to bronchodilators, his low weight, and the physical findings, I questioned the diagnosis of asthma. Also, his poor weight gain despite an excellent appetite suggested intestinal malabsorption. His sputum was thick and lacked eosinophils that might be expected in asthma. His clinical picture was consistent with cystic fibrosis,[250] an autosomal recessive genetic disease that leads to a defect in a transmembrane conductor regulator and hence to increased viscosity of respiratory, intestinal and pancreatic secretions. Cystic fibrosis was subsequently diagnosed by detecting an abnormally high concentration of chloride in his sweat.[250]

The second child, age 7 years, had (in addition to his lower airway symptoms) nasal polyps and recurrent episodes of otitis media and chronic sinusitis. These symptoms are not characteristic of asthma. Also, the child's attacks of bronchitis failed to respond to bronchodilating agents. Cystic fibrosis was unlikely, since the concentration of chloride in his sweat was normal. Using pattern recognition, my knowledge of known illnesses, and thinking about the pathophysiology behind the child's symptoms, I suspected that the child had immotile cilia syndrome,[251] a congenital defect in the structure and movement of respiratory cilia that leads to a failure to expel mucus from the upper and lower respiratory tracts. Confirming my suspicion, a biopsy of the child's nasal epithelium demonstrated that his nasal cilia did not beat. Electron micrographs of the biopsy showed that the dynein arms in the microtubules of the nasal cilia (dynein arms provide the energy through the enzyme ATPase to move the cilia) were absent.[252] That clinched the diagnosis of immotile cilia syndrome.

In both cases, after the diagnoses were corrected, the residents still signed out the patients as having asthma! When I asked them why, they said they did so because asthma had been repeatedly diagnosed during the past hospitalizations. When I reminded them that the diagnosis of asthma was now disproven and that the diagnoses were corrected, they reluctantly changed the diagnoses on the hospital medical charts. But they admitted that they were uncomfortable with the changes, since many other faculty members and residents had previously made the diagnosis of asthma. It was an example of the power of confirmation bias in the practice of medicine.

Possible Confirmation Bias in FDR's Case

Anyone unaware of our 2003 publication[2] likely accepts that FDR had paralytic polio. For those who have read our article and continue to believe the correct diagnosis is poliomyelitis, confirmation bias may have colored their opinions.

I have done my best to assure that confirmation bias did not creep into my thinking, by 1) making sure that I took all of FDR's clinical findings into account, not just a select few, 2) looking at all the facts, including the pathogenesis of paralytic polio and GBS, 2) relying on objective diagnostic and statistical methods, not unsubstantiated opinions, and 3) taking into account and learning from any criticisms that might be published.

I am used to the scientific method where new information can overturn old conceptions, and where published papers have to pass the gauntlet of the peer-review process. I am willing to accept new facts, because there is no use denying reality. However, as previously described in Chapter 20, the criticisms so far have failed to change the strong conclusion that FDR likely did not have paralytic polio.

I never wished to stir up a controversy. I was instead led to the problem by serendipity. And then it was necessary to thoroughly review the original documents concerning FDR's illness and to apply diagnostic reasoning to solve the question of the cause of his neurological malady.

The likelihood that FDR likely had GBS is strong, over 99%, even though we purposely used incidence rates and symptom probabilities to favor polio when there was any question. However, given the perhaps equally strong force of confirmation bias, it is not surprising that many would continue to believe what they grew up believing.

The conclusion in favor of GBS is also robust. Extreme, unrealistic alterations in symptom probabilities or incidence rates are required to make paralytic polio as likely as GBS.

The reconstruction of the pathogenesis of FDR's illness was consistent with GBS, but was inconsistent with paralytic polio. Based on our current knowledge of health and disease, FDR's symmetric ascending paralysis, facial paralysis, descending pattern of recovery from the paralysis, prolonged bladder and bowel paralysis, and prolonged hyperesthesia, strongly indicate that GBS is the most likely cause of his 1921 illness.

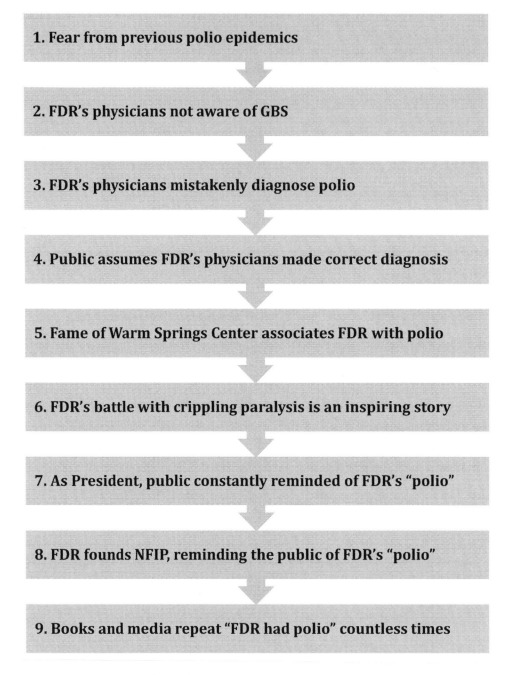

Figure 20. Causes of Confirmation Bias in FDR's Case.

The reality may be, however, more complicated. Some critics may have later changed their minds, but did not feel the need to publish a confirmatory study. In that respect, physicians in academic life or in private practice are pressed for time and have little opportunity to indulge in a project that does not aid their careers or add to their financial worth. Finally, historians in the main are not equipped to deal with medical controversies unless they are trained in medicine or relevant biological sciences.

For most historians and physicians, it is perhaps embarrassing to acknowledge that something they have always assumed to be true (that FDR had polio) is probably untrue. However, that is how science works. No "fact" should be off limits from investigation. The purpose of research reports should not be to "tell a story" to make us feel good (the "story" of how FDR had polio), but to ascertain the truth to the best of one's abilities. Especially in this case, there is no need to "tell a story", because Roosevelt's incredible accomplishments are not diminished by his having GBS instead of polio, since he was paralyzed in either case. And neither is the suffering of polio survivors diminished, regardless of the correct diagnosis of FDR's paralytic illness.

Escalation of Confirmation Bias in FDR's Case

The tenacity in which the diagnosis of paralytic polio is held becomes more understandable when the progress of confirmation bias in FDR's case is retraced (Figure 20, above).

1. First, severe epidemics of paralytic polio beset the region where FDR lived just a few years before his illness began. Thus, polio was generally feared, and on the mind of the public.

2. At that time and place, about the only known cause of non-traumatic flaccid paralysis was poliomyelitis. Therefore, most physicians in the United States probably assumed that flaccid paralysis was due to paralytic polio, regardless of the age of the patient or whether some symptoms were not consistent with polio.

3. FDR's physicians misdiagnosed his 1921 illness as paralytic polio, because they were experts in that disease and not familiar with GBS.

4. The public assumed that physicians would make the correct diagnosis, and many continue to believe that whatever FDR's physicians diagnosed must be right.

5. FDR became further identified with polio because of his creation of a rehabilitation center for victims of paralytic polio, and because of his direct participation in their rehabilitation.

6. His struggles to overcome paralysis make a dramatic and inspiring story that was repeated so many times that it attained the status of a popular myth.

7. FDR served four terms as President, constantly reminding the public of his physical disability and the polio diagnosis.

8. His link with poliomyelitis was further strengthened by his creation of the National Foundation for Infantile Paralysis that supported the development of a poliovirus vaccine that prevented the disease in most of the world.

9. Countless books, movies, TV shows, radio programs, speeches, newspaper articles, magazine articles, and other sources stated that FDR had polio, as a "fact". These many reiterations left an indelible impression upon the public and progressively strengthened the belief that FDR had paralytic polio.

Given that the belief in the diagnosis of paralytic polio came from so many different sources and for so many years, it is understandable why there is great reluctance to consider that FDR had a very different neurological disease in 1921.

Confirmation bias permeates our thoughts and actions so much that we are usually unaware of its presence. However, anyone who cares to look can readily see confirmation bias all around. For example, James Tobin writes, *"It seems to me that when I was growing up in the 1960s, everybody knew Franklin Roosevelt had been crippled. When I was no older than six or seven, my grandmother told me a tale of a heroic, crippled president who once had struggled bravely across a stage to give a speech.*" Like just about every other child growing up in the United States, he was constantly reminded that "FDR had polio". In Tobin's case, the seeds of confirmation bias were even more deeply planted, due to the influence of his grandmother's story. Certainly, I would cherish and want to believe something my grandmother might have told me at such a young age.

Tellingly, FDR's political advisor Louis Howe observed, *"If you say a thing often enough, it has a good chance of becoming a fact."*[253] Howe's aphorism is perhaps as good a definition of confirmation bias as any.

Almost any marketing book will devote space to confirmation bias, though perhaps not referring to it by that name. For example, Robert Cialdini, in his best seller *Influence, the Psychology of Persuasion*,[254] speaks of *"our nearly obsessive desire to be (and to appear) consistent with what we have already done"*. This is closely related or identical to confirmation bias.

Cialdini explains a main attraction of this kind of automatic consistency as, *"all we have to do when confronted with the issue is to turn on our consistency tape, whirr, and we know just what to believe, say, or do."* In the case of FDR's 1921 illness, the *"consistency tape"* plays back countless times saying *"FDR had polio"*. Cialdini observes, *"It (automatic consistency) offers us a way to avoid the rigors of continued thought"*.

Cialdini offers a second *"perverse"* attraction of this type of consistency, namely the sometimes harsh consequences of thoughtful activity. He states, *"Sometimes it is the clear and unwelcome set of answers provided by straight thinking that makes us mental slackers. There are certain disturbing things we simply would rather not realize. Because it is a preprogrammed and mindless way of responding, automatic consistency can supply a safe hiding place from those troubling realizations. Sealed within the fortress wall of rigid consistency, we can be impervious to the sieges of reason".*

To many people, the idea that a dramatic story, almost a national myth, is not true is highly disturbing. However, there is no reason to be disturbed by the truth. FDR still overcame paralysis to become President. As FDR said, *"the only thing we have to fear is fear itself".*

Movies and television programs depicting famous, iconic individuals have a powerful influence upon the public. This surely has been the case with the story of FDR's 1921 paralytic illness. What the public sees, they tend to believe, even when the documented history is to the contrary. The 2014 movie "Selma", which depicts the struggle for civil rights in the United States, is a case in point. In this otherwise excellent movie, President Lyndon B. Johnson is depicted as an opponent to the 1965 voting rights legislation and to King's plan to march from Selma to Montgomery. History refutes those contentions. Not surprisingly, the historical reality is more complex than the kind of fictionalized history often presented by the movie industry. But young, impressionable viewers may not know the difference, and may come to believe that Johnson was not an advocate for civil rights in 1964.

In the case of FDR's illness, confirmation bias and the power of movies and television (see Chapter 9) worked synergistically to imprint the diagnosis of paralytic polio firmly in the minds of the public.

Chapter 22. Epilogue

"Oh, there's just one more thing." ~ Lieutenant Columbo

As this book ends, I wish to expand upon certain take-home messages.

Beliefs Subject to Change

There are many examples in medicine and other fields where beliefs have had to be modified or replaced. In that spirit, I would not be disappointed if future scientific evidence proves that FDR had a disease other than GBS. All of us in medicine, or in other scientific disciplines, should be prepared to change a belief, if sufficient scientific evidence refutes it.

A Cautionary Tale

Roosevelt was born too soon to benefit from the specific diagnostic tests and therapeutic procedures for GBS that were developed in the latter part of the twentieth century. Little was known about Landry's ascending paralysis (GBS) by most American physicians when FDR became ill in 1921. Furthermore, it was misinterpreted by some of the leading medical authorities including FDR's physician, Dr. Lovett, that Landry's ascending paralysis was a clinical feature of paralytic polio. Given the state of medical knowledge at the time, it is understandable that a physician in the United States in 1921, presented with FDR's case, would have concluded that he had paralytic polio.

As I contemplated my medical career, it became clear that a great deal of medical science was not imagined at the time I was trained. In the same vein, it is likely that future physicians will look back at the current era and remark about how little we knew. Undoubtedly, there are many misconceptions in our understanding of certain aspects of medical diagnosis and clinical care. In that

sense, the misdiagnosis of FDR's 1921 neurological illness is a cautionary tale
for physicians.

Irony of the Misdiagnosis

Ironically, the misdiagnosis of FDR's 1921 neurological illness had a long-term
positive effect. Because of FDR's preoccupation with paralytic polio, he founded
(in 1938) the National Foundation for Infantile Paralysis that raised funds to
develop one of the major poliovirus vaccines. The vaccines brought the scourge
of paralytic polio to a halt in the United States and later helped to wipe out polio
in all but a few parts of the planet. If the diagnosis had been Landry's ascending
paralysis (later termed GBS), it is unlikely that FDR would have had the same
impact upon the prevention of poliomyelitis.

Prisoners of Time

As I reflected about the story of FDR's 1921 neurological illness, I thought more
about his physicians. Even though FDR's doctors did not make the correct
diagnosis, they were admirable in many ways. Bennet was a dedicated family
physician, deeply appreciated by the people of Lubec and the surrounding areas
for his meticulous patient care. In recognition of his devotion to patient care, in
1937, he received the "Annual Award for Outstanding Service as a Doctor" from
the Maine Medical Society.[255] Keen, Levine, Lovett, and Draper were excellent,
nationally recognized physicians who made significant contributions to the
science and practice of medicine. Lovett and Draper undoubtedly conducted
careful physical examinations. Furthermore, their clinical observations of FDR
were in close agreement. But like any medical professional, each of FDR's
physicians had certain shortcomings. Bennet lacked the special knowledge and
expertise needed to diagnose FDR's illness. Keen, although famous in the field
of neurosurgery, was not an expert in diagnosing non-surgical neurological
diseases. It is doubtful that Keen had cared for many victims of paralytic polio or

understood that FDR's physical findings pointed to Landry's ascending paralysis (GBS).

Levine was later widely respected for his work in the diagnosis of coronary thrombosis and of pernicious anemia, and for his dedication to medical education at Harvard Medical School. He was an excellent physician, but many of his ideas about paralytic polio, including the therapeutic value of doing a lumbar puncture, were incorrect. Furthermore, he did not consider the possibility of an alternate diagnosis.

Lovett was an outstanding orthopedist who devised innovative surgical procedures to ameliorate the crippling effects of paralytic polio and of scoliosis. He wrote an excellent book about poliomyelitis. But along with the vast majority of physicians who practiced medicine at that time, he apparently did not understand that Landry's ascending paralysis was due to a peripheral neuropathy, not to poliomyelitis. Also, Lovett's expertise lay in surgical rehabilitation, not in medical diagnosis. Remarkably, in his September 12, 1921 letter to Draper, he said *"I never feel that the history is of much value anyway"*.[21] This goes against everything we know about the importance of the history in determining the cause of an illness.

Draper was deeply interested in the origin, diagnosis, possible prevention, and early treatment of paralytic polio. But as previously discussed, he mistakenly believed that certain normal phenotypic variations were indicators of a susceptibility to paralytic polio. And again, there is no evidence that he was aware of GBS (Landry's ascending paralysis) as a separate disease.

All of FDR's physicians lived at a time when it was assumed that if an individual developed a sudden, non-traumatic flaccid paralysis, it was due to paralytic polio. GBS was either not known to FDR's physicians, or for unknown reasons they failed to consider it. Since the discoveries concerning GBS were made in Europe, it was much less likely that physicians in the United States would be aware of

GBS. Furthermore, the discovery by Guillain and his colleagues was made during the First World War, interfering with trans-Atlantic communication between physicians. It is perhaps difficult for those who live in the information-digital age to imagine what life was like in the absence of the internet that permits almost instantaneous, global access to information regarding all types of diseases regardless of their frequency or complexity. The concept of GBS as a separate disease was not widely accepted in the United States until after the Second World War, and the immunological basis of the disease would not be known until the 1990's.

I too am a prisoner of time, in that there is much that I do not know because of the period in which I live. If I was able to witness the future, I probably would be unable to comprehend what I was seeing. During my six decades in medicine, I have witnessed the accelerating pace of innovation in medical knowledge and technology. If I had lived in 1921, I could not have imagined the enormous changes in medical knowledge that happened in the nearly 100 years since, including the wealth of new discoveries concerning the origin, diagnosis, and treatment of GBS.

Today, the science of medicine is accelerating more rapidly than ever before. Trying to keep up with new medical knowledge takes a great deal of time and effort. Yet most physicians are so busy seeing patients, dealing with the increasing bureaucratic regulations required to practice medicine, and whatever other personal or family matters they are involved with, that they are hard pressed to keep up with new advances in medical science. In that respect, many physicians are "prisoners of time" in that they mostly rely upon knowledge learned years ago. Even when the physician finds time, learning new information can be difficult. Pick up a copy of an outstanding research journal such as *Science* or *Nature*, and you will probably find that few of the articles are understandable, unless they are in your area of interest.

In 1921, FDR's physicians faced the same basic problems modern day doctors face – what was wrong with the patient and what could be done to treat the patient. But physicians in 1921 had to contend with different handicaps. 1) They did not have ready access to foreign medical journals where GBS (Landry's ascending paralysis) had been reported. 2) They did not have the luxury of rapidly searching the medical literature via the Internet for clues to the causes and treatments of medical problems. 3) Finally, medical technology and medical therapeutics were in their infancy.

Anyone who studies or writes about FDR's illness must rely on the factually confirmed historical record concerning his clinical course. The historical record is far from perfect. For example, no hospital records are available. However, FDR was closely attended by family, a colleague, and physicians, so there are multiple letters and other accounts that make the clinical course reasonably clear, as has been presented in this book. The problem is that nobody previously thought to critically reexamine the historical record, and ask, "Did he really have polio?". Instead, each generation repeated the "fact" that FDR had polio. As the decades passed, the story achieved the status of a national myth, and confirmation bias grew ever stronger. However, impartially examining the evidence, as detailed in this book, leads to the conclusion that FDR likely had GBS.

Many historians have accepted as authoritative the diagnostic conclusions of Drs. Draper and Lovett. In their minds, if Draper and Lovett diagnosed polio, that should be absolutely trusted. I have taken a different approach. I neither accepted nor denigrated the diagnostic conclusions of any of FDR's physicians. Instead, I paid close attention to how they might have arrived at their conclusions. They were "all prisoners of time", doing their best given the relatively poor state of medical knowledge in 1921 and the difficult circumstances on remote Campobello Island.

The cause of FDR's illness is properly not based on what FDR's physicians concluded, but instead on what they observed and what we currently know concerning polio and GBS. FDR's physicians failed to even consider GBS as a possible diagnosis, likely because of their lack of awareness of that disease. Therefore, it is understandable that they arrived at the wrong diagnosis. It would likely have helped to ascertain the cause of the illness if a diagnostic lumbar puncture had been done early in the course of the illness. However, as explained in detail in this book, it appears that the procedure was not done, and could not have been done early enough in the course of the illness to provide useful information.

What If FDR Had Died?

FDR came close to dying during August 1921, because of the severity of his neurological disease and the medical complications that could have occurred. I have often wondered what would have happened if FDR had died. What would have happened to his family? Who would have been the thirty-second president of the United States? How would the Great Depression have been handled? Would our democracy have survived? What would have been the outcome of the Second World War? Would the United Nations have been created?

After FDR's death in 1945, Eleanor Roosevelt had many major roles in national and international affairs. She was a Delegate to the United Nations, the Chair of the United Nations Commission on Human Rights, the overseer of the drafting of the Universal Declaration of Human Rights, and the Chair of the Presidential Commission on the Status of Women during President Kennedy's Administration. But Eleanor's impact may very well have been far beyond those accomplishments, since she most likely saved the life of her husband Franklin, during his serious 1921 illness.

Why it Matters

Some ask why the cause of FDR's illness matters. Regardless of whether FDR had polio or GBS, the outcome (paralysis) was the same, and his accomplishments remain the same. So the argument goes, why waste time trying to correct the diagnosis?

It matters because history is not simply a made-up story, but instead a telling and analysis of what really happened. Saying "what does it matter?" can be a convenient rationalization for those who simply want to persist in their beliefs.

Even beyond the search for truth and historical accuracy, there is an important practical reason to correct the diagnosis of FDR's 1921 illness. Over many years, the "fact" that "FDR had polio" has been emphasized time and time again in the public media. Consequently, many members of the public and some physicians have come to believe that certain clinical features of GBS (symmetric ascending paralysis, prolonged progression of the paralysis, facial paralysis, dysesthesia, and regression of the paralysis in a descending fashion) are typical of paralytic polio. Thus, the correction of the diagnosis will clarify the clinical differences between paralytic polio and GBS for many members of the public and for some historians and physicians.

George Santayana, the famous philosopher and essayist (1863-1952), said, *"Those who cannot remember the past are condemned to repeat it"*,[256] often paraphrased as *"Those who do not know history's mistakes are doomed to repeat them"*. This certainly applies here. Comparison of FDR's symptoms with reported symptoms in case series of paralytic polio and GBS patients shows that FDR likely had GBS. However, since FDR is still by far the most famous case of "polio", many authors now base their understanding of polio symptomatology on FDR's case. For example, since FDR had prolonged hyperesthesia, prolonged hyperesthesia is supposedly characteristic of polio. This is a remarkable example of circular reasoning.

Therefore, besides simply getting the historical facts straight, it is important to get the diagnosis of FDR's illness right because as long as the misdiagnosis persists in the minds of historians and physicians, their understanding of polio will likely be incorrect.

Last Words?

The last words in this work concerning FDR's near fatal 1921 illness are from a friend, someone I have been close to for many years. After reading our first article on FDR's illness, he gently took me aside and remarked in a thoughtful way,

"Beware, my good fellow, beware, for I fear that your fanciful words, replete with the jargon of medicine, are but the coinage of your mind. For as you can see, your thoughts bear no relationship to the world round you – to what other members of your medical species believe. So beware, take care, for you might be declared as quite mad, even though in some sense we all are. But nonetheless, beware. For think about it – how is it that you and your small hardy band of colleagues found the way and the rest went astray?"

The words of my "friend" were in reality a conversation with myself. After thinking about it a bit more, I responded to myself in the following way.

"More than a decade ago, we were given a gift from an unlikely source,

And given the nature of the matter we had no other recourse

Than to investigate it in the best ways we knew.

In doing so, we examined every single clue.

And after we weighed and reweighed every symptom and sign,

We knew that the diagnosis of polio must be declined.

And in its place was an autoimmune disease,

That caused pain even to the slightest breeze.

And sparked a paralysis that crept up to the chest and arms,

And understandably caused great alarm.

For with a little more ascent, history would have changed forever,

But how it would have, I am not that clever."

So despite lingering doubts and over a decade since our initial analysis, Guillain-Barré syndrome remains the most likely cause of FDR's 1921 neurological illness. For in respect to matters of science, the majority opinion is not always correct. It is the best evidence that is decisive. But even so, the ultimate acceptance or rejection of a proposition concerning a controversial issue such as the nature of FDR's 1921 illness requires the test of time.

Time will tell whether our diagnostic reappraisal of FDR's 1921 neurological illness will be accepted by future historians, physicians, and medical investigators. Perhaps a future investigator will examine the primary sources of information pertaining to FDR's case and conduct a scientifically based diagnostic analysis of his 1921 illness, either confirming or refuting our findings. To date, this has not happened. Perhaps the powerful force of confirmation bias will win out, as new histories and documentaries repeat the message that FDR had polio. It is also possible that new archival information concerning his disease will be discovered, or some other novel approach will be taken.

But unless new evidence emerges, the most likely cause of FDR's 1921 illness remains Guillain-Barré syndrome. If so, then the case of Franklin Delano Roosevelt's 1921 neurological illness will be recorded in the annals of history as one of the most famous medical misdiagnoses of all time.

Appendix A. Bayesian Analysis Explained

Bayesian analysis is not required to make the case that GBS was the correct diagnosis for FDR's illness. Simply stated, FDR's age and symptoms were not generally consistent with paralytic polio, and are overall much more consistent with GBS.

However, Bayesian analysis quantifies clinical reasoning, and allows us to assign probabilities. So Bayesian analysis is helpful to make the analysis of FDR's illness more objective.

For those who wish to further explore Bayesian analysis, Appendix A and Appendix B show how Bayesian analysis was used in FDR's case. This discussion is placed in Appendices because it might otherwise interrupt the flow of the book, and because understanding the underlying math is not required to understand the usefulness of Bayesian analysis. Nate Silver's book *The Signal and the Noise* is recommended for those interested in reading more about applying Bayesian analysis to everyday thinking, and the math behind Bayes' Theorem.[261]

To help understand Bayesian analysis, an example is presented that calculates the likelihood (the "posterior probability") that FDR's illness was due to GBS or paralytic polio, given that FDR had facial paralysis.

Since this section uses math equations, we need to use variables, like X and Y. The names X and Y are not particularly informative. So we will start by defining some "user-friendly" variable names.

1) First, the "outcome variable", what we are calculating:

– `Post_Prob` is the posterior probability that FDR had GBS.

2) Next, the "input variables", the numbers fed into the Bayesian analysis:

– `Prior_GBS` is the prior probability of GBS (57%).

– `Prior_Polio` is the prior probability of paralytic polio (43%).

– `Symptom_GBS` is the % of GBS cases with the symptom (50%).

– `Symptom_Polio` is the % of paralytic polio cases with symptom (2%).

3) Next, two "intermediate" variables, to simplify the Bayesian equation:

– `G_Term` is the GBS contribution to the posterior probability.

– `P_Term` is the paralytic polio contribution to the posterior probability.

4) We calculate `G_Term` and `P_Term` as follows:

```
G_Term = Prior_GBS x Symptom_GBS = 0.57 x 0.50 = 0.2850

P_Term = Prior_Polio x Symptom_Polio = 0.43 x 0.02 = 0.0086
```

5) Finally, here is the Bayesian equation, and the calculated result:

```
Post_Prob = G_Term / (G_Term + P_Term)

Post_Prob = 0.2850 / (0.2850 + 0.0086) = 0.9707 ≈ 97%
```

So the posterior probability (best estimate) that FDR had GBS, based on the symptom of facial paralysis, is 97%. Thus, based solely on the incidence rates (the prior probabilities) and the presence of facial paralysis, it is 97% likely that FDR had GBS.

For most people, "Bayesian analysis" sounds difficult. But the above equations are just simple algebra. And it turns out that Bayesian analysis is so simple that it does not even require an equation! Figure 21 shows that basic counting and proportions can be used to easily carry out Bayesian analysis.

Figure 21. Bayesian Analysis Explained Without an Equation. If 10,000 adult cases of flaccid non-traumatic paralysis in 1921, with facial paralysis (FP), 2,850 / 2,936 are due to GBS, so the likelihood of GBS in such a case is 97%.

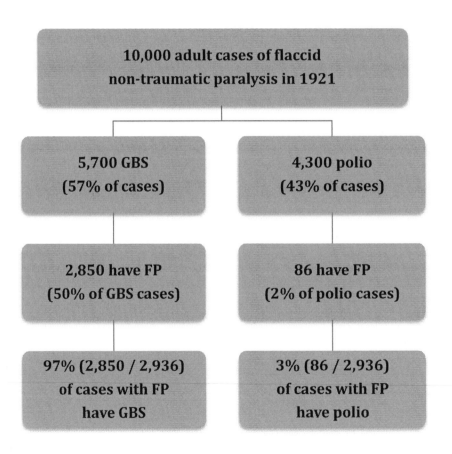

The following is an explanation of each step in Figure 21:

Start with 10,000 cases of non-traumatic flaccid paralysis, in 1921, in adults around FDR's age. We could use any number of cases, and get the same posterior probabilities. 10,000 is a convenient number of cases to use.

1. About 57% (a prior probability) of the 10,000 cases will be GBS (5,700 GBS cases).

2. About 43% (a prior probability) of the 10,000 cases will be paralytic polio (4,300 paralytic polio cases).

3. About 50% (a symptom probability) of the 5,700 GBS cases will have facial paralysis (FP) (2,850 GBS cases with the symptom).

4. About 2% (a symptom probability) of the 4,300 paralytic polio cases will have facial paralysis[92,106-109] (86 paralytic polio cases with the symptom).

Therefore, of 2,936 cases with facial paralysis (2,850 GBS + 86 paralytic polio), 97% of the cases (2,850 / 2,936) are due to GBS. It directly follows that for a case of non-traumatic flaccid paralysis and facial paralysis occurring in 1921 in an adult, it is 97% likely that the correct diagnosis is GBS.

If you have followed the above example, you can appreciate that Bayesian analysis is just a matter of simple proportions.

Appendix B. Overall Bayesian Probabilities

In Chapter 11, we introduced Bayesian analysis, a simple method that takes into account 1) "prior probabilities" (disease incidence rates) and 2) "symptom probabilities" (% of cases with a symptom) to produce 3) "posterior probabilities" (new best guess which disease is the correct diagnosis). In Chapter 15, we used Bayesian analysis to calculate the posterior probability of paralytic polio or GBS in FDR's case by looking at one symptom at a time. For example, given that FDR had dysesthesia, it is 98% likely that GBS was the cause of FDR's illness.

For six of FDR's eight symptoms, the posterior probabilities favored GBS. This indicates that FDR's illness was GBS. Furthermore, the majority of FDR's symptoms continued to favor GBS even when disease incidence rates and symptom probabilities were significantly changed to favor paralytic polio.

This is good evidence to confirm the impression from pattern recognition that FDR did not have paralytic polio. However, since FDR had a spectrum of symptoms, not just a single symptom such as dysesthesia, it would seem desirable to know the overall probability that FDR had paralytic polio or GBS, based on the total clinical picture. Thus, all (not just one) of FDR's symptoms might be taken into account to produce an overall numerical likelihood that FDR had paralytic polio or GBS.

Since FDR's symptoms did not fit with paralytic polio, that disease was unlikely. But how unlikely? This section answers that question by providing an overall probability number. We will present two ways for calculating an overall likelihood that FDR had paralytic polio or GBS.

First approach: The first overall approach is analogous to the way a physician might make a diagnosis. In FDR's case, the chief complaint was a non-traumatic flaccid paralysis.

First, the physician gathers information, by using the history, physical examination, laboratory tests, and other methods as needed. A physician can gather additional information at any point to assist in the diagnostic process. We gathered information by closely examining the historical record concerning FDR's case.

Next, with the information at hand, the physician chooses the most probable causes of the illness. As explained in Chapter 12, for FDR's case, the possibilities narrowed down to paralytic polio and GBS.

The physician, unconsciously using Bayesian thinking, or one could say using common sense, will consider more likely causes first. Based on the 56.5% prior probability that FDR had GBS (see Chapter 15 for how the figure was derived), a modern-day physician, transported back in time to 1921, would consider GBS slightly more likely than paralytic polio when confronted with a 39 year old with non-traumatic flaccid paralysis. Which disease is more likely as the physician takes FDR's symptoms into account?

As shown in Table 8, with the addition of each piece of information, the physician reassesses which potential cause is more likely. In Bayesian terms, the physician's probability estimate after considering new information is called the "posterior probability". In FDR's case, suppose the new information is "ascending, symmetric paralysis". After plugging the symptom probabilities (symptom occurs in 70% of GBS cases, 2% of paralytic polio cases) into the Bayesian equation, the posterior probability of GBS is 97.8%.

Table 8. Multi-Symptom Bayesian Analysis of FDR's Illness. In eight steps, each of FDR's symptoms was taken into account to produce an overall posterior probability for GBS and paralytic polio (PP).

FDR's Symptoms	Probability of Correct Diagnosis	
	Before Step GBS / PP	After Step GBS / PP
Ascending, symmetric paralysis	**0.565** / 0.435	**0.978** / 0.022
Permanent paralysis	**0.978** / 0.022	**0.932** / 0.068
Bladder / bowel paralysis ~14 days	**0.932** / 0.068	**0.993** / 0.007
No meningismus	**0.993** / 0.007	**0.999** / 0.001
Fever	**0.999** / 0.001	**0.938** / 0.062
Hyperesthesia / numbness	**0.938** / 0.062	**0.999** / 0.001
Descending recovery	**0.999** / 0.001	**1.000** / 0.000
Facial paralysis	**1.000** / 0.000	**1.000** / 0.000

Next, in the same way, the hypothetical physician factors in a second symptom, for example "permanent paralysis". A key point is that this time we use 97.8% (not the initial 56.5% value) as the prior probability of GBS, because 97.8% is our current best estimate. After running the Bayesian analysis with the new symptom probabilities (symptom occurs in 15% of GBS cases, 50% of paralytic polio cases), the posterior probability of GBS is 93.2%.

Again referring to Table 8, we continue the process until all of FDR's symptoms are factored in. At each step, we start with a prior probability (current best guess), factor in new information (one of the eight clinical findings), and end up with a posterior probability (our new best guess). The probability estimate becomes more reliable at each step, because it is based on more information.

At the end, after factoring in all of FDR's symptoms, the likelihood of GBS is 99.9998%. From pattern recognition and that six of eight symptoms favor GBS, it is not surprising that the overall analysis so overwhelming favored GBS, because FDR's symptoms are so atypical of paralytic polio.

It should be noted that the order in which the symptoms are examined makes no difference in the final outcome of Table 8. For example, if we switched "fever" and "facial paralysis" in the series of steps, the overall likelihood that GBS is the correct diagnosis still ends up 99.9998%.

What if the symptom probabilities reported in the literature are somewhat different from those existing in reality? To test that possibility, we artificially halved each GBS symptom probability (not shown). For example, instead of the best estimate that 50% of GBS cases have facial paralysis, we used a 25% figure. Even with these huge changes, the overall probability of GBS remained greater than 99.99%. This shows that the analysis is "sturdy", that it stands up to significant changes in input values.

As explained in Chapter 15, we selected disease incidence rates to give paralytic polio the "best chance to succeed". As a further way to tilt the odds in favor of polio, we artificially halved the GBS prior probability (from 56.5% to 28.3%), and accordingly adjusted the prior probability for paralytic polio to 71.7%. Even with this big change, the overall probability of GBS remained at nearly 100%. Again, this shows that the analysis is "sturdy".

Even adjusting the GBS initial prior probability by an incredible 100-fold factor, to 0.6%, and using a prior probability of 99.4% for paralytic polio, the result is an overall GBS posterior probability of 99.97%, as shown in Table 9. This phenomenon, called "swamping the priors", is a profound concept. With enough data, the posterior probability converges to the same value, regardless of the initial disease incidence rates. In this case, FDR's symptoms are typical of GBS, not of paralytic polio, so they overwhelm any initial prior probability.

Table 9. FDR's Symptoms Overwhelm any Initial Probability. Lowering the initial prior probability of GBS 100-fold still results in an overall probability of 99.97% in favor of GBS over paralytic polio (PP).

FDR's Symptoms	Probability of Correct Diagnosis	
	Before Step GBS / PP	After Step GBS / PP
Ascending, symmetric paralysis	0.006 / **0.994**	0.166 / **0.834**
Permanent paralysis	0.166 / **0.834**	0.056 / **0.944**
Bladder / bowel paralysis ~14 days	0.056 / **0.944**	0.374 / **0.626**
Descending recovery	0.374 / **0.626**	**0.954** / 0.046
No meningismus	**0.954** / 0.046	**0.995** / 0.005
Fever	**0.995** / 0.005	**0.697** / 0.303
Hyperesthesia / numbness	**0.697** / 0.303	**0.991** / 0.009
Facial paralysis	**0.991** / 0.009	**1.000** / 0.000

This is especially relevant to FDR's case, because some critics have argued that FDR led such a sheltered childhood that he was never exposed to the poliovirus, and was hence very likely to develop paralytic polio as an adult. As explained in Chapter 2, FDR was exposed to many others in his childhood, was certainly not anything like a "boy in a bubble". Nevertheless, for the sake of argument, assume that FDR really was at a much higher risk of polio, even at a nearly 100% risk compared with GBS, either because of a protected childhood or because polio rates were highest during the summer. It would not change the conclusion. FDR's symptoms were so at odds with paralytic polio that the likelihood he had that disease is very low.

Thus, even when symptom probabilities (see Table 7, page 127) or prior probabilities (see Table 9) were artificially "rigged" to greatly favor paralytic polio, GBS remained far and away the most probable diagnosis.

Second approach: Before explaining the second approach, which is somewhat more complex and technical than the first approach, we need to introduce another method sometimes used for making a medical diagnosis. In this method, a standard list of typical clinical findings for a specific disease is agreed upon. If some agreed upon combination of the findings is present in a patient (or often a medical chart), then the diagnosis of the specific disease can be made with a high degree of certainty. It is a variation on pattern recognition, the most commonly used method in medical diagnosis.

For example, the "modified Jones criteria for acute rheumatic fever" guideline has five "major criteria" (such as carditis, erythema marginatum, or a migratory polyarthritis,) and five "minor criteria" (such as fever, arthralgia, or leukocytosis). Without going into all the details, a diagnosis of rheumatic fever requires evidence of recent streptococcal infection (e.g., raised streptococcal antibody titer), along with either "two major criteria" or "one major and two minor criteria".[262] Another example is the criteria proposed for the diagnosis of systemic lupus erythematosis (SLE) by the Systemic Lupus Collaborating Clinics. Without going into all the details, the presence of 4 out of 17 possible criteria (such as characteristic skin lesions, arthritis, pleuritis, or pericarditis) is required to diagnose SLE.[263]

These "criteria-based" diagnostic methods are perhaps best suited to ensure consistency for research and surveillance purposes. The lists provide an objective standard for examining a medical chart and classifying a patient as having (or not having) a particular disease. We can apply the same kind of logic as an independent assessment of the probability that FDR had GBS or paralytic polio.

The overall idea is that if FDR more closely resembles a paralytic polio patient, then he more likely had paralytic polio. The same logic applies for GBS. It makes sense to define "closely resembles" as requiring that at least three to five symptoms match up. This is the same logic used in the rheumatic fever and lupus examples, where only some (not all) clinical findings have to match. We will take four to be a reasonable number of matches required to make a diagnosis.

Suppose there are 100 adults in 1921 with paralytic polio, and that we are somehow certain of the diagnosis. How many of them will have four or more of FDR's symptoms? Similarly, of 100 adults in 1921 with GBS, how many will have four or more of FDR's symptoms? The answer will help tell us whether FDR's symptoms are more consistent with paralytic polio or GBS, and help us calculate an overall likelihood for which one is the correct diagnosis.

Given the single symptom probabilities listed in Table 6 (page 125), the probability is 68.7% that a given patient with GBS has four or more of FDR's symptoms. So about 69 of the 100 GBS patients would resemble FDR's case. In contrast, the probability is only 0.75% that an adult with paralytic polio will have four or more of FDR's symptoms. So only about 1 of the 100 adult paralytic polio patients would resemble FDR's case.

A computer program was written to calculate these results (68.7% and 0.75%). For each combination of symptoms being present (or not present), a probability 'P' was calculated. If the combination had at least four of FDR's symptoms present, 'P' was added in to the overall probability of at least four symptoms being present. For example, what is the likelihood that a known GBS case has the first five symptoms in Table 6 (page 125), and is lacking the last three symptoms? Simple math tells us the answer is 0.7 x 0.5 x 0.5 x 0.5 x 0.99 x 0.99

x 0.3 x 0.85 = 2.19%. There are 256 such combinations. Of these 256, 163 have four or more of the eight symptoms. We simply add together the probabilities of those 163 combinations.

To ensure that the program was working correctly, we verified that it produced correct results with smaller data sets (two or three symptoms instead of eight), where the results could be compared with those calculated by hand.

Even without going further, we can already see a strong trend that FDR's case more closely resembles GBS, since only 0.75% of paralytic polio cases resemble FDR's illness. By applying Bayes' Theorem, we can quantify the trend even better.

Assuming that at least four symptoms are required to make a diagnosis, 68.7% (for GBS) or 0.75% (for paralytic polio) can be used as the overall symptom probability, and plugged into the Bayesian equation along with the prior probabilities for GBS and paralytic polio. This Bayesian analysis results in a posterior probability of 99.2% that FDR had GBS (0.8% posterior probability that paralytic polio was the correct diagnosis). Carrying out the same analyses with the assumption that at least three symptoms are required to match for a diagnosis of GBS (or paralytic polio), the overall posterior probability is 92.3% in favor of GBS. If five symptoms are required, the posterior probability is 99.9% in favor of GBS.

Why is there such a disparity (68.7% vs 0.75%) in the probability that a given patient with GBS (or paralytic polio) will have four or more of FDR's symptoms? The reason is obvious from Table 6. Only two of FDR's symptoms, permanent paralysis and fever, favor paralytic polio. It logically follows that it is rare (0.75%) to see a paralytic polio case with four or more of his symptoms. In contrast, six of FDR's symptoms are typical of GBS. So it makes sense that it is likely (68.7%) that a given GBS case will have four or more of his symptoms.

Bayesian analysis is used here to quantify something more or less obvious by simple reasoning. The 1921 incidence rates for paralytic polio and GBS in a 39 year old with a non-traumatic flaccid paralysis are about equal. Factor in FDR's symptoms, which strongly favor GBS, and the conclusion swings strongly away from paralytic polio. Exactly how far it swings is best determined by Bayesian analysis. It turns out the conclusion swings nearly 100% toward GBS. The analysis shows that it is very likely (around 99%) that FDR had GBS.

In Bayesian terms, why did FDR's physicians miss the diagnosis? Mostly, it was because their prior probabilities were totally off. Lovett was aware of Landry's ascending paralysis but believed it was due to polio. In addition, they never mentioned the 1916 report by Guillain and his colleagues. Therefore, instead of the correct prior probability of about 57% for GBS, they apparently assigned a zero likelihood, because GBS was not included in their differential diagnosis. We cannot say what prior probability they might have assigned for paralytic polio, but perhaps it was around 90%. The other causes considered by FDR's doctors (*"a heavy cold"* or *"a clot of blood from a sudden congestion"*) were even less consistent with FDR's symptoms.

A key fact: Bayesian analysis can never change a zero prior probability. Even a vanishingly small prior probability can be "swamped" by overwhelming evidence. But a zero prior probability can never be changed into a non-zero posterior probability, regardless of the evidence. If one believes something absolutely, or is unaware of a possibility, no amount of evidence can change the opinion. FDR's physicians were left with one diagnostic possibility – paralytic polio – so it is understandable that they came to that conclusion. They were "prisoners of time".

Appendix C. Pathogenesis Example

This appendix presents an actual case that demonstrates how reconstructing the pathogenesis can help to arrive at the correct medical diagnosis.

An 11-year old girl thought to have chickenpox, mumps, and measles in quick succession was admitted to the inpatient service at the medical school in Galveston. The illnesses occurred before the vaccines to those common viral infections were given routinely to infants. The referring and attending physicians believed that the quick occurrence of three different viral infections was due to an immunodeficiency. That was why I was asked to see the patient.

When I arrived on the ward, I watched the child and her mother from the hallway. The child was in bed avidly reading *Alice in Wonderland*. Her mother seemed anxious, but alert. I introduced myself and indicated that I was asked to help decide whether she had an immune deficiency. The girl asked what immunology was and what happened when you were deficient. I tried to explain it to her, but probably failed. Then she piped up and said, "*So immunology may be too much or too little.*" I nodded in agreement and she said, "*Golly, that's just like Alice in Wonderland.*" I asked her why. "*Well, Alice found things to eat that made her very small or very tall. I guess that's the way immunology is. You either got too much, too little or just enough.*" On that note, I ceased the mini-lecture, agreed with the child's analysis, and elicited the following history.

The child had been healthy, save for occasional upper respiratory infections. The mother volunteered that she thought it strange that her girl had mumps twice – once about three years ago and now at this time. That was of interest because the first recognized patient with a genetic immune deficiency, Bruton's disease (X-linked agammaglobulinemia, a severe deficiency in the production of all types of antibodies),[257,258] had recurrent mumps parotitis (a viral infection of one or more of the salivary glands). However, since Bruton's disease is almost always limited to males, I discounted that possibility.

I asked the mother when her daughter became ill, and what was the first indication of the illness. She said, "*The chickenpox began a little over two weeks ago.*" I asked her where it appeared. She said, "*It was on the left side of the face.*" And what did it look like? She answered, "*They were like little pimples, but then they got larger and drained some yellow pus.*"

And then what happened? The mother thought for a bit. "*That was when the mumps began*". And was it on both sides, or just on one? "*Oh, it was just on the left side.*" I asked her to show me where and she pointed directly in front of the child's external ear and just below the angle of the jaw. Was it tender or not? "*It hurt her quite a bit to touch it.*" The child nodded vigorously in assent.

Was anything else going on at that time? "*Well, she had some fever and the chickenpox on her face wasn't getting any better.*" Then what happened? "*After about a week, the measles started.*" Where did the measles first appear? "*I think it started first on her neck and face. Then it spread to the chest and back and then to the rest of the body. It itched some.*" The girl chimed in that she was glad the itching was over. Did she have any cough, runny nose, red eyes, or sore throat? "*No, she didn't. And you know Doctor, I thought that was strange because my two older children did when they had the measles.*"

How is she now? "*Well she seems better – the measles are about gone, but we are worried that she might get worse again.*" How are your other children? "*Oh, they are just fine, and you know, they haven't got the chickenpox from her yet. But the doctors all tell me that she had the chickenpox, so I guess they are right.*"

I asked about the rest of the family because it might have provided a clue to a possible genetic disease involving the immune system. There was no evident consanguinity (relationship by descent from a closely related common ancestor).

Aside from heart problems in some adults in the father's family and breast cancer in an elderly maternal aunt, the family history was unremarkable.

The child was well nourished and alert. She responded quickly to questions about her schoolwork and about what she was doing before she became ill. Her growth, development, and vital signs were normal. There were several small pustules on the left side of her face. The conjunctivae appeared normal. The tongue was somewhat reddened, but the rest of the mouth and throat, including the sublingual glands, the posterior pharynx, the tonsils, and the opening of the duct from the parotid gland into the side of the mouth appeared to be normal. Koplik spots (ulcerated mucosal lesions of the mouth that are an early pathognomonic sign of measles) were absent. The parotid glands were not palpable, but a tender lymph node was found in front of the left external ear. Red lines were present in the flexural creases of the elbows and armpits (axillae). The skin on the lower arms was peeling slightly. A few, normal-sized, non-tender subcutaneous lymph nodes were palpated in the cervical areas and axillae. The spleen was normal-sized by percussion (sounds produced by firm tapping with a finger pad). The rest of the physical examination was normal.

Did she have an immunodeficiency? Because of her benign past history, in particular few infections, an immunodeficiency was doubtful. The rapid occurrence of three unrelated common viral infections seemed highly improbable, because they were not known to occur in any immune deficiencies. And it was summer – an unlikely time for the occurrence of those viral infections. Also, the absence of conjunctivitis or coughing, and the initial sites of the skin lesions were not in keeping with measles.[259]

Recurrent mumps was improbable, since it had been reported in only one type of immunodeficiency disease (X-linked agammaglobulinemia). Also, as I remarked previously, her sex and her past medical history (only a few minor upper respiratory infections) were inconsistent with that disease. Furthermore, a stone or another type of obstruction in the left parotid duct could not account for the previous bilateral parotitis. Also, in a congenital or inherited immunodeficiency that gave rise to an increased susceptibility to viral infections, lymphoid atrophy would be expected. However, the patient had palpable subcutaneous lymph nodes. Moreover, the pharyngeal tonsils and posterior pharyngeal lymphoid tissues were normal-sized.

The possible pathogenesis of the illness was reconstructed. First, the pustules on the left side of her face may have been due to a bacterial infection, such as a staphylococcus or a streptococcus. Then the bacterial infection spread via regional lymphatics from the infected skin to the nearest lymph node – the one in front of the ear – the left preauricular lymph node.

I postulated that 1) the initial facial infection was due to *Streptococcus pyogenes*, 2) the swelling in front of her left ear was an enlarged lymph node, and 3) the generalized rash was not measles, but scarlet fever.[260] Indeed, the clinical features of the skin eruption were atypical of measles, whereas the distributions of the skin rash, residual red lines (Pastia sign), fading erythema of the tongue (possible residual of a "strawberry tongue"), and peeling skin lesions were in keeping with scarlet fever.

To test my hypothesis, pus from one facial skin lesion was examined microscopically, and pus from a separate facial lesion was cultured for bacteria. Microscopy revealed many neutrophils and chains of bacterial cocci that were consistent with *Streptococcus pyogenes*. Some bacteria were extracellular and others were phagocytosed by neutrophils. The ingested bacteria suggested that there were IgG antibodies to *Streptococcus pyogenes* that facilitated the uptake of those bacteria by neutrophils.

Back on the ward, I told the mother that I did not think that her child had an immune deficiency, and that I needed to discuss the case with her doctors. The residents and students gathered about the nurses' station to learn about my diagnosis and recommendations. When I told them what I found and what I thought happened, they seemed unconvinced. But they did not argue.

The specimen from the facial pustule was sent to the clinical laboratory to be cultured. A few days later, *Streptococcus pyogenes* was isolated from the culture.

Almost all cases of scarlet fever are due to streptococcal infections of the posterior pharynx or tonsils. To further confirm the diagnosis, a specimen of her venous blood was sent to the clinical laboratory to measure antibodies to one of the main streptococcal antigens, streptolysin O. A high titer of serum IgG antibodies against streptolysin O was found, confirming that a streptococcal infection had recently occurred.

Thus, the diagnosis was made by reconstructing the pathogenesis of the illness, deductive reasoning, and conducting a few confirmatory laboratory tests. It was interesting that the patient's immediate medical history, past medical history, family history, and the extent of the abnormal physical findings were not discovered by the residents or students assigned to her case. Perhaps that was due to their inexperience and a ready acceptance of the diagnoses made by the referring and attending physicians. I suspected that their acceptance interfered with their abilities to question the prior diagnoses made by senior physicians. As in FDR's case, once a patient is labeled with a diagnosis, the diagnosis is hard to remove even when it is wrong.

But the main message from the preceding case that pertains to FDR's case is how clinical information, knowledge of the basic and clinical sciences, and logic are used to reconstruct the pathogenesis and hence the cause of a perplexing illness. Chapter 16 shows how this method was used to help establish the diagnosis of FDR's neurological disease.

Appendix D. Letters and Telegrams

Despite the remote location of Campobello Island, there were a surprisingly large number of letters (and a few telegrams) sent back and forth during FDR's 1921 paralytic illness. Later, many more letters were sent. To make it easier for the reader to keep track of the communications, as an aid to other researchers interested in FDR, and to shine a light on what FDR, his doctors, Eleanor, and others actually said, I have included a chronological list of the communications that seem related to FDR's illness.

For each letter, the source is listed. For the Countway letters, the folder number is noted. For "FDRL", the source is the FDR Library folder marked "Family, Business, and Personal Matters - General Correspondence 1904-1928". In addition to the letters and telegrams below, there are notes kept by Lovett concerning the case (Figure 5, page 29), as well as Dr. Samuel Levine's "unpublished note" (Appendix E).

1. 1921-08-14 letter from Eleanor to Marguerite ("Missy") LeHand (FDRL) - *"Your letter has been so long unanswered because Mr. Roosevelt had a severe chill last Wednesday which resulted in fever & much congestion & I fear his return will be delayed."* Letter goes on to discuss Ms. Lehand's salary.

2. 1921-08-14 letter from Eleanor to James R. Roosevelt (FDRL) - *"We have had a very anxious few days as on Wed. evening Franklin was taken ill. It seemed a chill but Thursday he had so much pain in his back and legs that I sent for the doctor, by Friday evening he lost the ability to walk or move his legs but though they felt numb he can still feel in them. Yesterday a.m. Dr. Bennet and I decided we wanted the best opinion we could get quickly so Louis Howe (who, thank heavens, is here, for he has been the greatest help) went with Dr. Bennet to*

Lubec and they canvassed the nearby resorts and decided that the best available diagnostician was the famous old Dr. W. W. Keen of Philadelphia and he agreed to motor up and spend the night. He arrived about 7:30 and made a most careful, thorough examination and the same this morning and he thinks a clot of blood from a sudden congestion has settled in the lower spinal cord temporarily removing the power to move though not to feel. The doctor feels sure he will get well but it may take some months. . . . The doctor thinks absorption has already begun as he can move his toes on one foot a little more which is very encouraging. He [Keen] has told the doctor here [Bennet] just what medicines to give and what treatment to follow and we should know in the next ten days or two weeks how things are going."

3. 1921-08-14 letter from Louis Howe to Frederic Delano (missing) - It is generally agreed that on August 14th or 15th, Louis Howe wrote a letter to Frederic Delano, requesting that Delano find a specialist to quickly come see FDR. However, the consensus from several authors is that the letter has been lost. The FDR Library has no copy of the letter, as well as no copy of any return letter from Delano to Howe. However, there is a letter, dated August 20, 1921 (see below), which mentions both the letter from Howe to Delano, and an August 14th letter from Eleanor to Delano (also apparently missing).

4. 1921-08-17 letter from Eleanor to Marguerite ("Missy") LeHand (FDRL) - *"Mr. Roosevelt is improving but I fear it will be a slow business."*

5. 1921-08-18 letter from Eleanor to James R. Roosevelt (FDRL) - *"Yesterday and today his temperature has been normal and I think he is getting back his grip and a better mental attitude though he has of course times of great discouragement. We thought yesterday he moved his toes on one foot a little better which is encouraging. Dr. Keen wrote me a long letter saying that the longer he reflected the more he inclined to discard the clot and think the inflammation had caused a lesion in the spinal cord which might be a longer*

business than his first estimate. He also sent me his bill for $600! I dread the time when I have to tell Franklin and it wrings my heart for it is all so much worse to a man than to a woman but the 3 doctors agree he will be eventually well if nothing unfavorable happens in the next ten days or so and at present all signs are favorable, so we should be very thankful."

6. 1921-08-19 letter from Howe to Washburn (FDRL) - *"Your letter to Mr Roosevelt unfortunately arrived after he had been taken with a severe chill, the result of which has been to leave him very weak and under strict orders from the doctor not to so much as look at the postage stamp on a letter for some time. . . . I feel sure that Franklin would have been only too glad . . . helping you about the loan but of course it is utterly out of the question to even talk to him about it and will be, I am afraid, for some time to come."*

7. 1921-08-19 letter from Eleanor to Peabody (Groton) - *"Your letter reached Franklin sometime ago but he was taken ill here during his vacation & so as the doctor won't let him visit yet he has asked me to write you for him. He thinks your idea of a Father's dinner is splendid & he will gladly serve on the committee but he could not be chairman. . . . We have really had a very anxious time about Franklin, far more so than he knows, & I doubt if we get back to New York till sometime in September. The exact date of his return to hard work is not certain in my mind but of course I am not saying this to him & only to you because I do not want you to count on him too soon for any great activity."*

8. 1921-08-20 letter from Frederic Delano to Eleanor (FDRL) - *"I am so sorry that I did not get your Sunday letter till Thursday and Mr. Howe's till yesterday, but as soon as I did I acted promptly. In order to be nearer the scene of action and perhaps consult a Doctor who could go to Campobello, I came over on the Federal last night. The great Doctor Lovett was away . . . I called up the Peter Bent Brigham Hospital and they recommended Dr. Levine . . . as their best man on Infantile Paralysis. I saw Levine at 2.15 and read him your letter & Howe's*

letter and your last telegram. He said at once, as did Dr. Parker in Washington, that it was unquestionably Infantile Paralysis. Secondly, he said you should stop the manipulations & massages as unwise so early in the game. His argument is that the disease attacks the nervous system and you must give the patient rest to rebuild, etc. . . . This Dr. Levine has had a great deal of practice in this disease and as you probably know "Boston" has rather specialized on it. . . . You are aware too that the practice as to massage has changed and the Dr. says it is bad to begin it too soon - Let the patient have as much rest as possible for 4 to 8 weeks. My advice would be to send for this man and let him look F. over and a telegram to his office will get him. . . . The impression I get is that the only way to secure a complete cure without serious after effects is to follow a very strict regimen. I am afraid it will be a long grind, but I feel sure he will come out all right. Dr. Keen, all Doctors seem to know. He is a fine old chap, but he is a Surgeon and not a connoisseur on this malady. I think it would be very unwise to toast to his diagnosis, when the Inf. Paralysis can be determined by test of the spinal fluid. . . . I need not explain why the blood clot theory is not accepted. But the Doctors I have consulted both stated that could not be and gave their reasons. I realize your great anxiety and I wish I could be of more service to you. . . . Levine is a man of 30 or 32 and I don't think he will be unreasonable in his charges. He took great interest in the case as did Dr. Parker. As to possible other cases; Howe spoke of other symptoms felt by some of you. Don't let these be treated lightly, the disease is too serious to trifle with."

9. 1921-08-23 letter from Eleanor to James R. Roosevelt (FDRL) - *"The doctors agree that there is no doubt but that F. is suffering from the after effects of a congestion of the lower part of the spinal cord which was of unusually short duration so far as the acute symptoms. (His temp. has been a little subnormal the past few days but is up to 98 today.) It is too early yet to say positively if all this came from his chill and exposure which brought to a focus an irritation that had existed some time, or from an attack of Infantile Paralysis. The symptoms so far*

would be much the same. On Uncle Fred's urgent advice, which I feel I must follow on Mama's account, I have asked Dr. Keen to try to get Dr. Lovett here for a consultation to determine if it is I.P. or not. Dr. Keen thinks <u>not</u> but the treatment at this stage differs in one particular and no matter what it costs I feel and I am sure Mama would feel we must leave no stone unturned to accomplish the best results."

10. 1921-08-23 telegram from Lovett to Keen (Countway 27) - Lovett indicates his plan to come to Campobello to see FDR. Mentions that a spinal tap would be useful, but makes clear he cannot not do it. *"Leave Boston tonight Tuesday – proceed to Eastport and patients house – desirous to return Wednesday night. Have telegraphed wife of patient – unless already done spinal tapping, cell count, & globular reaction[§] would be useful. This I cannot do personally. Shall arrive at Harvard Club Boston tonight."*

11. 1921-08-23 telegram from Lovett to Eleanor (Countway 27) - *"Leave Boston tonight. Have telegraphed Keen. If possible please secure me lower berth or stateroom & Wednesday night train for Boston."*

12. 1921-08-24 letter from Eleanor to Lovett (Countway 35) - *"I enclose your notes as you requested & please allow me to thank you again for your kindness to me. It is a great satisfaction to feel that we know what is the trouble & are giving the right treatment."*

13. 1921-08-27 letter from Bennet to Lovett (Countway 06) - *"Mr. Roosevelt seems improved since Wednesday. Motion has increased somewhat. Wonderfully cheerful. . . . I am wondering about the transportation. . . . Now will some of the officials along the line of travel not <u>demand</u> proof that this man and family are not a menace to the public. I am anxious to help in any way possible, providing that by so doing I am not endangering <u>others</u>. Mr. House leaves tonight for Washington and that makes me wonder? Do you feel that this is the <u>right</u> course*

[§] "Globular reaction" means protein measurement.

to pursue, and can it <u>probably</u> be carried through? Is it a <u>safe</u> course so far as the <u>public</u> is concerned or are we heading toward <u>breakers</u>?"

14. 1921-08-28 letter from Eleanor to Peabody (Groton) - *"Dr. Keen & Dr. Lovett from Boston decided that Franklin had a mild but definite case of poliomyelitis (infantile paralysis). They think he has a very good chance for complete recovery & at the worst it will probably only mean slight lameness & almost certain after he reaches New York the latter part of September he will be able to take up the direction of his business and various other interests. They also assure me that the danger to the children is probably over some time ago & none of the children have been in Franklin's room since a few days after he was taken ill for I had thought about this as a possibility though it seemed incredible. Please do not talk of this as Franklin is anxious to be back in New York before it is generally known, though of course I have had to tell a number of people. . . . Franklin says to tell you he can still do lots of work on the committee he hopes!"*

15. 1921-08-28 letter from Frederic Delano to Eleanor (FDRL) - *"I am so glad you decided to have Dr. Lovett and bad though it is, it is better for all to know just what has happened and what must be guarded against. As soon as Dr. Parker in Washington said he feared Inf. Paralysis I decided I had better go to Boston so as to be nearer you and be able to assist in sending the right man. It is a hard blow to Franklin and to you and will require a good deal of intelligent care and exercise but it seems as though Franklin was making a good start in overcoming the trouble, and he ought to make a complete recovery. . . . the secret [FDR's illness] has been pretty well kept considering all the telegraphing, etc. . . . I want particularly to thank him [Howe] for his long and explicit letter in re Franklin of Aug 15th recd by me Aug 19th which gave me the data I required to present the matter to the Doctors . . . that letter was most helpful in getting a correct grasp of the situation."*

16. 1921-08-31 letter from Lovett to Bennet (Countway 22) - *"I think it would be wise and best to report the case at once. As to travel you will have to furnish a certificate that the affair is three or four weeks old which is a written admission of failure to report and might make trouble all around if looked into. . . . With a certificate there should be no trouble about transportation or change of boats, and three or four weeks is accepted everywhere as adequate. There is no epidemic in the east and no panic."*

17. 1921-08-31 telegram from Bennet to Lovett (Countway 06) - *"Atrophy increaseing [sic] power lessening causing patient much anxiety attributed by him to discontinuance of massage can you recommend anything to keep up his courage and make him feel the best is being done or tell him those changes are unavoidable his wife anxious to avoid worry on his part"*

18. 1921-09-01 letter from Bennet to Lovett (Countway 06) - *"Mr. Roosevelt seemed a little unnerved yesterday. The last few days have shown some falling off which has disturbed him somewhat. Is still unable to urinate. Bowels the same. Is less motion in feet. Especially the left. The muscles are more flabby. Sensation as you saw it. Desire for food fair. He attributes the loss in muscular tone to discontinuance of "massage" or rather he wonders if that is the real cause. . . . He seems to feel that perhaps something more might be going on. It is easy to imagine how he feels. . . . The thigh muscles show some hyperesthesia. Temp - practically normal. When you stated that the improvement in 2 weeks would be considerable, did you mean above or below waist line? If the former it is working and correctly, if the latter not so. Will it be better to tell him frankly that these changes must come and not to be discouraged. I am anxious about his being moved to New York. It would appear that a statement to the effect that Mr. Roosevelt and family were not now a menace to the public; signed by the physicians in attendance would permit him to pass. Otherwise they will surely have trouble."*

19. 1921-09-01 letter from Frederic Delano to Levine (Reference 218) - *"Referring to my visit and my consultation with you in regard to Mr. Franklin Roosevelt, Dr. Keene of Philadelphia adhered very strenuously to his diagnosis of blood clot or congestion of the spinal cord, but finally said that he would be glad to call in Dr. Lovett in consultation. He personally sent for Dr. Lovett to come to Eastport and the two doctors met there and, as you may suppose, Dr. Lovett not only convinced himself, but convinced Dr. Keene (I think) that the case was really infantile paralysis. Although Mr. Roosevelt is getting along as well as could be expected and will probably be moved to New York about the middle of this month, we all realize that it is a very serious matter."*

20. 1921-09-02 letter from Lovett to Bennet (Countway 22) - *"Letter received. Cannot add anything to my letter or telegram. Regard case as routine and would advise against additional treatment. Prefer to leave treatment by drugs to you. Do not consider it in any way important. Slight variations in power have no significance. Certificate matter dealt with in my letter to you."*

21. 1921-09-03 letter from Lovett to Bennet (Countway 22) - *"With regard to travel, I shall be glad to send a certificate of my opinion if the legal requirements of New Brunswick have been complied with, but you see as Chairman of the Harvard Infantile Paralysis Commission I would have to be very careful. . . . The atrophy amounts to nothing, but any considerable loss of power in the legs should not occur. It may be due to over-exercising the muscles in the patient's effort to see how they are. There is a progressive type, but it is not like this as a rule, and I am not worried unless the loss of power is really marked and rapid. The bladder symptoms accompany all grades, and as I said, I do not recall ever having seen permanent trouble. . . . Massage will prolong hyperaesthesia and tenderness, and the thigh sensitiveness should be watched from this point of view. There is nothing that can be added to the treatment, and this is one of the hardest things to make the family understand. The use of hot baths should I think now be considered again, as it is really helpful and will encourage the patient, as he can*

do so much more under water with his legs. There is likely to be mental depression and sometimes irritability, as you heard me say to Mrs. R. I would have the patient sit up in a chair as soon as it can be done without discomfort."

22. 1921-09-03 letter from FDR to Langdon Marvin (FDRL) (written by Eleanor, probably from dictation) - *"After many consultations among the med. fra. my case has been diag by Dr. Lovett as one of poly. otherwise inf. paral. Cheerful thing for one with my gray hairs to get. I am wholly out of com. as to my legs but the doctors say that there is no question that I will get their use back ag. though this means several months of treatment in N.Y."*

23. 1921-09-04 letter from Frederic Delano to FDR (FDRL) - *"I spent a restless night last night and thought a good deal about you, wondering how I could be of some service and as a result of that cogitation, I came to the conclusion that I might give you some "Fatherly" advice. It won't do any harm and it may do some good! I do not remember the school book definitions of philosophy, but since I passed 40, I have worked out ideas of my own on the subject. To my mind Philosophy means in substance, "making the best of the situation", or in other words taking things as they are, analyzing the facts, above all not fooling yourself, and by intelligent reasoning determining the next course to pursue. I never worry, I accept things as they are, I "look forward and not back". I realize that you are up against a hard problem, and hard cruel facts, and yet I feel the utmost confidence that you will emerge a better and stronger man. It will give you time for reflection and that alone is worth a great deal! In your rushing and busy life you have not had that. . . . My philosophy does not at all exclude the supernatural power of our Heavenly Father, but I do think there is more truth than poetry in the Saying "God helps those who helps themselves"! . . . Marvellous "cures" have been effected by men I know, in consumption, paralysis, etc., by the will and determination of the patient, and I feel so confident of your background of health and good habits and of your courage and good temper, that I refuse to be cast down. . . . Among these [books], I have come*

upon a book on "breathing" (vitallic breathing it is called) which I have found very helpful and when you get back home and settled down to "hard work", I will send it to you for it is just the thing to do in bed when none of the family is about."

24. 1921-09-06 letter from Bennet to Lovett (Countway 07) - *"Since Sunday 4th Mr. Roosevelt has developed some temp. 4th 99.5 5th 99.6 am 100 pm 6 am 100.3. The urine continues a goodly number of leukocytes - otherwise negative. Evidently some disturbance here, which seems to be the only apparent cause for rise in temp. Appetite not quite so good, sleep fair, otherwise much the same. We would like to have your opinion about the trip to New York. . . . I hope he can be moved as planned Sept 14th as I feel that a longer stay here would not be to his advantage, which is the important point."*

25. 1921-09-07 letter from Lovett to Eleanor (Countway 22) - *"I had a telegram from Dr. Peabody yesterday, asking me if it would be safe for your boy to go back on September 20th. I telegraphed back that it was safe in every way. This is, however, on the proviso that the boy wears clothing which he did not wear at Campobello, that he puts on fresh under clothing, and that he takes a bath and washes his hair immediately before leaving, and he should not of course go if there is any question of personal illness of any nature."*

26. 1921-09-08 letter from Bennet to Lovett (Countway 07) - *"I have had word from the Provincial Board of Health . . . It will be all right with them. I believe Mr. James Roosevelt has arranged, or is arranging to have Franklin go by Special Car from Eastport direct to N.Y. . . . The Maine Board of Health are willing for him to come in, etc. etc. Mr. Roosevelt has been more comfortable for past two days".*

27. 1921-09-08 letter from Earl Harding to Eleanor (FDRL) - Harding thanks Eleanor for her letter dated August 31 that indicated that FDR was very ill. In addition, Harding thanks her for shouldering the burden as secretary and nurse.

28. 1921-09-09 letter from Draper to Lovett (Countway 08) - *"Mrs. James Roosevelt came in to see me yesterday about Franklin, and said that he was to be brought to town and that you had very kindly suggested that he be put under my care here in New York. Her history of the case was very vague . . . If you could let me have a complete a story as possible of the early stages of this unfortunate malady and any directions which you have to give in the matter of temporary splinting, or massage, or rest, please include it in the letter, so I shall have it before he arrives. It is indeed a most distressing affair, and I was glad to hear Mrs. Roosevelt say that you felt he would make a hasty recovery."*

29. 1921-09-09 letter from Keen to Lovett (Countway 11) - *"I have a letter from Dr. Bennet as to Mr R. He seems not to be gaining. His muscles Dr. B. says are more flabby & he himself (Mr R) "misses the massage" & "feels that more ought to be going on.". I confess I did not see first why it was better to stop the massages . . . I am writing Dr B. that I have referred the question [about the massages] to you to decide. . . . Dr B. wants to know whether I would be willing to sign a certificate stating that Mr R. would not be a menace to those whom he would meet on his way home. . . . I would be willing to sign such a document but again I defer to your better judgment."*

30. 1921-09-09 letter from Lovett to Bennet (Countway 23) - *"In view of your letter of September 8th I fancy there is nothing you want of me. I am, however, sending you a certificate which may or may not be used . . ."*

31. 1921-09-09 certificate letter from Lovett (Countway 23) - *"To Whom it May Concern: Mr. Franklin Roosevelt had a mild attack of poliomyelitis some weeks ago and was seen by me in consultation on August 25th."*

32. 1921-09-09 letter from Eleanor to Lovett (Countway 35) - *"Both my husband and I want to thank you . . . Dr. Bennet has told you how he is so I will only say that to me his general health seems to improve, after a slight setback, & he is wonderfully cheerful."*

33. 1921-09-10 letter from Keen to Lovett (Countway 11) - *"I have written Bennet confirming your views and enclosing a Ctf. [certificate] which I hope will be effective."*

34. 1921-09-12 letter from Lovett to Keen (Countway 11) - *"I am very much interested in your question about the massage, and my experience with it is this - I found that following massage, in early cases that came under my care some years ago, the tenderness increased."*

35. 1921-09-12 letter from Lovett to Draper (Countway 24) - Lovett provides a detailed description of the medical findings in FDR's case and his diagnosis of infantile paralysis, with no mention of a spinal tap being done. *"With regard to Mr. R., I was called to see him in Campobello and I saw him with Dr. W. W. Keen of Philadelphia who had seen him. There was some uncertainty in their minds about the diagnosis, but I thought it perfectly clear as far as the physical findings were concerned and I never feel that the history is of much value anyway. He went down there very tired, took a bath and stayed in the water a good while. He ran home in his wet bathing suit, and subsequently had chills, high temperature and pain. Questioning, however, showed that there had been some hyperaesthesia of the legs preceding the bath for a day or two. He was tender when I examined him, but not excessively so, so that my examination had to be more or less superficial. He had I thought some facial involvement, apparently no respiratory, but a weakness in the arms, not very severe and not grouped at all. There was some atrophy of the left thenar eminence, and so far as I could see pretty normal abdominal muscles. His bladder was paralyzed but infection had been kept away. There was a scattered weakness in the legs, most marked in the hips when I saw him, very few muscles were absent, and in those that were recovering there was a pretty fair degree of power at the end of two weeks. No deformities were present, and the general aspect of the thing was a mild, rather scattered attack without excessive tenderness, coming on promptly and not in a sneaking way, with spontaneous improvement beginning most at*

once and progressing. It seems to me that it was a mild case within the range of possible complete recovery. I told them very frankly that no one could tell where they stood, that the case was evidently not of the severest type, that complete recovery or partial recovery to any point was possible, that disability was not to be feared, and that the only out about it was the long continued character of the treatment. It is dangerous to speak from impressions at the end of the second week, but my feeling about him was that he was probably going to be a case where the conservation of what muscular power he has may be very important, and it looked to me as if some of the important muscles might be on the edge where they could be influenced either way - toward recovery, or turn into completely paralyzed muscles. I was as non committal as I could be about who should conduct the treatment, and I asked them to put themselves in your hands and follow your advice. I did this, not because I wanted you to refer them back to me, but because I honestly do not know who in New York is taking the most interest in the matters. I trust that you will be successful with Mrs. Millett, whom I found quite difficult and one might almost say skeptical about the value of therapeutic measures as advocated in America."

36. 1921-09-14 letter from Keen to Lovett (Countway 11) - *"I confess I was puzzled to conceive a reason why massage should not be used from the start in such a case as Mr. Roosevelt's. But you may remember the old Latin maxim, pronounced, however, in the old fashioned way in which I was brought up - "Experientia docit" - translated as "Experience does it". Whatever our theories may be, the facts as you state are very interesting to me, and I confess quite novel. Of course, in the case of Mr. R., if his pain is increased by the massage, I take it that you will stop it. . . . I also emphasized again the need of the utmost aseptic care, never to be relaxed for a moment, in the use of the catheter, the most dangerous instrument in surgery. I also suggested to Dr. Bennet that Urotropin was the best urinary disinfectant that I knew and that its administration would not interfere with anything else that was being done."*

37. 1921-09-19 letter from Bennet to Lovett (Countway 07) - *"His trip to New York was uneventful . . . It seems very unfortunate that this came on when Mr. Roosevelt was away from home, where he would have been in reach of the best in the line of treatment . . . Dr. Draper spoke of having treated successfully a number of acute cases, with a serum prepared from the blood of convalescent patients. This was new to me. Is it of real value?".*

38. 1921-09-20 letter from Lovett to Bennet (Countway 23) - Indicates that there is little if any evidence that convalescent immune serum is successful in the treatment of polio. *"I heard from George Draper about Mr. Roosevelt and he asked me if I would come on and see him within a few days. He seemed to think he was in good condition and said his bladder was better. . . . With regard to the serum from convalescent cases, we used it in the epidemic in Massachusetts in 1916. We thought we got good results from it, especially in preparalytic cases. Dr. Francis Peabody who had charge of it, however, analyzed all the cases to whom it had been given that year and compared them with controlled cases in the same series to whom it was not given, and came to the conclusion that the cases without it did as well as the cases with it. That material was published in the Boston Medical and Surgical Journal August 11th, 1921. This was the intraspinal method. Dr. Amoss and Dr. Draper believe in the intraspinous and intravenous method at the same time. In 1920 we had an epidemic of about 1800 cases in and about Boston, and the Harvard Infantile Paralysis Commission had to decide what to do in the matter of treatment. Dr. Peabody and Dr. Rosenau after a careful survey of all the facts at their disposal did not feel there was enough definite about the serum to justify us in using it and so we did not use it in last years cases."*

39. 1921-09-24 letter from Draper to Lovett (Countway 08) - Requests a report concerning Lovett's findings in FDR's case.

40. 1921-09-26 letter from Lovett to Draper (Countway 24) - *"When I saw Mr. R. I found a very definite involvement of both arms, but it seemed to me slight and scattered, which of course is a good matter in prognosis. The involvement of the bladder is almost always associated with abdominal weakness and often the girdle type of both abdomen and back. I agree with you that there is no use in seeing him until his tenderness has gone . . . I have found immersion in a strong saline bath of value at this stage, as I believe it hastens the disappearance of the tenderness and allows some muscular action. We also find the use of electric light seems to hasten the disappearance of the tenderness".*

41. 1921-10-11 letter from Draper to Lovett (Countway 08) - *"I think it would be a good thing if you could come over to see Franklin R. toward the end of this week. He hinted to me that he understood that you sometimes came over to this town [NYC] anyway and rather hoped that it might be on one of those occasions, feeling a little, I think, that to summon you for his case alone might mean an enormous expense. . . . We have had him in the hot tub every other day for the past week and a half with very definite benefit I believe . . . He still has a little tenderness in his ham strings. I was delighted to find that he had much more power in the back muscles than I had thought, but I must say that the pelvic girdle and thighs and, indeed, most of the leg muscles are in poor shape."*

42. 1921-10-17 letter from Lovett to Bennet (Countway 23) - *"I saw our patient F. R. yesterday and found him much improved. He was in the Roosevelt Hospital in good spirits, is just able to sit up but is still tender in spots. He is cheerful and doing an hour or so of business each day. He had been in a chair once and I recommended pushing him around, and letting him go home when he wanted to. There is power in practically all of the hip muscles and when he starts on muscle training I believe that things will start along."*

43. 1921-10-23 letter from Bennet to Lovett (Countway 07) - *"I am indeed greatly pleased to know Mr. Roosevelt is improving and trust he may get well up to normal in time."*

44. 1921-10-24 letter from Draper to Lovett (Countway 09) - *"I should like to have it clear in my mind just what the relationship is between Miss Simpson, who came to me a few days ago offering her services, and Mrs. Kathleen Lake, whom Miss Simpson spoke of as her assistant. It makes no difference to me which one of these ladies I engage to work with Mr. R., but I should hate to be involved in serious diplomatic problems."*

45. 1921-10-25 letter from Lovett to Draper (Countway 24) - Discusses which nurses (Miss Simpson and/or Mrs. Lake) might care for FDR once he goes home.

46. 1921-11-19 letter from Draper to Lovett (Countway 09) - *"The patient is doing very well - has been moved to his house and navigates about successfully in a wheel chair. He is exceedingly ambitious and anxious to get to the point where he can try the crutches, but I am not encouraging this."*

47. 1921-12-02 letter from Lake to Lovett (Countway 13) - Provides details on FDR's treatments and condition. *"Things are going as well as can be expected".*

48. 1921-12-17 letter from Lake to Lovett (Countway 14) - Lake gives a follow-up on her efforts to help FDR with his physical therapy and indicates FDR's reluctance to use crutches.

49. 1922-01-04 letter from Lake to Lovett (Countway 15) - Lake briefly indicates FDR's progress.

50. 1922-01-13 letter from Lake to Lovett (Countway 16) - Lake is not satisfied with FDR's progress and wants Lovett to see him.

51. 1922-01-22 letter from Lake to Lovett (Countway 17) - Lake provides many details concerning FDR's progress or lack of progress.

52. 1922-01-31 letter from Lovett to Krida (Countway 28) - *"I am impressed with the necessity of preventing hip flexion contraction as the important feature in the case now. . . . every effort ought to be concentrated on getting those legs out straight."*

53. 1922-02-02 letter from Krida to Lovett (Countway 12) - *"I have begun the progressive gradual correction of the slight knee joint contracture . . . Progress in this direction seems to be satisfactory . . . We are also stretching the tissues on the front of the hip joint region for one hour daily, with good result."*

54. 1922-02-02 letter from Lovett to Draper (Countway 24) - *"Do not bother about the tank. It is a very good thing, but not absolutely necessary and not worth bothering about. . . . I shall not charge what I did when I went to New York last, but a good deal less."*

55. 1922-02-12 letter from Lake to Lovett (Countway 18) - Lake gives a follow-up on her efforts to help FDR with his physical therapy.

56. 1922-03-17 letter from Lake to Lovett (Countway 19) - Lake writes about FDR's ideas to spend time between NYC and Hyde Park.

57. 1922-03-20 letter from Lovett to Draper (Countway 24) - *"How is FR getting on, and is he walking, and is the hip flexion better? The correction of the hip flexion I regard as crucial."*

58. 1922-03-25 letter from Draper to Lovett (Countway 09) - *"F. R. is getting on apparently very well. He is walking quite successfully and seems to be gaining power in the hip muscles. The quadriceps are coming a little, but they are nothing to brag of yet. Below the knee I must say it begins to look rather hopeless . . . There has a situation arisen . . . The patient has gotten the idea into his head that he must economize this Summer, and proposes, consequently, to rid himself of his nurses and have his wife take over the joint duties of Mrs. Lake and Miss Rocky. Obviously this is an impossible plan. In the first place Mrs. R. is pretty*

much at the end of her tether with the long hard strain she has been through, and I feel that if she had to take on this activity, that the whole situation would collapse. . . . Mrs. Lake does not seem to fit perfectly smoothly into the picture. . . . I think Miss Rocky occasionally gets on the nerves of Mrs. R. . . . What I want your support for chiefly, is to combat the patient's absurd plan to have his wife do the work."

59. 1922-03-28 letter from Lovett to Draper (Countway 25) - A brief note indicating that the nurse was quite able to help FDR carry out the exercises. *"I should thoroughly disapprove of his wife doing them."*

60. 1922-05-02 letter from Draper to Lovett (Countway 09) - *"She [Mrs. Lake] thinks Mr. Roosevelt is a little tired, more with his mental activities, which are incessant, than with the leg activities. I agree with her. . . . Now the patient feels that unless Mrs. Lake sees him every day, he will stop advancing. . . . I think I shall suggest to him not to put quite so much steam into his brain work. I also would like to have you see him toward the end of this month to outline a general plan for the Summer as regards the use of his legs. I must say I am a little discouraged at the outlook."*

61. 1922-05-03 letter from Lovett to Draper (Countway 25) - *"I'm afraid I was a little unsatisfactory over the phone . . . I was having a depressed stage in which my lot seemed more than I could bear. I feel better now. . . . The patient in question is a very important one, the outcome is of great importance to you and me as well as to him, and nothing can go wrong. I am not awfully keen of course about the trip, but I will come [to see FDR] any time."*

62. 1922-05-05 letter from Lovett to Draper (Countway 25) - Plans to see FDR and Draper on May 20, 1922.

63. 1922-05-06 letter from Lake to Lovett (Countway 20) - Lake indicates that there was a possibility that she would be taken off the case.

64. 1922-05-08 letter from Draper to Lovett (Countway 10) - *"It would be a little better . . . to see the patient on Friday afternoon, the 19th . . . concern about trying to have you come over when you had other patients to see, because of her fear of the great expense when you come alone."*

65. 1922-05-10 letter from Lovett to Draper (Countway 25) - Trying to make an alternate time to see FDR.

66. 1922-05-23 letter from Lovett to Lake. (Countway 29) *"Counsel him not to try new methods with his muscles, but to trust us to give him the maximum dose that he can stand for, and above all things advise him to look out for hip flexion contraction, which is the keynote in many cases. He cannot be too careful."*

67. 1922-05-24 letter from Lake to Lovett (Countway 21) - Lake gives a detailed description of FDR's progress and various things that happened.

68. 1922-06-01 FDR's medical record from Lovett (Countway 38) - Mostly detailed information concerning FDR's muscular functions.

69. 1922-06-04 letter from Eleanor to Lovett (Countway 36) - *"I hear on all sides how much my husband is improving & I am so glad you think he can really learn to go up & down steps alone for that will mean getting in & out of a motor with ease."*

70. 1922-06-05 letter from Lovett to Krida (Countway 28) - *"Mr. Roosevelt arrived here in good shape . . . I meant to speak to you when I was in New York about the reason that I thought he had better come on here, and I asked Dr. Draper to explain the thing to you verbally rather than to write."*

71. 1922-06-05 letter from Lovett to Draper (Countway 26) - FDR has been improving at Phillips House. Miss Wright has been helping him. New braces are being made.

72. 1922-06-05 letter from Lovett to Eleanor (Countway 31) - Comment that FDR is doing well with his rehabilitation.

73. 1922-06-07 letter from Lovett to Lake. (Countway 29) *"He is getting out and getting a change of scene, he looks better, and everything goes extremely well."*

74. 1922-06-07 letter from Lovett to Eleanor (Countway 32) - Commented on FDR's progress during his stay at Phillips house. Also encouraged her to spend a few days there and to speak with him (Lovett) about her husband's situation. *"The news I shall have for you will be all to the good."*

75. 1922-06-09 letter from Draper to Lovett (Countway 10) - *"We wasted so much time this Winter in all this bad management. . . . I am rather disappointed in Krida's brace work. I purposely saw very little of him [FDR] during the winter. . . . I was able to see with a better perspective the intense and devastating influence of the interplay of these high voltage personalities one upon another. It has been a great comfort, having you in the background all the time."*

76. 1922-06-21 letter from Lovett to Draper (Countway 26) - Discusses FDR's progress in handling himself, problems with his old braces, many efforts to fix the problems, and the new braces that were made.

77. 1922-06-21 letter from Lovett to Eleanor (Countway 31) - General comments about FDR's condition.

78. 1922-06-22 letter from Draper to Lovett (Countway 10) - *"He [FDR] seems to be very cheerful, and I should say had gained considerably in the tricks of handling himself. The new braces are, of course, infinitely better than the others, which I must say were an absolute failure."*

79. 1922-06-24 letter from Eleanor to Lovett (Countway 36) - A thank you note and general comments.

80. 1922-08-02 letter from Bennet to Lovett (Countway 07) - *"I am anxious to know how much real progress Mr. Franklin D. Roosevelt has made since his return home last Sept."*

81. 1922-08-04 letter from Lovett's Assistant to Bennet (Countway 05) - *"Dr. Lovett is away for the summer . . . I will hold your letter until his return."*

82. 1922-08-14 letter from Lovett to FDR (Countway 03) - *"I had the pleasure of seeing Mrs. Roosevelt here the other day . . . I rather inferred from what she said that you had not been using your crutches and splints as much as I think you ought to. I probably mislead you by telling you the splints were not a treatment for your paralysis, which is perfectly true, but I think it is very important for you to do all the walking that you can within your limit of fatigue, with a view of your activities next winter."*

83. 1922-09-22 letter from FDR to Lovett (Countway 01) - *"I am glad to be able to report that I have faithfully followed out the walking and am really getting so that both legs take it quite naturally, and I can stay on my feet for an hour without feeling tired. I think the balance is coming back also, and though I can negotiate stairs if I have a hand rail I cannot get up steps with only the crutches, and I doubt if this feat can be accomplished for a long time."*

84. 1922-10-14 letter from Lovett to Draper (Countway 26) - Says FDR had *"improved a lot during the summer, not only in general, but in walking."*

85. 1922-10-18 letter from Draper to Lovett (Countway 10) - *"He [FDR] looks a little fat and pasty in the face, I do not think quite so hard as he was when he left in the Spring, but this may have only been a chance impression. I am glad to hear you think he is coming on, but his wife told me on the side that she did not feel very sanguine. I saw his legs in bed today & feel sure that there is a very real advance of power".*

86. 1922-11-12 letter from Rockey to Lovett (Countway 34) - *"I feel Mr. Roosevelt has not attempted any of your suggestions to date, all this lovely fall has gone with only a few minutes devoted to walking, not every day. Several days ago he was compelled to walk about one quarter of a mile which completely took him off his feet for about four days."*

87. 1922-11-15 letter from Lovett to Rockey (Countway 30) - *"I am much obliged for the suggestions contained in your letter, which will be of use to me."*

88. 1923-04-27 letter from FDR to Lovett (Countway 01) - *"I am back after a highly successful trip to Florida waters, during which time I did not go ashore at all from the boat, but got plenty of swimming and fishing. The result has been most satisfactory and I am convinced that there is a vast improvement in the leg muscles. Mrs. Lake, who has been in today, is highly enthusiastic. . . . I am tremendously keen about life on a boat, especially in Florida waters. Memorandum for Dr. Lovett: The following suggestions may prove of value in other cases as they proved useful on a small houseboat in Florida this winter. . . . [getting up and down stairs] . . . [navigating passageways too narrow for crutches] . . . [going swimming, as the water was 10 feet below the deck] . . . [rocking chair to exercise quadriceps] . . . [catching large fish]"*

89. 1923-06-01 letter from Lovett to Eleanor (Countway 31) - Indicates that he is well satisfied with FDR's progress.

90. 1924-02-11 letter from Draper to Lovett (Countway 10) - *"I saw F.D.R. a day or two ago before he went south and I am very much disheartened about his ultimate recovery. I cannot help feeling that he has almost reached the limit of his possibilities. I only hope that I may be wrong in this."*

91. 1924-10-11 entire letter from FDR to Egleston (FDRL)

"Please excuse my delay in replying to your letter which has been forwarded to me down here in your neighboring state where I am spending a few weeks

swimming and getting sunlight for my legs.

I am very glad to tell you what I can in regard to my case and as I have talked it over with a great many doctors can, I think, give you a history of the case which would be equal to theirs.

First symptoms of the illness appeared in August, 1921, when I was thoroughly tired from overwork. I first had a chill in the evening which lasted practically all night. The following morning the muscles of the right knee appeared weak and by afternoon I was unable to support my weight on my right leg. That evening the left knee began to weaken also and by the following morning I was unable to stand up. This was accompanied by a continuing temperature of about 102 and I felt thoroughly achy all over. By the end of the third day practically all muscles from the chest down were involved. Above the chest the only symptom was a weakening of the two large thumb muscles making it impossible to write. There was no special pain along the spine and no rigidity of the neck.

For the following two weeks I had to be catheterized and there was slight, though not severe, difficult in controlling the bowels. The fever lasted for only 6 or 7 days, but all the muscles from the hips down were extremely sensitive to the touch and I had to have the knees supported by pillows. This condition of extreme discomfort lasted about three weeks. I was then moved to a New York hospital and finally moved home in November, being able by that time to sit up in a wheel chair, but the leg muscles remained extremely sensitive and this sensitiviness [sic] disappeared gradually over a period of 6 months, the last remaining point being the calf muscles.

As to treatment—the mistake was made for the first 10 days of giving my feet and lower legs rather heavy massage. This was stopped by Dr. Lovett of Boston who was, without doubt, the greatest specialist on infantile paralysis. In January,

1922, 5 months after the attack he found that the muscles behind the knees had contracted and that there was a tendency to foot-drop in the right foot. These were corrected by the use of plaster casts during 2 weeks. In February, 1922, braces were fitted on each leg from the hips to the shoes and I was able to stand up and learned gradually to walk with crutches. At the same time gentle exercises were begun, first every other day, then daily, exercising each muscle 10 times and seeking to avoid any undue strain by giving each muscle the correct movement with gravity. These exercises I did on a board placed on the bed.

The recovery of muscle paralysis began at this time, though for many months it seemed to make little progress. In the summer of 1922 I began swimming and found that this exercise seemed better adapted than any other because all weight was removed from the legs and I was able to move the legs in the water far better than I had expected. Since that time, i.e. for the last two years, I have as far as possible in connection with my work and other duties, carried out practically the same treatment with the result that the muscles have increased in power to a remarkable extent and the improvement in the past six months has been even more rapid than at any previous time.

I still wear braces, of course, because the quadriceps are not yet strong enough to bear my weight. One year ago I was able to stand in fresh water without braves when the water was up to my chin. Six months ago I could stand in water up to the top of my shoulders and today can stand in water just level with my armpits. This is a very simple method for me of determining how fast the quadriceps are coming back. Aside from these muscles the waist muscles on the right side are still weak and the outside muscles on the right leg have strengthened so much more than the inside muscles that they pull my right foot outward. I continue corrective exercise for all the muscles.

To sum up I would give you the following "Don'ts." Don't use heavy massage but use light massage rubbing always towards the heart. Don't let the patient over-exercise any muscle or get tired. Don't let the patient feel cold, especially the legs, feet or any other part affected. Progress stops entirely when the legs or feet are cold. Don't let the patient get too fat.

The following treatment is so far the best judging from my own experience and that of hundreds of other cases which I have studied. 1) Gentle exercises especially for the muscles which seem to be worst affected. 2) Gentle skin rubbing— not muscle kneading—bearing in mind that good circulation is a prime requisite. 3. Swimming in warm water—lots of it. 4) Sunlight—all the patient can get, especially direct sunlight on the affected parts. It would be ideal to lie in the sun all day with nothing on. This is difficult to accomplish but the nearest approach to it is a bathing suit. 5) Belief on the patient's part that the muscles are coming back and will eventually regain recovery of the affected parts. There are cases known in Norway where adults have taken the disease and not been able to walk until after a lapse of 10 or even 12 years.

I hope that your patient has not got a very severe case. They all differ, of course, in the degree in which the parts are affected. If braces are necessary there is a man in New York whose name I will send you if you wish when I get back to New York, who makes remarkable light braces of duraluminum. My first braces of steel weighed 7 lbs. apiece—my new ones weigh only 4 lbs. apiece. Remember that braces are only for the convenience of the patient in getting around—a leg in a brace does not have a chance for muscle development. This muscle development must come through exercise when the brace is not on—such as swimming, etc."

92. 1925-05-09 letter from FDR to Ober (Countway 02) - FDR observed that he is able to stand in the waters of Warm Springs with his *"shoulders 4 inches out of water"*. He considers the pool the best after-care treatment for *"polyo"*.

93. 1925-05-15 letter from Ober to FDR (Countway 04) - Ober thanks FDR for his letter concerning Warm Springs.

94. 1926-12-15 letter from Plastridge to Ober (Countway 33) - General note indicating that FDR is improving and plans to return to Warm Springs.

95. 1931-04-20 letter from Williams to Ober (Countway 37) - Confidential request for information concerning FDR's muscular activity.

96. 1931-04-23 letter from Ober to Williams (Countway 37) - Ober declines William's request dated April 20, 1931.

Appendix E. Dr. Levine's "Unpublished Note"

1421

<u>The Early Days of President Franklin D. Roosevelt's</u>

<u>Attack of Poliomyelitis</u>

One Saturday morning in late August of 1921 while I was at the
Peter Bent Brigham Hospital, I received a telephone call from a Mr.
Frederick A. Delano from Washington, D.C. He said he wanted to see
me on a very important matter concerning his nephew, Franklin D.
Roosevelt. Although I had planned to work at the hospital that day,
the problem seemed quite serious, and I therefore arranged to confer
with him in my office, which at that time was at 21 Bay State Road.

I quickly learned from Mr. Delano that FDR was critically ill
at Eastport, Maine. He had been well and had come up from Baltimore
or Washington to his summer house. Soon after arriving on August 10,
he developed pains in his back and limbs on returning from a swim.
Fever and chills ensued, and the next day he lost the use of both
arms. Mr. Delano began to receive letters and telegrams about the
President's sudden illness. At first, no doctors could be reached,
but soon Dr. W.W. Keene, a well-known elderly retired surgeon from
Philadelphia who was relatively close by, was called to examine the
patient. He attributed the symptoms to a "clot on the brain," i.e.,
a cerebral stroke. Later reports sent to Mr. Delano alluded to the
possibility of poliomyelitis, since at that time a severe epidemic
of infantile paralysis had become prevalent in the northeastern part
of the country.

Realizing that the diagnosis remained puzzling, Mr. Delano quickly
left Washington and on reaching Boston contacted the Harvard Infantile

-2-

Paralysis Commission Office. This commission consisted of Dr. Francis W. Peabody, who was in charge of the medical or clinical aspects of the problem, Dr. Robert Lovett, in charge of surgical or orthopedic aspects, and Dr. Milton J. Rosenarr, in charge of the public health and epidemiologic problems involved. The commission had been formed when cases of poliomyelitis became widespread in Massachusetts in the summer and fall of 1916. During this devastating epidemic, a call was made for two young medical volunteers to see patients on an emergency basis in any part of the state. Dr. John Wentworth and I, who were both working at the Brigham at that time—he as an assistant resident and I as a medical intern—volunteered to do this work. For about two months, day and night, we were both busily engaged in answering frantic calls and seeing many children and some young adults who had contracted or were suspected of having poliomyelitis. As a result, I had the opportunity to see about 300 cases of infantile paralysis. I tell this long introductory tale to explain how a student of cardiology came to be involved in a celebrated case of acute poliomyelitis.

On inquiring at the Commission Office, Mr. Delano learned that Dr. Lovett was in Newport, Rhode Island, and that Dr. Peabody and Dr. Rosenarr were also out of town for the summer. He was told that Dr. Samuel A. Levine had done a good deal of the field work and had examined many polio patients, providing medical care for those with acute cases during the epidemic of 1916 (five years before). In fact, I was the only one involved in the work of the commission who was in town at that time to offer Mr. Delano any advice.

-3-

On reading through the letters and telegrams that Mr. Delano had received and hearing the content of the various telephone conversations that had taken place between Eastport and Washington, it seemed clear to me that Mr. Roosevelt was suffering from acute poliomyelitis. I explained to Mr. Delano that the initial general malaise and limb pains followed by weakness and then paralysis of the limbs, the low-grade fever that subsided in a few days, and the fact that an epidemic of poliomyelitis was still raging made this diagnosis quite certain. The possibility of a cerebral stroke suggested by Dr. Keene could definitely be dismissed. (This was no reflection on the retired professor of surgery, who was then over 80 years old and probably had had little if any experience with acute poliomyelitis.)

At this point, Mr. Delano asked me if there would be any point in my traveling to Campobello immediately. Had this question been put to me differently or had I answered it more wisely, FDR's health might not have suffered so severely. Transportation by airplane had not yet become available, and it would have taken at least 24 to 36 hours to get there by train, boat, and motor car. Since the advice I intended to give could be transmitted by telephone, I replied that my presence was not really essential and urged that a physician be called from Bangor to perform a lumbar puncture. This procedure could be carried out that very day (Saturday), thereby saving at least 24 hours.

One might ask why I regarded the lumbar puncture to be so important under the circumstances. I had performed this procedure many times during the polio epidemic of 1916. Often I found that the cerebrospinal pressure was markedly elevated, and the fluid sample spurted out,

-4-

quickly filling the test tube. More importantly, removal of some of the fluid relieved the intense pressure and in some cases resulted in an immediate improvement in the patient's clinical condition. In one patient a severe headache might suddenly be dispelled, another might show a prompt reduction in fever, and still another might regain lost motor function. I recall seeing one young girl begin to wiggle her toes as I finished the procedure although they had been completely immobile just before the puncture. It appeared that the relief of pressure alone permitted some local nerve fibers to function. In fact, a good many of the patients my colleagues and I had seen were definitely in the preparalytic stage, and after the lumbar puncture had been performed to confirm the diagnosis, paralysis never developed.

Thus, there was two reasons for recommending that the President, who was still in the acute stage of the illness, undergo a lumbar puncture. First, if the pressure was found to be elevated, the relief might actually mitigate the paralysis that had already occurred or prevent further paralysis. Second, it would establish the diagnosis, which until now had remained questionable. Therefore, rather than delaying the procedure for two days while I traveled to Campobello, I urged that the puncture be performed by a physician in the vicinity. Little did I anticipate what would actually take place. If Mr. Delano had insisted that I go up there immediately, naturally I would have gone, but time was precious and I did not want to appear to be better equipped to perform the puncture than some other physician close by.

Thus ended the conference with Mr. Delano but not the particular episode in which I was engaged. Two days later, I received a telephone

-5-

call from Dr. Robert Lovett, who was anxious to have a conference with
me. Arrangements were made for him to have dinner with me at the
Harvard Club. He had finally been reached by telephone in Newport and
was on his way up to see the President. I told him all that I learned
from Mr. Delano concerning FDR's condition and expressed no doubt about
the diagnosis of poliomyelitis. To my surprise he asked me how one
could distinguish the paralysis associated with cerebral thrombosis or
hemorrhage (Dr. Keene's presumptive diagnosis) from that of poliomyelitis.
Inasmuch as Dr. Lovett had been my teacher in an undergraduate course
on orthopedic surgery, I wondered whether he was now testing me about
the neurologic findings in these two types of paralysis. I replied
that in poliomyelitis (in which peripheral motor neurons are involved)
motor reflexes are decreased or absent, whereas in a cerebral lesion
(with upper motor neuron involvement) reflexes are exaggerated, and one
might elicit a positive Babinski sign or an ankle clonus. Since Dr.
Lovett's practice was concerned mainly with orthopedic reconstruction,
which is generally begun some weeks after the onset of an illness, he
had had little opportunity to study or care for patients during the
early stage of acute poliomyelitis. Most likely he wanted to be apprised
of some of the features characterizing the acute phase of this disease.
In any event, I added that I had urged that a lumbar puncture be performed
but had not been informed of the result.

Some days later I received a letter from Mr. Delano dated September
1, 1921, with the following note: "Referring to my visit and my
consultation with you in regard to Franklin Roosevelt, Dr. Keene of
Philadelphia adhered very strenuously to his diagnosis of blood clot or

-6-

congestion of the spinal cord, but finally said that he would be glad

to call in Dr. Lovett in consultation. He personally sent for Dr.

Lovett to come to Eastport, and the two doctors met there and, as you

may suppose, Dr. Lovett not only convinced himself, but convinced Dr.

Keene (I think) that the case was really infantile paralysis. Although

Mr. Roosevelt is getting along as well as could be expected and will

probably be moved to New York about the middle of this month, we all

realize that it is a very serious matter...."

By the time Dr. Lovett saw the patient, the lumbar puncture had

still not been done. At last, on Wednesday the procedure was carried

out—four days after I had advised it. It was never made clear to me

whether my suggestion was not relayed by Mr. Delano, whether no one

was available to carry out my instructions? or possibly whether the local physicians

believed this maneuver to be inadvisable. During those several days

of delay, however, further paralysis had taken place, and it never

will be known whether more prompt removal of the spinal fluid would

have altered the course of the disease.

As I mentioned earlier, if the spinal fluid was under increased

pressure, clinical experience warrants the opinion that progress of

the disease might well have been influenced favorably and that the

final outcome might have been less disabling.

A practical lesson may be learned from this experience. My advice

was not followed. Realizing the gravity of the situation, I should

have been less timid and self-effacing and should have replied to Mr.

Delano that I would telephone directly myself, giving the orders to

the household to call in a physician (possibly from Bangor) to perform

-7-

the puncture. Furthermore, I should have resolved to leave immediately

to go and see the patient, even though I could not have reached him in

less than 24 hours. On the other hand, at that time I was inexperienced

and had not been practicing medicine for very long. This difficulty

would have been solved if Mr. Delano had stated that he wanted me to go

up there as soon as possible rather than leaving the decision up to me

and asking whether I should go. (Such things were not mentioned in

William Osler's Textbook of Medicine.) Perhaps the President's tragic

illness could be considered a blessing in disguise, acting as the

stimulus for the wonderful accomplishments of Franklin Roosevelt and

his wife Eleanor.

References

1. Gallagher HG. FDR's Splendid Deception: The Moving Story of Roosevelt's Massive Disability – And the Intense Efforts to Conceal It from the Public. New York: Dodd, Mead, 1985.

2. Goldman AS, Schmalstieg EJ, Freeman DH Jr., Goldman DA, Schmalstieg FC Jr. What was the cause of Franklin Delano Roosevelt's paralytic illness? J Med Biography 2003; 11:232-40.

3. Racaniello VR, Baltimore D. Molecular cloning of poliovirus cDNA and determination of the complete nucleotide sequence of the viral genome. Proc Natl Acad Sci U S A 1981; 78:4887–91.

4. Kitamura N, Semler B, Rothberg P, Larsen GR, Adler CJ, et al. Primary structure, gene organization and polypeptide expression of poliovirus RNA. Nature 1981; 291:547-53.

5. Goldman AS, Schmalstieg EJ, Dreyer CF, Schmalstieg FC Jr, Goldman DA. FDR's 1921 neurological disease revisited. The most likely diagnosis remains Guillain–Barré syndrome. J Med Biography 2016; 24:452-9.

6. Morgan T. FDR – A Biography. New York: Simon and Schuster, 1985.

7. Smith JE. FDR. New York: Random House, 2007.

8. Keene JD. World War I. Westport, Conn: Greenwood Press, 2006.

9. Boghardt T. The Zimmermann Telegram: Diplomacy, Intelligence, and The American Entry into World War I. Working Paper Series. Washington DC: The BMW Center for German and European Studies, Edmund A. Walsh School of Foreign Service, Georgetown University, 2003.

10. Vincent CP. The Politics of Hunger: Allied Blockade of Germany, 1915-1919. Athens, Ohio: Ohio University Press, 1985.

11. Lay Navy Scandal to F.D. Roosevelt. New York Times. July 20, 1921,p. 4.

12. Looker E. This Man Roosevelt. New York: Brewer, Warren & Putnam, 1932.

13. Pinet PR. Invitation to Oceanography, Fifth Edition. Sudbury, Mass: Jones and Bartlett Publishers, 2009.

14. Roosevelt FD. Letter to Dr William Egleston, 11 October 1924, reproduced from the South Carolina Medical Association 1946; 42. Located in: Personal correspondence of Franklin D Roosevelt and his family, Franklin D Roosevelt Library, Hyde Park, New York, USA.

15. Roosevelt E. Letter to James R. Roosevelt, 14 August 1921. Located in: Personal correspondence of Franklin D Roosevelt and his family. Franklin D Roosevelt Library, Hyde Park, New York, USA.

16. Keen WW. The Surgical Operations on President Cleveland in 1893. Philadelphia: G W Jacobs & Co, 1917.

17. United States Department of Labor, Bureau of Labor Statistics. CPI Inflation Calculator. http://www.bls.gov/data/inflation_calculator.htm web page.

18. Levine HJ. Samuel A. Levine (1891-1966). Clin Cardiol 1992; 15:473-6.

19. Delano FA. Letter to Eleanor Roosevelt, 20 August 1921. Located in: Personal correspondence of Franklin D Roosevelt and his family, Franklin D Roosevelt Library, Hyde Park, New York, USA.

20. Lovett RW. The Treatment of Infantile Paralysis. Philadelphia; P Blakiston's Sons, 1917.

21. The Robert W Lovett papers, Boston Medical Library, in the Francis A Countway Library of Medicine, Boston, MA, USA.

22. Lewers AHN. Half of a broken glass catheter removed from the bladder. Proceedings Royal Society Med (Obstetr-Gyn Section) 1912; 5:300-1.

23. d'Abreu AL. Dangers of the glass catheter. Br Med J 1934:2:1174.

24. Holick MF, Garabedian M. Vitamin D: Photobiology, Metabolism, Mechanism of Action, and Clinical Applications. In: Favus MJ, editor. Primer on the Metabolic Bone Diseases and Disorders of Mineral Metabolism. 6th ed. Washington, DC: American Society for Bone and Mineral Research; 2006.

25. Crandon JH, Lund CC, Dill DB. Experimental human scurvy. NEJM 1940; 223:353–69.

26. Cook BW. Eleanor Roosevelt. New York: Viking Press, 1992.

27. Roosevelt E. You Learn by Living: Eleven Keys for a More Fulfilling Life. Louisville, KY: Westminster John Knox Press, 1960.

28. Roosevelt J, Shalett S. Affectionately, F. D. R. New York: Harcourt, Brace, & Company, 1959.

29. Roosevelt E, Brough J. An Untold Story; The Roosevelts of Hyde Park. New York: GP Putman's Sons, 1973.

30. Doctor George Draper, F. D. Roosevelt Ill Of Poliomyelitis. New York Times, September 16, 1921.

31. Draper G. Infantile Paralysis. New York City: Appleton - Century, 1935.

32. Morris E. Theodore Rex. New York: Random House, 2001.

33. Gould JA. A Good Fight: the story of FDR's Conquest of Polio. New York: Dodd, Mead and Company, 1960.

34. Minchew KL. Troup County Archives. Roosevelt Warm Springs Institute for Rehabilitation. New Georgia Encyclopedia. Athens. GA, University of Georgia Press, 2013.

35. Roosevelt E. (ed). F.D.R.: His Personal Letters 1905-1928. New York: Duell, Sloan and Pearce, 1950.

36. Beecher HK. The powerful placebo. JAMA 1955; 159:1602–6.

37. de la Fuente-Fernández R. The placebo-reward hypothesis: dopamine and the placebo effect. Parkinsonism Relat Disord 2009; 15 (Suppl 3):S72-4.

38. Marx R. The Health of the Presidents. New York: GP Putman's Sons, 1960.

39. Kiewe A. The body as proof: Franklin D. Roosevelt's preparations for the 1932 Presidential campaign. Augmentation and Adocacy 1999; 36:88-100.

40. Haymaker W, Kernohan JW. The Landry - Guillain - Barré syndrome: a clinicopathological report of fifty fatal cases and a critique of the literature. Medicine 1949; 28:59-141.

41. Burns TM. Guillain-Barré syndrome. Semin Neurol 2008; 28:152-67.

42. Lelyveld, J. His Final Battle: The Last Months of Franklin Roosevelt. New York: Alfred A. Knopf, 2016.

43. Gould SJ. Full House. The Spread of Excellence from Plato to Darwin. New York: Three Rivers Press, 1996.

44. Fine PEM. Herd immunity: history, theory, practice. Epidemiological Reviews 1993; 15: 265-302.

45. Landsteiner K. Über Agglutinationserscheinungen normal menschlichen Blutes. *Wiener Klinischw Wochenschrift* 1901; 14:1132-4.

46. Landsteiner K, Popper E. Übertragung der Poliomyelitis acuta auf Affen Zeitschrift für Immunitatsforschung 1909; 2:377–90.

47. Landsteiner K, Levaditi C. La transmission de la paralysie infantile aux singes. Comptes Rendus des Séances de la Société de Biologie et de ses Filiales 1909; 67:592–4.

48. Landsteiner K, Levaditi C. La paralysie infantile expérimentale. Comptes Rendus des Séances de la Société de Biologie et de ses Filiales 1909; 67:787–90.

49. Flexner S, Lewis PA. The transmission of acute poliomyelitis to monkeys. JAMA 1909; 53:1639.

50. Flexner S, Lewis PA. The transmission of epidemic poliomyelitis to monkeys: A further note. JAMA 1909; 53:1913.

51. Paul JR. A History of Poliomyelitis. New Haven: Yale University Press, 1971.

52. De Jesus NH. Epidemics to eradication: the modern history of poliomyelitis. Virology J 2007; 4:70.

53. Chamberlain, HS. Die Grundlagen des Neunzehnten Jahrhunderts (in German), Munich, Germany: Munchen: Bruckmann F, 1899.

54. Lavinder CH, Freeman SW, Frost WH. Epidemiologic Studies of Poliomyelitis in New York City and the Northeastern United States During the Year 1916. Public Health Bulletin No. 91. Washington, DC: US Government Printing Office, 1918.

55. Wyatt HV. The 1916 New York City epidemic of poliomyelitis: Where did the virus come from? Open Vaccine J 2011; 4:13-7.

56. Emerson HA. Monogram on The Epidemic of Poliomyelitis (Infantile Paralysis). New York: Arno Press, 1977.

57. Ansari AA. Clinical features and pathobiology of Ebolavirus infection. J Autoimmun 2014; 14: 00130–9, S0896-8411.

58. Chan, M. Ebola virus disease in West Africa – no early end to the outbreak. New England Journal Medicine 2014; 371:1183–5.

59. Kolmer JA. An improved method of preparing the Kolmer poliomyelitis vaccine. Am J Public Health Nations Health 1936; 26:149-57.

60. Gould T. A Summer Plague: Polio and Its Survivors. New Haven: Yale University Press, 1995.

61. Sabin AB, Ward R. The natural history of human poliomyelitis. I. Distribution of virus in nervous and non-nervous tissues. J Exp Med 1941; 73:771–93.

62. Enders JF, Weller TH, Robbins FC. Cultivation of the Lansing strain of poliomyelitis virus in cultures of various human embryonic tissues. Science 1949; 109:85–7.

63. Enders JF, Kane LW, Cohen S, Levens JH. Immunity in mumps. J Exp Med 1945; 81:93-117.

64. Enders JF, Robbins FC, Weller TH. The cultivation of the poliomyelitis viruses in tissue culture. nobelprize.org/nobel_prizes/medicine/laureates/1954/enders-robbins-weller-lecture.pdf Nobel Lecture, December 11, 1954.

65. Marks HM. The 1954 Salk poliomyelitis vaccine field trial. In: 100 Landmark Clinical Trials. New York: John Wiley and Sons, 2008.

66. Francis T Jr, Napier JA, Voight RB, et al. Evaluation of the 1954 field trial of poliomyelitis vaccine: final report. Ann Arbor, MI: Edwards Brothers, 1957.

67. Offit PA. The Cutter Incident: How America's First Polio Vaccine Led to the Growing Vaccine Crisis. New Haven: Yale University Press, 2005.

68. Thrupp LD, Forester HER, Brody JA. Poliomyelitis in the United States, 1957. Public Health Rep 1959; 74:535-45.

69. Surveillance of poliomyelitis in the United States, 1958-61. Public Health Rep 1962; 77:1011–20.

70. Plotkin SA, LeBrun A, Courtois G, Koprowski H. Vaccination with the CHAT strain of type 1 attenuated poliomyelitis virus in Leopoldville, Congo 3. Safety and efficacy during the first 21 months of study. Bull World Health Organ 1961; 24:785-92.

71. Horstmann D. The Sabin live poliovirus vaccination trials in the USSR, 1959. Yale J Biol Med 1991; 64:499-512.

72. Sabin AB. Oral poliovirus vaccine: History of its development and the current challenge to eliminate poliomyelitis from the world. J Infect Disease 1985; 151:420-36.

73. Shell M. Polio and Its Aftermath. The Paralysis of Culture. Boston, Mass: Harvard University Press, 2005.

74. Itzhak Perlman. en.wikipedia.org/wiki/Itzhak_Perlman web page.

75. Cowie PJ. Coppola: A Biography. New York: Da Capo Press, 1994.

76. Polio Strikes Los Angeles. The West Australian (Perth, WA) August 14, 1954.

77. Alda A. Never Have Your Dog Stuffed: And Other Things I've Learned. London: Hutchinson, 2006.

78. Dinah Shore. en.wikipedia.org/wiki/Dinah_Shore web page.

79. Lardner, George. Mitch McConnell: The man who makes money talk. Washington Post. September 7, 1997; p. A01.

80. Schraff AE. Wilma Rudolph: The Greatest Woman Sprinter in History. Berkeley Heights, New Jersey: Enslow Publishers, 2004.

81. Troyan M. A Rose for Mrs. Miniver: The Life of Greer Garson. Lexington: University Press of Kentucky, 1999.

82. "The Waltons": The Easter Story (1973 TV Episode) - imdb.com/title/tt0743724/ web page.

83. Bayes T. An essay towards solving a problem in the doctrine of chances. Philosophical Transactions Royal Soc London 1763; 53:370–418.

84. Stigler SM. The History of Statistics. Boston, Mass: Harvard University Press, 1986.

85. Dawson-Saunders B, Trapp RG. Basic and Clinical Biostatistics (2nd edition). Norwalk, Conn: Appleton and Lange, 1994, pp 68–9.

86. Moore M, Kaplan MH, McPhee J, Bregman DJ, Klein SW. Epidemiologic, clinical, and laboratory features of Coxsackie B1-B5 infections in the United States, 1970-79. Public Health Rep 1984; 99:515-22.

87. Noah DL, Drenzek CL, Smith JS, Krebs JW, Orciari L, et al. Epidemiology of human rabies in the United States, 1980 to 1996. Ann Intern Med 1998; 128:922-30.

88. Tunkel AR, Glaser CA, Bloch KC, Sejvar JJ, Marra CM, et al. Infectious Diseases Society of America. The management of encephalitis: clinical practice guidelines by the Infectious Diseases Society of America. Clin Infect Dis 2008; 47:303-27.

89. Gutzwiller FS, Steffen R, Mathys P, Walser S, Schmid H, Mütsch M. Botulism: prevention, clinical diagnostics, therapy and possible threat. Dtsch Med Wochenschr 2008; 133:840-5.

90. Gibson K, Uwineza JB, Kiviri W, Parlow J. Tetanus in developing countries: a case series and review. Can J Anaesth 2009; 56:307-15.

91. Claveigero FS. Storia della California, Venezria, 1789. Cited by Marsh CD, Claswon AB, Roe AC. Coyotillo (Karwinskia humboldtiana) as a poisonous plant. USDA Tech Bull 1928; 29.

92. Marx A, Glass JD, Sutter RW. Differential diagnosis of acute flaccid paralysis and its role in poliomyelitis surveillance. Epidemiol Rev 2000; 22:298–316.

93. Eisen A. Amyotrophic lateral sclerosis: A review. BCMJ 2002; 44:362-6.

94. Froin G. Inflamations méningees avec chromatique, fibrineuse et cytologique du liquide céphalo-rachidien. Gazette des hôpitaux, Paris 1903; 76:1005-6.

95. Clarke NE. Loculated meningitis with the syndrome of Froin in the cerebrospinal fluid. Arch NeurPsych 1924: 12:173-86.

96. Mirza S, Adams WM, Corkhill RA. Froin's syndrome revisited, 100 years on. Pseudo-Froin's syndrome on MRI. Clinical radiology 2008; 63:600-4.

97. Kwon S-K, KIM M-W. Pseudo-Froin's syndrome, xanthochromia with high protein level of cerebrospinal fluid. Korean J Anesthesiol 2014; 67:S58-9.

98. Albers JW, Fink JK. Porphyric neuropathy. Muscle Nerve 2004; 30:410–22.

99. Chamberlin SL, Narins B (eds.). The Gale Encyclopedia of Neurological Disorders. Detroit: Thomson Gale, 2005.

100. McGrogan A, Madle GC, Seaman HE, de Vries CS. The epidemiology of Guillain-Barré syndrome worldwide. A systematic literature review. Neuroepidemiol 2009; 32:150-63.

101. Russel WR. Poliomyelitis: the pre-paralytic stage, and the effect of physical activity upon the severity of the paralysis. Br Med J 1947; 2:1023-8.

102. Hargreaves ER. Poliomyelitis: effect of exertion during the pre-paralytic stage. BMJ 1948; 2:1021-2.

103. Horstmann DM. Acute poliomyelitis: relation of physical activity at the time of the onset to the course of the disease. JAMA 1950; 142:236-41.

104. Francis T Jr., Krill CE, Toomey JA, Mack WN. Poliomyelitis following tonsillectomy in five members of a family. An epidemiological study. JAMA 1942; 119:1392-6.

105. Papenbarger RS Jr, Wilson VO, Engler JI, Kennedy RLJ. McBride OW. The effect of prior tonsillectomy on the incidence and clinical type of acute poliomyelitis. American Journal of Hygiene 1957; 64:131-50.

106. Mulder DW. Clinical observations on acute poliomyelitis. Ann New York Acad Sciences 1995; 753:1–10.

107. Dietz V, Lezana M, Garcia Sancho C, Montesano R. Predictors of poliomyelitis case confirmation at initial clinical evaluation: implications for poliomyelitis eradication in the Americas. International J Epidemiology 1992; 21:800–6.

108. Jubelt B, Miller JR. Viral infections. In: Rowland LP, ed. Merritt's Textbook of Neurology (9th edition). Baltimore: Williams & Wilkins, 1995.

109. Kidd D, Manji H, Brown D, Howard RS. Acute paralytic disease. Postgraduate Med J 1996; 72:699-701.

110. Yohannan MD, Ramia S, al Frayh AR. Acute paralytic poliomyelitis presenting as Guillain-Barré syndrome. J Infection 1991; 22:129-33.

111. Chomel A-F: De épidémie actuellement régnante à Paris. J Hebd Méd 1828; 1:331–8.

112. Viets HR. History of peripheral neuritis as a clinical entity. Arch NeuroPsych 1934; 32:377-94.

113. Landry O. Note sur la paralysie ascendante aigue. Gazette Hebdomadaire de Médecine et de Chirurgie. 1859; 6:472-4, 486-8.

114. Duménil L. Paralysie peripherique du mouvement et du sentiment portant sur les quatgre membres. Atrophie des rameaux nerveux des parties paralysées. Gazette Hebdomadaire de Médecine et de Chirurgie 1864; 1:203-9.

115. Leyden E von. Über poliomyelitis und Neuritis. Zeitschrift für klinische Medizin 1879/80; 472:486-93.

116. Oppenheim H. Lehrbuch der Nervenkrankheiten für Ärzte und Studierende. Fifth edition, Berlin:Verlag Von S. Karger 1908.

117. Guillain G, Barré JA, Strohl A. Sur un syndrome de radiculo-nevrite hyperalbuminose du liquide cephalorachidien sans reaction cellulaire: remarques sur les caractères cliniques et graphiques des réflexes tendineux. Bulletins et Mémoires de la Société Médicale des hôpitaux de Paris 1916; 40:1462-70.

118. Hughes RAC. Guillain-Barré Syndrome. London: Springer-Verlag, 1990.

119. Löffel NB, Rossi LN, Mumenthaler M, Lütschg J, Ludin HP. The Landry–Guillain– Barré syndrome: complications, prognosis and natural history in 123 cases. J Neuro Sci 1977; 33:71–9.

120. Samantray SK, Johnson SC, Mathai KV, Pulimood BM. Landry–Guillain–Barré–Strohl syndrome: a study of 302 cases. Med J Australia 1977; 2:84–91.

121. Kennedy RH, Danielson MA, Mulder DW, Kurland LT. Guillain–Barré syndrome: a 42 year epidemiologic and clinical study. Mayo Clinic Proceedings 1978; 53:93–9.

122. Schoenberg BS. Epidemiology of Guillain–Barré syndrome. Advances Neurology 1978; 19:249–58.

123. Asbury AK, Cornblath DR. Assessment of current diagnostic criteria for Guillain–Barré syndrome. Annals Neurology 1990; 27 (suppl):S21–4.

124. Ropper AH. The Guillain–Barré syndrome. NEJM 1992; 326:1130–6.

125. Lange DJ, Latov N, Trojaborg W. Acquired neuropathies. In: Rowland LP, ed Merritt's Textbook of Neurology (9th ed). Baltimore: Williams & Wilkins, 1995.

126. Adams RD, Victor M, Ropper AH. Principles of Neurology (9th edition). New York: McGraw-Hill, 1997.

127. Hughes RA, Rees JH. Clinical and epidemiologic features of Guillain–Barré syndrome. J Infectious Dis 1997; 176 (suppl 2):S92–8.

128. Barohn RJ, Saperstein DS. Guillain–Barré syndrome and chronic inflammatory demyelinating polyneuropathy. Seminars Neurology 1998; 18:49–61.

129. van Dorn PA. Diagnosis, treatment, and prognosis of Guillain–Barré syndrome. Presse Med 2013;42(6 Pt2):e193-201.

130. Sakakibara R, Uchiyama T, Kuwabara S, Mori M, Ito T, et al. Prevalence and mechanism of bladder dysfunction in Guillain–Barré Syndrome. Neurourology Urodynamics 2009; 28:432–7.

131. Ruts L, Drenthen J, Jongen JL, Hop WC, Visser GH, Jacobs BC, van Doorn PA. Pain in Guillain–Barré syndrome: a long-term follow-up study. Neurology 2010; 75:1439-47.

132. Adams T. Global eradication of poliomyelitis: Is the end of the campaign in sight? J Paediatr Child Health 2010; 46:619-22.

133. Levinson A. Cerebrospinal fluid in health and disease. St Louis: Mosby, 1923.

134. He Y, Mueller S, Chipman PR, Bator CM, Peng X, et al. Complexes of poliovirus serotypes with their common cellular receptor, CD155. J Virol 2003; 77:4827-35.

135. Robinson CM, Jesudhasan PR, Pfeiffer JK. Bacterial lipopolysaccaride binding enhances viron stability and fitness of an enteric virus. Cell Host Microbe 2014; 15:38-46.

136. Ohka S, Matsuda N, Tohyama, K, Oda T, Morikawa M, Kuge S, Nomoto A. Receptor (CD155)-dependent endocytosis of poliovirus and retrograde axonal transport of the endosome. J Virol 2004; 78:7186–98.

137. Hill AB, Knowelden J. Inoculation and poliomyelitis. BMJ 1950; 2:1-6.

138. Wyatt HV. Provocation of poliomyelitis by multiple injections. Trans R Soc Trop Med Hyg 1985; 79:355-8.

139. Sutter RW, Patriarca PA, Suleiman AJ, Brogan S, Malankar PG, et al. Attributable risk of DTP (diphtheria and tetanus toxoids and pertussis vaccine) injection in provoking paralytic poliomyelitis during a large outbreak in Oman. J Infect Dis 1992; 165:444–9.

140. Ren R, Rancaniello VR. Poliovirus spreads from muscle to the central nervous system by neural pathways. J Infect Dis 1992; 166: 747-52.

141. Ohka S, Yang WX, Terada E, Iwasaki K, Nomoto A. Retrograde transport of intact poliovirus through the axon via the fast transport system. Virology 1998; 250:67-75.

142. Autret A, Martin-Latil S, Mousson L, Wirotius A, Petit F, et al. Poliovirus Induces Bax-dependent cell death mediated by c-Jun NH2-terminal kinase. J Virol 2007; 81:7504–16.

143. Ponnuraj, John TJ, Levin MJ, Simoes EAF. Cell-to-cell spread of polioviruses in the spinal cord of bonnet monkeys (*Macaca radiata*). J General Virology 1998; 79:2393-403.

144. Blondel B, Colbère-Garapin F, Couderc T, Swirotius A, Guivel-Benhassine F. Poliovirus, pathogenesis of poliomyelitis, and apoptosis. CTMI 2005; 289:25-56.

145. Nathenson N. The pathogenesis of poliomyelitis: what we don't know. Adv Virus Res. 2008; 71:1-50.

146. Jacobs BC, Rothbart PH, Van der Meché FGA, Herbrink P, Schmitz PI, de Klerk MA, van Doorn PA. The spectrum of antecedent infections in Guillian–Barré syndrome: a case-control study. Neurology 1998; 51:1110–5.

147. Ilyas AA, Willison HJ, Quarles RH, Jungalwala FB, Cornblath DR, Trapp BD, et al. Serum antibodies to gangliosides in Guillain–Barré syndrome. Ann Neurol 1988; 23:440-7.

148. Yuki N, Yoshino H, Sato S, Miyatake T. Acute axonal polyneuropathy associated with anti-GM1 antibodies following *Campylobacter* enteritis. Neurology 1990; 40:1900-2.

149. Wirguin I, Suturkova-Milosevic L, Della-Latta P, Fisher T, Brown RH Jr, Latov N. Monoclonal IgM antibodies to GM1 and asialo-GM1 in chronic neuropathies cross-react with *Campylobacter jejuni* lipopolysaccharides. Ann Neurol 1994; 35:698-703.

150. Hughes RA, Hadden RD, Gregson NA, Smith KJ. Pathogenesis of Guillain–Barré syndrome. J Neuroimmunology 1999; 100:74-97.

151. Yuki N, Yamada M, Koga M. Animal model of axonal Guillain-Barré syndrome induced by sensitization with GM1 ganglioside. Ann Neurol 2001; 49:712-20.

152. lla I, Ortiz N, Gallard E, Juarez C, Grau JM, Dalakas MC. Acute axonal Guillain-Barré syndrome with IgG antibodies against motor axons following parenteral gangliosides. Ann Neurol 1995; 38:218-24.

153. Schwartz-Albiez R, Monteiro RC, Rodriguez M, Binder CJ, Shoenfeld Y. Natural antibodies, intravenous immunoglobulin and their role in autoimmunity, cancer and inflammation. Clin Exp Immunol 2009; 158(Suppl 1):43-50.

154. Schonberger LB, Bregman DJ, Sullivan-Bolyai JZ, Keenlyside RA, Ziegler DW, et al. Guillain-Barré syndrome following vaccination in the National Influenza Immunization Program, United States, 1976--1977. Am J Epidemiol 1979; 110:105-23.

155. Nachamkin I, Shadomy SV, Moran AP, Cox N, Fitzgerald C, et al. Anti-ganglioside antibody induction by swine (A/NJ/1976/H1N1) and other influenza vaccines: insights into vaccine-associated Guillain-Barré syndrome. J Infect Dis 2008; 198:226-33.

156. Cao-Lormeau V-M, Blake A, Mons S, Lastère S, Roche C, et al. Guillain-Barré Syndrome outbreak associated with Zika virus infection in French Polynesia: a case-control study. Lancet 2016; 387:1931-9.

157. Lopez PH, Zhang G, Zhang J, Lehmann HC, Griffin JW, et al. Passive transfer of IgG anti-GM1 antibodies impairs peripheral nerve repair. J Neurosci 2010; 30:9533-41.

158. Ryan KJ, Ray CG. Sherris Medical Microbiology, 4th edition. New York: McGraw Hill, 2004.

159. Nachamkin I, Szymanski CM, Blaser J. Campylobacter (3rd edition). Washington, DC: ASM Press, 2008.

160. Walusinski O. Pioneering the concept of stereognosis and polyradiculoneuritis: Octave Landry (1826-1865). Eur Neurol 2013: 70:281-90

161. McKhann GM, Cornblath DR, Griffin JW, Ho TW, Li CY, et al. Acute motor axonal neuropathy: a frequent cause of acute flaccid paralysis in China. Ann Neurol 1993; 33:333-42.

162. Ho TW, Mishu B, Li CY, Gao CY, Cornblath DR, Griffin JW, Asbury AK, Blaser MJ, McKhann GM. Guillain-Barré syndrome in northern China. Relationship to Campylobacter jejuni infection and anti-glycolipid antibodies. Brain 1995; 118 (Pt 3):597-605.

163. Tang J, Dai Y, Li M, Cheng M, Hong S, Jiang L, Cai F, Zhong M. Guillain-Barré syndrome in Chinese children: a retrospective analysis. Pediatr Neurol 2011; 45:233-7.

164. Nachamkin I, Arzarte Barbosa P, Ung H, Lobato C, Gonzalez Rivera A, Rodriguez P, et al. Patterns of Guillain-Barre syndrome in children: results from a Mexican population. Neurology 2007; 69:1665-71.

165. Jackson BR, Zegarra JA, López-Gatell H, Seivar J, Arzate F, et al. Binational outbreak of Guillain–Barré syndrome associated with *Campylobacter jejuni* infection, Mexico and USA, 2011. Epidemiology Infection 2013; 7:1-11.

166. Willison HJ, Yuki N. Peripheral neuropathies and antiglycolipid antibodies. Brain 2002; 125 (pt. 12): 2591-625.

167. Willison HJ. The immunobiology of Guillain-Barré syndromes. J Peripher Nerv Syst 2005; 10:94–112.

168. Yuki N. Human gangliosides and bacterial lipo-oligosaccharides in the development of autoimmune neuropathies. Methods Mol Biol 2010; 600:51-65.

169. Crump JA. Salmonella Infections (Including Typhoid Fever). In: Goldman's Cecil Medicine. Ed, Goldman L, Schafer AI. 24th Edition. Philadelphia: Saunders Elsevier, 2008.

170. Ahmed SM, Hall AJ, Robinson AE, Verhoef L, Premkumar P, Parashar UD, Koopmans M, Lopman BA. Global prevalence of norovirus in cases of gastroenteritis: a systematic review and meta-analysis. Lancet Infect Dis 2014; 14:725–30.

171. Fisher M. An unusual variant of acute idiopathic polyneuritis (syndrome of ophthalmoplegia, ataxia and areflexia). NEJM 1956; 255:57–65.

172. Mori M, Kuwabara S, Fukutake T, Yuki N, Hattori T. Clinical features and prognosis of Miller Fisher syndrome. Neurology 2001; 56:1104-6.

173. Odaka M, Yuki N, Hirata K. Anti-GQ1b IgG antibody syndrome: clinical and immunological range. J Neurol Neurosurg Psychiatry 2001; 70:50-5.

174. Bickerstaff ER. Mesencephalitis and rhombencephalitis. BMJ 1951; 2:77–81.

175. Etienne M, Weimer LH. Immune-mediated autonomic neuropathies. Current Neurol Neurosci Rep 2006; 6:57-64.

176. Vernino S, Hopkins S, Wang Z. Autonomic ganglia, acetylcholine receptors antibodies, and autoimmune ganglionopathy. Auton Neurosci 2009; 146:3-7.

177. Vanasse M, Rossignol E, Hadad E. Chronic inflammatory demyelinating polyneuropathy. Handb Clin Neurol. 2013; 112:1163-9.

178. Sherwood RJ. Obituaries: Philip Drinker 1894–1972. Annals Occupational Hygiene 1973: 16:93-4.

179. P.C. Rossin College of Engineering and Applied Science. Philip Drinker '17. Distinguished Alumni: Great Talents & Bright Minds. Bethlehem, Pennsylvania: Lehigh University, 2011.

180. Gorham, J. A medical triumph: the iron lung. Respiratory Therapy 1979; 9:71–3.

181. Geddes, LA. The history of artificial respiration. IEEE Engineering in Medicine and Biology Magazine: the Quarterly Magazine of the Engineering in Medicine & Biology Society 2007; 26:38–41.

182. Weil MH, Shoemaker WC. Pioneering contributions of Peter Safar to intensive care and the founding of the Society of Critical Care Medicine. Crit Care Med 2004; 32 (2 Suppl):S8-10.

183. van den Berg B, Walgaard C, Drenthen J, Fokke C, Jacobs BC, van Doorn PA. Guillain–Barré syndrome: pathogenesis, diagnosis, treatment and prognosis. Nature Reviews Neurology 2014; 10:469–82.

184. Plasmapheresis and acute Guillain–Barré syndrome. The Guillain–Barré Syndrome Study Group. Neurology 1985; 35:1096-104.

185. Plasma Exchange/Sandoglobulin Guillain–Barré Syndrome Trial Group. Randomized trial of plasma exchange, intravenous immunoglobulin, and combined treatments in Guillain–Barré syndrome. Lancet 1997; 349:225-30.

186. Hughes RA, Raphaël JC, Swan AV, van Doorn PA. Intravenous immunoglobulin for Guillain-Barré syndrome. Cochrane Database Syst Rev 2006; CD002063.

187. O'Sullivan SB. Physical Rehabilitation 5th ed. Philadelphia: FA Davis, 2006.

188. Khan F, Pallant JF, Amatya B, Ng L, Gorelik A, Brand C. Outcomes of high- and low-intensity rehabilitation programme for persons in chronic phase after Guillain-Barré syndrome: A randomized controlled trial. J Rehab Med 2011; 43:638-46.

189. Molteni R, Zheng J-Q, Ying Z. Voluntary exercise increases axonal regeneration from sensory neurons. Proc Natl Acad Sci 2004; 101:8473-8.

190. Parambil JG, Savci CD, Tazelaar HD, Ryu JH. Causes and presenting features of pulmonary infarctions in 43 cases identified by surgical lung biopsy. Chest 2005; 127:1178-83.

191. Pawlak R, Parrott SJ, Raj S, Cullum-Dugan D, Lucus D. How prevalent is vitamin B12 deficiency among vegetarians? Nutr Rev 2013; 71:110-7.

192. Lanska DJ. Chapter 30: Historical aspects of the major neurological vitamin deficiency disorders: the water-soluble B vitamins. Handb Clin Neurol 2010; 95:445-76.

193. Ropper AH. Severe acute Guillain–Barré syndrome. Neurology 1986; 36:429–32.

194. Bliss M. Harvey Cushing: A Life in Surgery. Oxford: Oxford University Press, 2005.

195. Cushing H. War Diary (Base Hospital No. 5). Medical Historical Library of the Yale University School of Medicine.

196. Reich SG. Harvey Cushing's Guillain-Barré syndrome: an historical diagnosis. Neurosurg 1987; 21:135-41.

197. Macher BA, Klock JC, Fukuda MN, Fukuda M. Isolation and structural characterization of human lymphocyte and neutrophil gangliosides. J Biol Chem 1981; 256:1968-74.

198. Heller J. Catch-22 New York: Simon & Schuster, 1961.

199. Heller J, Vogel S. No Laughing Matter, New York: G. P. Putnam's Sons, 1986.

200. Goldman D. Our Genes, Our Choices. How Genotype and Gene Interactions Affect Behavior. Waltham, Massachusetts: Elsevier/Academic Press, 2012.

201. Coker JW. Franklin D. Roosevelt: A Biography. Westport, Connecticut: Greenwood Press, 2005.

202. Winkler AM. Franklin D. Roosevelt and the Making of Modern America. New York: Pearson Educational, Inc, 2006.

203. Brands HW. Traitor to His Class: The Privileged Life and Radical Presidency of Franklin Delano Roosevelt. New York: Doubleday, 2008.

204. Tobin J. The Man He Became. How FDR Defied Polio to Win the Presidency. New York: Simon & Schuster, 2013.

205. Oshinsky D. Polio. An American Story. New York: Oxford University Press, Inc, 2005.

206. Peters ST. Epidemic: The Battle Against Poliomyelitis. New York: Benchmarks Books, 2005.

207. Wilson DJ. Living with Polio: The Epidemic and Its Survivors. Chicago: University of Chicago Press, 2005.

208. Parry G, Steinberg J. Guillain-Barré Syndrome: From Diagnosis to Recovery. New York: Demos Medical Publishing, 2007.

209. Friedenberg ZB. Franklin D. Roosevelt: his poliomyelitis and orthopaedics. J Bone Joint Surg (Am) 2009; 91:1806-13.

210. Shreve SR. Warm Springs: Traces of a Childhood at FDR's Polio Haven. Boston: Houghton Mifflin Company, 2007.

211. Lomazow S. http://fdrsdeadlysecret.blogspot.com/2010/01/my-paper-on-fdr-in-journal-of-medical.html (January, 2010)

212. Ditunno JF Jr, Becker BE, Herbison GJ. Franklin Delano Roosevelt: The diagnosis of poliomyelitis revisited. PM R. 2016; 8:883-93

213. Brenner IK, Castellani JW, Gabaree C, Young AJ, Zamecnik J, Shephard RJ, Shek PN. Immune changes in humans during cold exposure: effects of prior heating and exercise. J Appl Physiol 1999; 87:699-710.

214. Peake J, Peiffer JJ, Abbiss CR, Nosaka K, Okutsu M, et al. Body temperature and its effect on leukocyte mobilization, cytokines and markers of neutrophil activation during and after exercise. Eur J Appl Physiol. 2008; 102:391-401.

215. Goldberg RT. The Making of Franklin D. Roosevelt: Triumph Over Disability. Lanham, Maryland: University Press of America, 1984.

216. Samuel Levine papers (H MS c448) Harvard Medical Library in the Francis A. Countway Library of Medicine (accession 2015-051).

217. Darras BT, Jones HR Jr, Ryan MM, De Vivo DC. Neuromuscular Disorders of Infancy, Childhood, and Adolescence. A Clinician's Approach. Second Edition. Waltham, Massachusetts: Academic Press, 2014.

218. Letter from Frederic Delano to Dr. Samuel Levine, dated September 1, 1921, and relating that Dr. Lovett had "convinced himself . . . that the case was really infantile paralysis". Scanned image of letter provided by Mrs.Sandra Levine on November 13, 2014.

219. Hogle JM, Chow M, Filman DJ. Three-dimensional structure of poliovirus at 2.9 Å resolution. Science 1985; 229:1358-65.

220. Witte JJ, Henderson DA. The cerebrospinal fluid in type 3 poliomyelitis. American J Epidemiol 1966; 83:189-95.

221. Link H, Wahren B, Norrby E. Pleocytosis and immunoglobulin changes in cerebrospinal fluid and herpesvirus serology in patients with Guillain-Barré syndrome. J Clin Microbiol 1979; 9:305-16.

222. Flexner S. A note on the serum treatment of poliomyelitis (infantile paralysis) JAMA 1916: 8:583-4.

223. Hammon W. Passive immunization against poliomyelitis. Monogr Ser World Health Organ 1955; 26:357–70.

224. Rinaldo C. Passive immunization against poliomyelitis: The Hammon Gamma Globulin Field Trials, 1951–1953. Am J Public Health 2005; 95:790–9.

225. Ivar Wickman, (Wickman I. Die akute Poliomyelitis bzw. Heine-Medinsche Krankheit. Mit zwölf Textabbildungen und zwei Tafeln, Berlin 1911.

226. Paul JR. Poliomyelitis: early diagnosis and early management of acute cases. Ann Intern Med 1949; 30:1126-33.

227. Silverstein A, Silverstein V, Nunn LS. Polio. Diseases and People. Berkeley Heights, NJ: Enslow Publishers, 2011.

228. Kidd D, Williams AJ, Howard RS. Poliomyelitis. Postgraduate Med J 1996; 72:641-7.

229. Weinstein L, Shelokov A, Seltser R, Winchell GD. A comparison of the clinical features of poliomyelitis in adults and children. New Engl J Med 1952; 246:297-302.

230. Weinstein L, Aycock WL, Feemster RF. The relationship of sex, pregnancy and menstruation to susceptibility in poliomyelitis. New Engl J Med 1951; 251:54-8.

231. Bernsen RJAM, de Jager AEJ, van der Meché FGA, Suurmeijer TPBM. How Guillain-Barré patients experience their functioning after 1 year. Acta Neurol Scand 2005; 112:51-6.

232. Moulin DE, Hagen N, Feasby TE, Amireh R, Hahn A. Pain in Guillain–Barré syndrome. Neurology 1997; 48:328–31.

233. Sánchez-Guerra M, Infante J, Pascual J, Berciano J. Severe backache in Guillain–Barré syndrome. Muscle Nerve 2002;25: 468.

234. Toscano A, Rodolico C, Benvenga S, Girlanda P, Laurà M, Mazzeo A, Nobile-Orazio E, Trimarchi F, Vita G, Messina C. Multifocal motor neuropathy and asymptomatic Hashimoto's thyroiditis: first report of an association. Neuromuscul Disord 2002; 12:566-8.

235. Lovett RW. The diagnosis, prognosis and early treatment of poliomyelitis. JAMA 1922; 78: 1607-11.

236. Wein AJ. Neuromuscular dysfunction of the lower urinary tract. In Walsh PC, Retik AB, Stamey TA, Vaughan ED Jr eds, Campbell's Urology, 6th edn. Philadelphia: WB Saunders, 1992: 573–642.

237. Chermansky CJ1, Moalli PA. Role of pelvic floor in lower urinary tract function. Auton Neurosci 2016; 200:43-8.

238. Andersson K-E, Arner A. Urinary bladder contraction and relaxation: physiology and pathophysiology. Physiological Reviews 2004; 84:935-86.

239. Zochodne DW. Autonomic involvement in Guillain-Barré syndrome: a review. Muscle Nerve 1994; 17:1145-55.

240. Bernsen RAJAM, de Jager AEJ, van der Meché FGA, Suurmeijer TPBM. How Guillain–Barre patients experience their functioning after 1 year. Acta Neurol Scand 2005: 112:51–6.

241. Darley JM, Gross PH. A hypothesis-confirming bias in labeling effects. J Personality Social Psychology 1983; 44:20-33.

242. Nickerson RS. Confirmation bias: a ubiquitous phenomenon in many guises. Review of General Psychology 1998; 2:175-220.

243. Bacon F. Novum organum. Original work published in 1620. In: Burtt EA, ed, The English philosophers from Bacon to Mill. New York: Random House, 1939, pp 24-123.

244. Blondlot P-R. On a new species of light. Comptes Rendus. The Proceedings of the Académies des Sciences 1903; 136:284.

245. Collins P. Banvard's Folly: Thirteen Tales of Renowned Obscurity, Famous Anonymity, and Rotten Luck. New York: Picador, 2002.

246. Blondlot P-R. 'N' Rays. Translated by Garcin J. London: Longmans, Green & Co., 1905.

247. Lagemann RT. New light on old rays: N rays. American Journal Physics 1977; 45: 281–4.

248. Wood RW. The N-Rays. Nature 1904; 70:530-1.

249. Devlin J. Webster's New School and Office Dictionary. Halifax, Canada: The New World Publishing Company. pp. 496, 1946.

250. Rosenstein BJ, Cuttings JR. The diagnosis of cystic fibrosis: a consensus statement. Cystic Fibrosis Foundation Consensus Panel. J Pediatr 1998; 132:589-95.

251. Goldman AS, Schochet SS Jr, Howell JT. Discovery of defects in respiratory cilia in the immotile cilia syndrome. J Pediatr 1980; 96:244-7.

252. Howell JT, Schochet SS, Goldman AS. Ultrastructural defects of respiratory tract cilia associated with chronic infections. Arch Path Lab Med 1980; 104:52-5.

253. Alter J. The Defining Moment. FDR's Hundred Days and the Triumph of Hope. New York: Simon & Schuster, 2007.

254. Cialdini RB. Influence, the Psychology of Persuasion. New York: HarperBusiness, 2006.

255. Roosevelt E. My Day. September 11, 1944, Copyright 1944 by United Feature Syndicate, Inc.

256. Santayana G. The Life of Reason. Reason in Common Sense, Volume 1, New York: Charles Scribner's Sons p. 284, 1905.

257. Bruton OC. Agammaglobulinemia. Pediatrics 1952; 9: 722–8.

258. Broides A, Yang W, Conley ME. Genotype/phenotype correlations in X-linked agammaglobulinemia. Clin Immunol 2006; 118:195–200.

259. Orenstein WA, Perry RT, Halsey NA. The clinical significance of measles: a review. J Infect Dis 2004; 89 (suppl 1): s4-s16.

260. Bialecki C, Feder HM Jr, Grant-Kels JM. The six classic childhood exanthems: a review and update. J Am Acad Dermatol 1989; 21(5 Pt 1):891-903.

261. Silver N. The Signal and the Noise. Why So Many Predictions Fail - But Some Don't. New York: Penguin Press, 2012.

262. Burke RJ, Chang C. Diagnostic criteria of acute rheumatic fever. Autoimmun Rev 2014; 13:503-7.

263. Yu C, Gershwin ME, Chang C. Diagnostic criteria for systemic lupus erythematosus: a critical review. Journal of Autoimmunity 2014; 48-49:10-3.

264. Letter from Eleanor Roosevelt to Headmaster of the Groton School, Reverend Endicott Peabody 28 August 1921. From the Library of The Groton School, Massachusetts.

Glossary

Acute intermittent porphyria - A rare autosomal recessive, genetic disease due to a deficiency in the enzyme porphobilinogen deaminase. It was ruled out in FDR's case.

Anaerobe - An organism that does not require oxygen for growth. A pertinent example is *C. jejuni,* the commonest cause of Guillain-Barré syndrome.

Anesthesia - A lack of pain or touch sensation, such as was experienced by FDR during the start of his 1921 illness.

Antigen - The region of a foreign agent or self-component that is recognized by antibodies or by T cells. Examples are *C. jejuni* lipopolysaccharides.

Antibody - A protein produced by plasma cells that combines with foreign objects such as bacteria and viruses, but less commonly reacts with self-antigens. Autoantibodies cause Guillain-Barré syndrome.

Apoptosis - Programmed cell death, where the cell essentially self-destructs. The process occurs in motor neurons invaded by polioviruses.

Asthenic - A slender body build. George Draper believed that an asthenic body type increased the susceptibility to paralytic polio.

Autoantibodies - Antibodies directed against self-antigens such GM1 gangliosides as found in Guillain-Barré syndrome

Autoimmunity - Immunological reactions against self-antigens. It is the basis of autoimmune diseases, one of which probably occurred in FDR.

Autonomic nervous system - The part of the nervous system that operates below the level of consciousness. It controls the function of viscera such as the heart, gastrointestinal tract, and urinary tract. Some of this system became disabled in FDR during his 1921 illness.

Autosomal inheritance - Refers to inheritance where the gene is not on the X or Y chromosome. Most hereditary disorders are autosomal – that is are due to genes on non-sex chromosomes.

Bayesian analysis - A statistical method used to help determine the most likely cause of FDR's 1921 paralytic illness, based on symptom probabilities and disease incidence rates.

Botulism - A serious paralytic illness caused by a nerve toxin produced by the bacterium *Clostridium botulinum*. It was ruled out in FDR's case.

Bulbar poliomyelitis - A deadly form of poliomyelitis that strikes cranial motor nerves. It was ruled out in FDR's case.

Bulbospinal poliomyelitis - A deadly form of poliomyelitis that strikes spinal and cranial motor nerves. It was ruled out in FDR's case.

Campobello - A Canadian island in the Bay of Fundy close to Maine. FDR developed a severe neurological illness there in 1921.

Campylobacter jejuni (C. jejuni) - A bacterium that colonizes the intestinal tract of domesticated animals and frequently causes a mild enteritis in humans. It is the most common microbial trigger of Guillain-Barré syndrome.

CD155 - A protein that is the cellular receptor for polioviruses. The poliovirus binds to the CD155 receptor prior to entering the cell.

Cerebrospinal fluid - CSF. Clear colorless fluid in passageways in the brain and spinal cord. CSF findings help to distinguish paralytic polio from GBS.

Cilia - Minute, hair-like structures that protrude from respiratory tract epithelium. Cilia beat in a synchronous pattern to sweep secretions from the respiratory system. Cilia are dysfunctional in immotile cilia syndrome.

Confirmation bias - The tendency to selectively seek out or interpret information that confirms preconceptions and ignore or reinterpret reasonable evidence to the contrary. Confirmation bias is likely a factor in the long-standing belief that FDR had paralytic polio.

Coyotillo - *Karwinskia humboldtiana*. A tree that grows in the arid regions of Northern Mexico and Southwestern United States. Its fruit contains a neurotoxin that causes a neuropathy that resembles Guillain-Barré syndrome. FDR was not exposed to coyotillo toxin.

Cystic fibrosis - An autosomal recessive genetic disease that leads to an increased transport of chloride and sodium across epithelium, resulting in thickened secretions of the respiratory tract, pancreas, liver, and intestines.

Cytopathic - "Cell killing". Live polioviruses are cytopathic, which allows them to be detected in tissue cultures.

Decubitus ulcers - Pressure sores. They were a potential threat to FDR during his 1921 illness.

Dynein arms - A motor protein within cells. Involved in transport of the poliovirus and in the movement of cilia.

Dysesthesia - Unpleasant distorted sensations that occur to the slightest touch. Dysesthesia occurred in FDR's 1921 illness.

Dysphagia - Difficulty in swallowing. It occurs in some types of autoimmune neuropathies, but not in classical Guillain-Barré syndrome.

Dysphonia - Difficulty in speaking due to a physical disorder of the mouth, tongue, throat, or vocal cords.

Encephalitis - Inflammation of cerebral cortex often due to viral infections. It was ruled out in FDR's case.

Enteritis - Inflammation of the intestines. It frequently occurs in enteric bacterial infections such as those due to *C. jejuni*, the principal microbial trigger of Guillain-Barré syndrome.

Epidemic - The rapid spread of an infectious disease to a large number of people within a region, for example the 1916 polio epidemic.

Flexner, Simon - A research physician who confirmed in 1908 Landsteiner's discovery that poliovirus could be experimentally transferred to non-human primates.

Formalin - The agent used to inactivate polioviruses by Salk for the creation of the first successful poliovirus vaccine. Consists of an aqueous solution of formaldehyde with a small amount of methanol.

Ganglioside - A glycosphingolipid with one or more sialic acids. The molecule is present on motor and sensory nerves. It is the target for autoantibodies in Guillain-Barré syndrome.

Guillain, Georges - French neurologist. He, Barré and Strohl found that CSF findings in patients with Landry's ascending paralysis (now called Guillain–Barré syndrome) were different from those in paralytic polio, and that nerve conduction was decreased in those patients.

Guillain–Barré syndrome (GBS) - An autoimmune neuropathy principally due to autoantibodies to GM1 gangliosides. It was the most likely cause of FDR's 1921 neurological illness.

Hyperesthesia - Abnormal sensitivity to touch, pain, or other sensory stimuli. Pain to the slightest touch occurred in FDR's 1921 illness.

Immunodeficient - Deficient in some part of the immune system.

Immunogen - An antigen that elicits the formation of specific antibodies.

Intercostals - The muscles between the ribs that cause voluntary respirations when they contract. Those muscles were in all likelihood partially dysfunctional during FDR's 1921 neurological illness.

Koplik spots - Ulcerated mucosal lesions of the sides of mouth that occur in measles, a consideration in one of the illustrative cases in this book.

Landry, Octave - A French physician who described in 1859 ten adult patients with a symmetric, ascending paralysis and other evidence of a peripheral neuropathy.

Landry's ascending paralysis - An ascending, symmetric paralysis due to an autoimmune neuropathy, now called Guillain–Barré syndrome.

Landsteiner, Karl - An Austrian physician who first discovered that polioviruses could be experimentally transmitted to non-human primates.

Lipopolysaccharides - Large molecules found in the outer membrane of Gram-negative bacteria. Certain types of lipopolysaccharides operate in the pathogenesis of Guillain–Barré syndrome by eliciting antibodies that cross-react with certain self antigens (GM1 gangliosides).

Lubec - A town on the northern coast of Maine close to Campobello Island. Dr. Bennet, the first physician to see FDR during his illness, practiced in Lubec.

Lumbar puncture - Also called a spinal tap. A special needle is inserted into the subarachnoid space between lumbar vertebra three and four or four and five to collect cerebrospinal fluid for diagnostic studies.

Medulla oblongata - The brain stem, which contains many cranial nerve nuclei. It is involved in bulbar and bulbospinal poliomyelitis.

Miller Fischer syndrome - A rare autoimmune neuropathy caused by auto-antibodies and involving cranial nerves. It was ruled out in FDR's case.

Myelin - An electrically insulating fatty layer surrounding the axon of a neuron. Myelin speeds up transmission of nerve signals and forms a tract for nerve regeneration. It is damaged in Guillain-Barré syndrome.

Neuropathy - Damage to peripheral nerves due to viral, immunological, or metabolic disorders. Guillain-Barré syndrome is an autoimmune neuropathy.

Neuron - A cell that transmits and receives nerve impulses. Polioviruses invade axons of motor neurons, and are transported to the cell body in the spinal cord. In GBS, autoantibodies attach to the surface of neurons, leading to damage.

Nerve - A bundle of peripheral axons, along with protective and supportive structures. Each nerve contains many axons, either motor, sensory, or both.

Newport Sex Scandal - The sex scandal arose in 1919 from the United States Navy's investigation of illicit sexual behavior by Navy personnel in Newport, Rhode Island. FDR was rebuked in July 1921 by a Senate Subcommittee for permitting such behavior. The charge was dropped.

Neurotropic - Having an affinity for nervous tissue. The poliovirus is neurotropic.

Neutrophil - A type of white blood cell, involved in certain types of inflammation.

Opisthotonus - Severe hyperextension of the back and neck, in certain severe injuries to the brain such as cerebral palsy and tetanus. This severe problem occurred in certain individuals at risk for paralytic polio who were treated with injections of human serum into the subarachnoid space.

Phagocytosis - Ingestion of small particles by white blood cells such as neutrophils, monocytes, and macrophages, by infolding of the cell membrane and protrusion of cytoplasm until the particle is surrounded and engulfed.

Pandemic - An epidemic that occurs over a wide geographic area and affects a large proportion of the population, such as the 1918 influenza pandemic.

Paresthesia - Tingling, tickling, prickling, pricking, or burning sensations of the skin that often occur with neuropathies such as Guillain-Barré syndrome.

Pathogenesis - The steps leading to the development of a disease starting with initiating causes and ending with final clinical manifestations. It is a main diagnostic approach and was used in the analysis of FDR's case.

Pathognomonic - A clinical feature that is diagnostic of a particular disease. For example, Koplik spots are pathognomonic for measles (rubeola).

Pattern recognition - The most common diagnostic strategy. The patient's clinical findings are compared to the clinical features found in those diseases that most closely fit the patient's illness.

Plasmapheresis - A method of depleting blood plasma. Blood is separated into plasma and red blood cells. The plasma is discarded and the red blood cells are reinfused into the donor. The procedure is used to treat Guillain-Barré Syndrome by lowering serum concentrations of IgG autoantibodies.

Phrenic nerves - Two nerves, left and right, originating at the cervical C3-C5 level. The phrenic nerves signal the thoracic diaphragm to contract. When both phrenic nerves are damaged, respiratory failure ensues.

Poliomyelitis - Also called polio. An infectious disease caused by the poliovirus. The disease primarily struck young children during the summer months. It is widely believed that FDR contracted paralytic polio.

Poliovirus - An enterovirus responsible for many epidemics of paralytic disease in the 19th and 20th centuries. Poliovirus was initially believed to cause FDR's 1921 neurological illness.

Probability - The likelihood of something happening. Bayesian analysis is a way of predicting probabilities.

Reverse causality - The confusion of cause with effect. An example occurred with George Draper's belief that an asthenic body type increased the susceptibility to paralytic polio.

Serendipity - Finding valuable or agreeable things that are not sought for. An aptitude for making fortunate discoveries by accident. It was the initial event in the discovery of the cause of FDR's 1921 neurological illness.

Serotype - An antigenic variation within a species of bacterium, fungous or virus such as poliovirus.

Spinal tap - More appropriately called a lumbar puncture.

Springwood - The Roosevelt Estate at Hyde Park, New York.

Subarachnoid space - The space between the arachnoid membrane and the pia mater of the brain and spinal cord that contains cerebrospinal fluid.

Thenar eminence - The muscle mass in the palm of the hand at the base of the thumb. The muscles were temporarily paralyzed in FDR's case.

Transverse myelitis - An inflammatory process involving a single segment of the spinal cord. It was ruled out in FDR's case.

Typhoid fever - A serious intestinal infection caused by *Salmonella typhi*. FDR was thought to have had typhoid fever in 1913.

Vaccine - A biological preparation that increases immunity to a particular infectious disease, for example the poliovirus vaccine.

Von Leyden, Ernst - A German physician who determined in 1879 the pathological differences between paralytic polio and Landry's ascending paralysis (Guillain-Barré syndrome).

Warms Springs - A site in Georgia where FDR rehabilitated from his 1921 neurological illness and where he later created a rehabilitation center.

Zika Virus - A mosquito-borne virus that can cause microcephaly in infants born to infected pregnant mothers, and that may occasionally cause GBS.

Index

Made in the USA
Columbia, SC
16 January 2023

10419421R00193